GREEN
IS THE
COLOUR

Copyright © Peter Byrne 2012

First published in 2012 by
Carlton Books Limited
20 Mortimer Street
London W1T 3JW

A CIP catalogue record for this book is available from the British Library

10 9 8 7 6 5 4 3 2 1

ISBN: 978-0-233-00366-5 (hardback)
ISBN: 978-0-233-00357-3 (paperback)

Editor: Martin Corteel
Project Art Editor: Luke Griffin
Picture Research: Paul Langan
Production: Maria Petalidou

Printed in Great Britain by CPI Group (UK) Ltd, Croydon, CR0 4YY

GREEN
IS THE
COLOUR
THE STORY OF IRISH FOOTBALL

PETER BYRNE

ANDRE
DEUTSCH

Acknowledgements

It is with deep gratitude that I acknowledge the work of earlier historians in tracing the evolution of football in Ireland since the formation of the Irish Football Association in 1880. I am indebted in particular, to my good friend, Malcolm Brodie, widely regarded as one of the foremost authorities on the game in these islands and a constant source of astonishment to those who have worked with him down through the years.

Thanks is also owing to Neal Garnham for his splendid work, Association Football and Society in Pre-Partition Ireland, and Sean Ryan, never less than meticulous in researching the development of the game in the Republic of Ireland.

I would also like to put on record the contributions of senior football officials on both sides of the Irish border, the players, past and present, who gave so willingly of their time in the preparation of the book, those who provided historic photographs and, not least, the many librarians who facilitated my research. I trust the end product justifies the goodwill I experienced along the way.

Primary Published Sources

Irish Times, Irish Independent, Irish Press, Cork Examiner, Freeman's Journal, Irish Field, Dublin Evening Mail, Dublin Evening Telegraph, Sport, Irish Sportsman, Sunday Independent, Sunday Chronicle, Belfast Telegraph, Ireland's Saturday Night, Irish News, Belfast Newsletter, The Times, Press Association, Daily Express, Derry Journal, Londonderry Sentinel, Irish Worker, Sunday World, Sunday News, Munster Express, Limerick Leader, Dundalk Democrat.

Picture Credits

The publishers would like to thank the following sources for their kind permission to reproduce the pictures in this book.

First Plate Section
Page 1: (top) Private Collection; (bottom) Popperfoto/Getty Images
Page 2: (both) Popperfoto/Getty Images
Page 3: (both) Private Collection
Page 4: (top) Popperfoto/Getty Images; (bottom) Private Collection
Page 5: (both) Private Collection
Page 6: (top) Central Press/Getty Images; (bottom) Popperfoto/Getty Images
Page 7: (top) DPA/Press Association Images; (bottom) Colorsport
Page 8: (top) Private Collection; (bottom) Central Press/Getty Images

Second Plate Section
Page 1: (top) Colorsport; (bottom) Bob Thomas/Getty Images
Page 2: (both) Bob Thomas/Getty Images
Page 3: (both) Bob Thomas/Getty Images
Page 4: (top) Witters/Press Association Images; (bottom) Bob Thomas/Getty Images
Page 5: (both) Bob Thomas/Getty Images
Page 6: (top) Claudio Onorati/AFP/Getty Images; (bottom) Mike Hewitt/Getty Images
Page 7: (top) Paul Faith/Press Association Images; (bottom) Laurent Zabulon/Gamma/Getty Images
Page 8: (top) Michael Steele/Getty Images; (bottom) Peter Muhly/AFP/Getty Images

Contents

Foreword

by Jack Charlton

I wasn't long into my football education when I discovered that for a relatively small country, Ireland packs a helluva punch. And now that I find myself at the other end of the age spectrum, I am more convinced than ever of that fact.

Football has always been the game of the masses, and it follows that those countries with large populations are invariably expected to do well in the major competitions. What makes the game extra special is that in spite of the disadvantage of having to operate with limited resources, the smaller countries can still, occasionally, stand logic on its head and come up with results which grab international headlines. Ireland makes that point better than most.

When I was a lad listening to old timers recalling great players and great days, I remember I used to hear them mention names like Johnny Carey and Peter Doherty with the same kind of awe as legends such as Stan Matthews, Tommy Lawton and other marvellous England players in the post-war years. The first Irish player I actually got to know was Wilbur Cush in his time with Leeds United. He was only a little 'un, but I tell you something, nobody dared cross him. If you got on the wrong side of Wilbur Cush, you could expect a bit of bother.

There wasn't much of Johnny Giles either when he came to the club some time later, but he too could always compete when the going got tough. A brilliant passer of the ball was Johnny, both for Leeds and the Republic of Ireland, and I'm sure there were times, many times, when Sir Alf Ramsey wished he had the option of putting him in his England teams. Because of their involvement in the home international championship, Northern Ireland teams were pretty well known across the Irish Sea, and while high-profile individuals such as Peter McParland, Harry Gregg and the Blanchflower brothers, Danny and Jackie, were gone by the time I made it into England's team, I got to play against and respect players of the quality of Pat Jennings, Terry Neill and, of course, the incomparable George Best.

It was different with the Republic of Ireland. I mean you seldom read or heard about their teams in the north-east of England in those days, and when Gilesy went off to play for them, we usually didn't know how they got on until he made his way back to Elland Road. That's the way it was in the English newspapers at the time and it was a pity they didn't take more interest, for men like Charlie Hurley, Noel Cantwell and Andy McEvoy were serious players in English club football in the 1960s. I played for the Football League against the League of Ireland on a couple of occasions, but that, of course, wasn't quite the same as facing a full-strength international team.

All of which is by way of saying that when I was offered the chance of managing the Republic of Ireland's international team, I didn't know an awful lot about them. As it turned out, it was one of the best decisions I ever made in football and it gave me more job satisfaction that I could possibly have imagined when I met Des Casey, the FAI President, for the first time and became aware that the Irish job was on offer.

It took a while, of course, for some people to realise what Maurice Setters and I were about as we devised a method of getting the best out of the players we inherited. I soon went out to strengthen the squad by bringing the likes of John Aldridge, Ray Houghton and, later, Andy Townsend on board, and from this base we built a team which went on to demand respect from the best in Europe and beyond. As a player, I had known the delight of winning a World Cup medal with England, and for anybody involved in football that has to rate as a career high, but the sense of fulfilment I got from managing Ireland in two World Cup finals as well as the finals of the European championship in Germany in 1988, was enormous.

What made my time in Ireland extra special was the rapport I developed with the team's supporters. We may never have won any important silverware but I tell you something, we had the best fan base in the world. Thousands of people came with us when we played abroad, but the real joy was in noting the way the whole country got behind us during the World Cup finals. Those who travelled with the squad knew how to enjoy themselves. They also knew how to behave, and I think it's no exaggeration to say that they did much to enhance the image of Ireland and its people, anywhere we went.

A good proportion of our supporters came from Northern Ireland, and I'm told much the same happened in reverse when Northern Ireland took part in the World Cup finals in Spain in 1982 and again in Mexico four years later. And it proved that when you boil it all down, there is no better way of branding the image of Ireland abroad than through the mechanism of football. Of course, we've had our moments of tension, not least when we went to Belfast on that unforgettable evening in November 1993, looking for the point which would qualify us for the finals of the World Cup in America the following summer.

For me, that was an extraordinary occasion – and I'm not just referring to the fact that I got into a spat with my old friend Billy Bingham on the touchline. I had known Billy from a long way back, having gone to the same coaching courses at Lilleshall, and it's amusing now to reflect that for a couple of colourful minutes, we were trading some choice expressions that night. It didn't need the two managers to fire up the crowd in Windsor Park, but it just went to show that when it comes to football, the Irish are as passionate as any people in the world.

The pages of this book are testament to that passion. The relationship between north and south in football hasn't always been cordial in the last hundred years or so, but who knows what will happen in the future? Of one thing we can be certain. For millions of people around the world, the quality of the international teams sent out by Dublin and Belfast will continue to showcase Ireland and define the quality of the race like no other medium.

Introduction

As a young boy who prized sport above all else, I was frequently fascinated by the reaction of older people on the terraces in the days when the old Inter-City Cup competition was the biggest show in town.

It was one thing to go to Dalymount Park to watch Bohemians take on their arch-rivals, Shamrock Rovers, or venture down to Tolka Park in the hope of cheering Drumcondra to victory against the powerful teams Cork United put on the pitch in the 1940s. You had only to look at the passion on the faces of the paying customers, however, to realise that when teams like Linfield, Glentoran and Distillery travelled south, the agenda was vastly different.

On those occasions people who were normally separated by local club loyalties had no difficulty in bonding to support the home team, and I was assured that it was no different when southern teams crossed the border – they encountered the same solid wall of opposition on their travels.

Over a span of 65 years, that situation still obtains in Irish club football. And yet having been part of the media entourage which covered both Northern Ireland and the Republic of Ireland on their World Cup escapades in that period, I never cease to be amazed by the fact that as soon as they set down in a foreign clime, the fans are as one in supporting the team in green.

All sport, they say, is tribal, and once the parochial issues are parked, the representative teams sent out by the two national football bodies on the island have invariably enjoyed the goodwill of all sections of the community in the task of showcasing the special qualities of the Irish, in sport just as in commerce. Football in particular has played an important role in projecting Ireland's image abroad, and in a very real way it helped to keep morale high at times when the island was at the centre of international attention for very different reasons.

It was the sheer intensity of those early Inter-City games which attracted me to the north–south divide in football; and inevitably, perhaps, it got me interested in the origins of the fissure which in time would grow into the most notorious split in Irish sport. Much later, I was privileged to meet with many of the men who had been involved in the troubled politics of

Introduction

Irish football in the first half of the twentieth century. Now, at the start of a decade which marks the centenary of so many important events in the making of the new Ireland, I judged it was opportune to revisit the notes of some of those meetings before embarking on the task of writing the first history of Irish football, on a 32-county basis.

In doing so, I have tried to shine a spotlight on some of the contentious issues which have perhaps become blurred with the passage of time and, in the process, debunk some of the myths perpetrated by those who have, on different occasions, sought to dismiss Irish football as a legacy of British rule throughout the island.

That type of rationale ought to have no place in modern Ireland, and if this book assists in clarifying the situation as well as apportioning credit to those who fostered the game in Ireland in its early formative years, it will have served its purpose.

Chapter One

A Difficult Start

In common with the other two major Irish sporting organisations, the Gaelic Athletic Association and the Irish Rugby Football Union, the Irish Football Association was born into a turbulent era for Ireland and Irish people on 18 November 1880. The deprivations of the Great Famine some thirty years earlier were still casting a long shadow over the country, socially and economically, and renewed evidence of strident nationalism suggested even bigger problems in the making for the garrison forces of the British Empire.

The IRFU, formed in 1874 by the middle classes for the middle classes, began as a divided organisation, with a separate administration overseeing the early development of the game north of the border, before the practicalities of the situation demanded a pragmatic fusion of common interests in Dublin and Belfast.

The GAA, with its predominantly rural base, embraced an all-Ireland ethos from its inception in 1884, but its antipathy towards the substantial unionist community in the north-east of the island effectively meant that it, too, was a flawed body for much of its first hundred years in existence.

How ironic it was, then, that the Irish Football Association, the organisation with potentially the broadest mass appeal of the three major power brokers in Irish sport, should split apart relatively quickly and, in a very real sense, mirror the traumatic political developments which brought about the shaping of modern Ireland in 1921. And for all the attempts to reach reconciliation, football politics in Dublin and Belfast were to prove every bit as intransigent as those in Leinster House and Stormont for the remainder of the century.

Research shows that a form of football was played in the Fingal area of north Co Dublin as early as the 1690s. The more popular pastime of the period was Cad, a ball-carrying game which would later be influential in the sequence of events which saw William Webb Ellis introduce the discipline we now know as rugby in 1823.

In England, with the formation of the Football Association in 1863, association football, or soccer, quickly took over as the discipline with the largest following, appealing in the main to working-class people but sufficiently attractive to woo leading educational establishments and, ultimately, the professional classes by the end of the nineteenth century.

Where England had ventured, Scotland soon followed in 1867, and with the formation of the Football Association of Wales in 1877, the structure of the modern game was in place. When football eventually spread across the Irish Sea, the predominant influence was Scottish, rather than English as one might have imagined. The story of how the founding father of the game in Ireland, J.A. McAlery, became interested in football after watching it for the first time during his honeymoon in Scotland, is well documented.

Less evident is the fact that even before the first recorded game in Ireland, at a Belfast venue on 24 October 1878, members of Dublin University rugby club had tried and failed to arrange an exhibition game against Scottish opposition, because they were unable to secure a ground with a playing surface suitable for the new, more skilful game which put a premium on nimble footwork. A second attempt to put down roots for the game in Dublin, again through the primary agency of the Scottish Football Association, also failed. Subsequently the SFA changed focus and the captain of the Caledonians club in Glasgow, J.A. Allen, acting in concert with McAlery, arranged for his club to play another Scottish team, Queen's Park, in an exhibition game at the grounds of the Ulster Cricket Club in Belfast. McAlery, manager of the Irish Tweed Company in the city, was suitably encouraged by the public response, and in his capacity as the motivator-in-chief of the newly formed Cliftonville club, he summoned a meeting in the Queen's Hotel in Belfast, to explore the possibility of establishing a governing body for the code in Ireland.

Two of the four clubs represented at the talks, Cliftonville and Knock, were based in Belfast, with Moyola Park and Banbridge Academy representing Derry and Down respectively. The rules of the Scottish FA were adopted and, for good measure, the Scots donated a sum of £5 to purchase a trophy for the Irish Senior Cup competition. The meeting, it seems, went on longer than expected, and it may have been a portent when the licensing laws of the day forced those present to change rooms, to enable the business of the night to be concluded.

Six years later, the number of clubs affiliated to the IFA had risen to almost forty, and regional associations had been established in Antrim, Down and Derry as well as a mid-Ulster divisional body catering for Tyrone and Armagh. McAlery, a competent player when he wasn't officiating, had reason to be pleased with the progress of the game in the north-eastern corner of the country. The formation of the Irish League championship in 1890 appeared to consolidate that development, although the inclusion of just one provincial team, Milford in Co Armagh, as opposed to seven from Belfast, in the inaugural competition, bespoke the problems encountered by the founding fathers in promulgating their gospel of a new, exciting field game for all classes and creeds.

Nowhere were those difficulties more acute than in Dublin. As the capital city of the country, the willingness of the local citizenry to embrace the new code was central to the prospects of its overall success on the island, a point duly recognised by the Scottish FA in their efforts to concentrate their initial recruitment on Liffeyside. Even at that stage, Trinity was fulfilling its charter as a university which matched academic achievement with a proud sporting tradition, by taking a lead role in the early tortuous advance of the game in Leinster. For all the dedication of that small band of enthusiasts, however, it was not until 1883 that they found worthy opposition in the capital.

That followed the formation of the Dublin Association club at a meeting in Tyrone Place, now Cathedral Street, and the newcomers proved that they were not merely making up the numbers by defeating the university team 4–0 in the first ever Dublin derby on 7 November 1883. Both Trinity and Dublin Association entered the Irish Cup at the start of the 1884–85 season, but as it transpired, they had still much to learn from the better-organised northern teams and failed to advance beyond the first round of the competition.

Sadly, however, Dublin Association disbanded within seven years of their foundation, following a bitter dispute with the governing IFA authorities in Belfast. Seeking to become the first Dublin team to reach the final of the Irish Cup in 1880, they lost 3–2 to Cliftonville in a highly competitive semi-final tie in Belfast, but succeeded in having the game replayed on the grounds that one of the match officials was, in fact, a member of the Cliftonville club. They appealed again after losing the replay 4–2, citing more hometown decisions by the replacement officials, but on this occasion the authorities flatly rejected their claims. Incensed, Dublin Association stated that because of a northern bias by the Belfast authorities, they saw no future for the IFA as it was constituted, and were disbanding.

It was the first public manifestation of the differences between Dublin and Belfast which would ultimately lead to the most notorious split in Irish sport. Right from the start, the composition of the IFA, dominated as it was by personnel from Belfast and district, was regarded as suspect by those who sought to promote the game in the southern part of the country.

Major Spencer Chichester, the first IFA President, whose grandson James would, in time, become Prime Minister of Northern Ireland, was regarded as an affable landed gentleman with little regard for conventional politics. The third son of the Marquess of Donegall, his decision to allocate part of his estate to the Moyola Park club, to enable them to participate in the first Irish Cup competition, was seen as sufficiently magnanimous to warrant his appointment to the highest position in the new organisation.

Chichester's subsequent contribution confirmed him as a well-intentioned individual whose influence was limited to his local area, but the same could not be said of the man who succeeded him in 1897, the Marquess of Londonderry. In what was seen as a nakedly political act, the IFA chose a man who had served as the Lord Lieutenant in Ireland some ten years earlier and was at the forefront of opposition to the second Home Rule Bill in 1893. He was also said to have facilitated the ratification of several agreements between Ulster Tories and Liberal Unionists.

It was seen by the Home Rule lobby as another highly provocative political statement by the IFA who, in 1892, had also vetoed moves to appoint Thomas Sexton, Nationalist MP for West Belfast, as the vice-president of the Association on the grounds that it would send out the wrong signals to those grimly determined to preserve the old order. The effect was to deepen the distrust felt by those in Dublin who believed that, essentially, it was a pro-British organisation.

There is a fallacious belief that the early development of football in Dublin derived exclusively from British garrison forces deployed in the city. Unquestionably, British soldiers played the only field sport they knew on their arrival in Ireland, but not in sufficient numbers to make any real impact on competitive football in either Dublin or Belfast for the remainder of the nineteenth century. More influential was the influence of those Britons who settled in Ireland for commercial reasons and, to an even greater degree, of those in authority in the educational institutions. The latter interpreted the arrival of the new code as an opportunity to foster the physical wellbeing of students who, in many instances, had been denied even the most basic facilities to complement their academic endeavour.

Inevitably, Trinity College was at the heart of this campaign. Initially, cricket was the only sport available to the privileged students at the university, but in 1853 a rugby club was founded there, making it the second oldest in the world. Now, thanks to a decision taken by the authorities, Trinity College embraced football in its Athletic Union in 1883 and joined Dublin Association as the city's representatives in the Irish Cup.

Equally important were the decisions, taken by popular demand, to introduce football to the students at St Vincent's College at Castleknock and Clongowes Wood College in Co Kildare. The importance of educational establishments in promoting the game had been recognised by the IFA from the outset and, a year before Castleknock and Clongowes became involved, it was agreed to institute an Irish Schools Cup competition in 1884. Four of the five participating schools were based in the north-east of the country, with the other in Co Monaghan. Owing to this narrow geographical spread, the opportunities for expansion were limited and the competition lapsed in 1888.

Fortunately, the influence of the two Leinster colleges, joined later by St Helen's, Booterstown, would last much longer. Both had been active as rugby-playing institutions before the arrival of football in Ireland, but they quickly established themselves as equally skilled practitioners in the round-ball game. And, critically, both would contribute significantly to the foundation and development of Bohemians AFC in 1890 after the groundwork had been done by graduates of another educational institution, Kerr's Academy on Dublin's north side.

A second important factor in the dissemination of the gospel of football in Dublin in the latter part of the nineteenth century was the number of privileged young men who attended public schools in England. On their return home, they became active in promoting the new game and helped bestow on it an elitist status which, initially, put it on a collision course with rugby in the challenge of attracting the best of the emerging young sporting talent in the city. Nor should the input of the Boys Brigade in Dublin and Belfast be understated in a long, unbroken term of membership.

In time, the sporting emphasis at both Castleknock and Clongowes colleges would revert to rugby, reflecting a wider trend which saw the middle and upper classes mostly tending to associate themselves with the oval-ball code, and leaving football to recruit its membership primarily from lower down the social order. One of the side effects was to develop a better understanding between officials of the two organisations, but the same could not be said of the interaction with the GAA.

In 1886, just two years after the birth of the organisation in Thurles, GAA delegates voted, unanimously, not to engage in competition with teams operating outside GAA rules. This decision was reversed some nine years later, but the relevant rule was restored in 1902 and stayed in place until its removal in 1971 at the annual Congress in Belfast – an acclaimed shift in stance which was interpreted as an indication of the changed and changing face of the new Ireland.

Even more significant would be their historic decision in 2007 to permit football and rugby games to be played in Croke Park during the construction of the new National Stadium at Lansdowne Road. This was, by far, the most significant gesture in the campaign for sporting ecumenism and, while undoubtedly influenced in part by commercial considerations, it was widely interpreted as a triumph for common sense.

By the end of the 1880s, the IFA could boast that their membership had expanded to 124 clubs, the vast majority of which were based in and around Belfast. Progress was markedly less spectacular in Dublin, where in spite of the limited support of the garrison forces and the first signs of interest by educational establishments, the uptake was at first disappointing.

When the tide turned, the change could be attributed in some measure to the fallout from the Charles Stewart Parnell scandal. Parnell had originally been named as one of the three patrons of the GAA and, in the turmoil which ensued from the affair, the majority of those involved in Gaelic Games in the capital left the organisation to devote their energies to the fledgling football code.

The other, more significant development for sport in Dublin at the time was the foundation of Bohemians AFC, which took place at a meeting in a gate lodge at the Phoenix Park in 1890. While Clongowes and Castleknock colleges could justifiably claim to have been at the heart of the club's early history, there was also a northern influence, testimony to the fact that even at that stage there was a substantial migration from Belfast to Dublin.

If Dublin Association was the first southern club to make significant progress in the Irish Senior Cup, it was Bohemians (or the Gypsies, so named because of their search for a permanent home before settling down at Dalymount Park) who first offered a concerted challenge to the major powers in the north, such as Linfield, Cliftonville, Glentoran and Belfast Celtic. Bohemians were among the first of the Dublin clubs to host an English club team, suffering a heavy reverse against Liverpool in the process, and although an amateur club for the first eighty years of their existence, were also the first to employ the services of a professional coach, John Divers, a former Scotland international player, in 1904.

Freebooters FC rivalled Bohemians for a time as a fortress of the amateur game in Dublin but, unlike their great north city rivals, their influence was relatively short-lived. It was not until 1895, and the launch of Shelbourne FC, that there was a serious threat to Bohemians' reputation as the team northern clubs needed to beat to maintain the status quo in the IFA's pecking order. Born of a meeting at a public house in Ringsend, Shelbourne would in time establish a whole new power base for the game south of the Liffey and beat their arch-rivals to the honour of becoming the first Dublin club to lift the Irish Cup after their 2–0 win over Belfast Celtic in 1906.

As time went on, Shelbourne sought to match the greater cohesion and skills of the more successful northern teams by registering professional players, and in 1912 they emulated the example of Distillery, Belfast Celtic and Glentoran, among others, by forming a limited liability public company with the specific aim of building a stadium capable of accommodating 25,000 spectators. Sadly, the goal was not achieved, and the Shelbourne Sports Company, under the chairmanship of Tom Rowan, was wound up just 11 years later, the first of several failed ventures to improve ground facilities in the capital. No less than Bohemians, however, Shelbourne would make a huge contribution to the game in Dublin, an enviable record flawed only by the strange train of events which saw them suspended from the Irish Free State League in the mid-1930s.

Until the formation of the Leinster Football Association in 1892 eventually began to mobilise political opinion in the greater Dublin area, it was inevitable that the power base of the national structure would remain with the County Antrim Association. And Dublin was not alone in their belief that the numbers issue needed to be addressed. At that point, the North West Association was the third largest constituent body in the IFA, and they too sensed the need for reform. Soon, Derry was joining forces with Dublin in a significant move to threaten the North East monopoly.

The new alliance thought they had made the big breakthrough in the spring of 1900 when, at a conference held in Belfast, the composition of the Council of the IFA was revamped to give the County Antrim Association just six of the 12 seats, with the remainder split evenly between Leinster and the North West. J.F. Sheehan, one of the senior administrators in the Dublin area, was sufficiently impressed by this move to advocate hasty acceptance of the new deal. Speaking at the annual general meeting of the LFA on 6 May 1901, he complimented the IFA chairman A.H. Thompson on the manner in which he had conducted the talks and urged everybody with the best interests of Leinster football at heart to support the amended rule. What wasn't immediately apparent, however, was that the County Antrim Association would continue to have the casting vote in a tied situation, and soon Dublin's lack of faith in the ability of Belfast to legislate on a fair and equitable basis was being articulated more persistently at Council meetings.

Chapter Two

Dublin Awakening

Ironically, it was in Belfast in 1890, in the course of a discussion during the annual general meeting of the Irish Football Association, that the concept of a new organisation to administer the game in Leinster was first mentioned as a practical means of growing football outside of Ulster.

Unimpressed by the take-up numbers in the capital following the formation of the IFA ten years earlier, some northern delegates expressed the opinion that a more intense recruitment drive was needed in the province. That, inevitably, provoked the response from Dublin that football in the capital needed a greater sense of autonomy if it was to thrive, and eventually the County Antrim Association conceded that a separate divisional association, located in Dublin and affiliated to the Belfast-based parent body, would be a positive step in this direction.

In the light of the train of events which would see Dublin pull the plug on the uneasy alliance of north and south some thirty years later, that show of support by the County Antrim Association could be seen as having dramatic consequences, but the reality is that even without this northern intervention and the donation of £50 by the IFA to assist in financing the new structure, the birth of the Leinster Football Association in 1892 would still have happened.

Leinster Nomads, the club born of the demise of Dublin Association FC in 1890, had already echoed the need for a greater voice for Dublin before the topic became current elsewhere; and their delegate Tom Kirkwood Hackett, who was introduced to football during his time as a boarder in a public school in England, was never slow to voice his frustration concerning the existing structures, in addressing north–south issues at Council meetings.

Speaking in the aftermath of a heavy defeat sustained by Ireland in their meeting with England in the British international championship, he upset many of his fellow delegates with the charge that "all this has come upon us because of the prejudice of five men who select the teams, preventing anyone outside the Belfast area being chosen to represent his country".

In making that leading statement, Kirkwood Hackett was no doubt influenced by the fact that his club had eliminated Moyola Park, then a formidable force in the competition, in the first round of the Irish Cup. And while they crashed 6–0 to Distillery in their semi-final tie, Leinster Nomads were sufficiently buoyed to mobilise other clubs in the Dublin area and call a meeting in the Wicklow Hotel to chart a way forward. Those talks on 27 October 1892 brought about the formation of the Leinster Football Association, the biggest single development in the game in Ireland since the launch of the IFA itself, 12 years earlier.

Five senior clubs, Leinster Nomads, Bohemians, Montpelier, St Helen's School and Dublin University, were represented at the meeting, but in addition to the military teams stationed in barracks in the greater Dublin area, a number of smaller clubs also operated on a regular basis in the capital. A further meeting was arranged for 29 November 1892 when, with the Revd Canon Morley of St Helen's School in the chair, the proposed rules of the new Association were approved and permission was granted for the inauguration of a new competition, the Leinster Challenge Cup, in the province.

Among other things, the birth of the LFA resulted in marginally more Dublin players being selected for Ireland teams, but accusations that the national team selectors were prejudiced in favour of players attached to northern clubs would continue for some time. Just two years into the Association's activities, a Leinster Senior League championship was inaugurated, and this was followed soon afterwards by the launch of a Leinster Junior Alliance competition. In the space of just three years, the structure of an efficient, well-ordered organisation had been put in place and, as a consequence, the list of affiliations grew dramatically.

In 1894, thanks in part to the support of clubs in Leinster, the IFA voted by a 64–30 majority to legalise professionalism, but it would be another 11 years before the LFA chose to follow suit. In deciding to make it legal for clubs to pay some of their top players, the parent body said they were doing so in order to rid the game of the practice of clubs making covert payments. It was also thought that it would help to raise the standards of the local game.

With a degree of naivety which astonished many, the IFA reasoned that legitimate payments would stem the flow of players to England. Given the greater funding available in the game in Britain, that was never a realistic prospect. Additionally, the move to legalise payments hinted at problems down the road for clubs which, even before the new legislation was passed, were experiencing difficulties in making ends meet.

Curiously, the players who had moved to English clubs from the North of Ireland were never selected for international duty in those early years. And when they eventually made it into the side, there were, almost certainly, occasions when they wished they hadn't. Even in Belfast, many people were fiercely opposed to men being paid to play football. And it was on the professionals that they vented their anger on those frequent occasions when Ireland were outclassed by their England counterparts. For example, when the Irish team disembarked from the ferry in Belfast after suffering an embarrassing 13–2 defeat by England in the first international game to be played in Sunderland, they found that the number 13 had been scrawled on their travel bags by irate supporters.

Ireland's disappointing record in those early, tortuous years of the IFA's development was made even more unpalatable for Dublin enthusiasts by virtue of the fact that they had to travel to Belfast to watch "home" international games. In all, 27 international fixtures were played in the northern capital before the IFA condescended to entrust the Leinster Association with the responsibility of organising the game against England on St Patrick's Day, 1900.

With no suitable ground of their own, the Leinster authorities saw fit to hire the rugby stadium at Lansdowne Road to showcase the biggest football attraction to be staged in Dublin to that point. The match would later be recalled as a watershed in the evolution of the game in the south, and the degree of excitement it generated can be gauged from a story in the *Freeman's Journal*. This is how the paper set the scene for the big attraction: "As the day fast approaches for the last of Ireland's international matches for the present season against England, interest in the event increases. The game in which his Excellency, Earl Cadogan, Lord Lieutenant of Ireland, has graciously consented to give his patronage, will be the first ever association international played in Dublin and takes place at Lansdowne Road. Judging by the manner in which the tickets for both the stands and the ground are being disposed of, the attendance promises to rival in extent any previously recorded for a similar match in Ireland.

"As to the game, there can be no disguising the fact that it promises to provide the best exhibition of classic football ever witnessed in Dublin. Both teams are good ones – Matthew Reilly, the matchless Portsmouth goalkeeper, Archie Goodall, the Derby County half back, and Gara, the Preston forward, being included in the Irish side, but it must be said that the English team possesses a decided superiority. Mr G.O. Smith, the world's best centre forward, captains the English team."

Apart from Reilly, a former Gaelic footballer and the first Leinster player to sign professional forms for an English club, the only other southern-born player in the team was Dr George Sheehan of Bohemians, and to redress the apparent imbalance, the selectors awarded him the captaincy.

The Irish team wore St Patrick's blue jerseys with a shamrock crest – colours which the Irish Football Association retained until 1931 – and to facilitate people watching the Lord Mayor's parade in Dublin, the kick-off was delayed until 4 p.m. Eventually, some 10,000 spectators made their way to Lansdowne Road but sadly, there was to be no fairytale ending for the Irish. After a game described by the *Irish Times* as the best exhibition of football ever witnessed in Dublin, England triumphed 2–0 and the moulds of history had been set.

A measure of the importance attached to the Boys Brigade in the campaign to popularise the game was the LFA's decision to award them honorary membership. Football was first embraced by the Boys Brigade in Belfast in 1888, and when companies of the Brigade were formed in Dublin three years later, it gave the game on Liffeyside an immediate fillip. Influential, too, in those early years of development, was the role of the British Army garrison forces. At times the relationship between the military and civilian clubs was fraught with tension, the latter claiming that military teams enjoyed an unfair advantage in having so much time to train and practise in facilities attached to their barracks.

Military clubs were formed at the Curragh barracks, the biggest in the country, in 1884, but did not figure initially in any of the Leinster competitions. It wasn't until the dawn of the twentieth century that military teams began to impact on the closing stages of the Leinster Cup, with the Manchester Regiment team, beaten 2–0 by Bohemians in 1912, the last of five Army sides to lose in the final of the competition.

After Leinster Nomads had won the inaugural staging of the Leinster Cup by beating Dublin University 2–1 in the final, Bohemians and Shelbourne took control of the competition and, for the next 24 years, one or other lifted the trophy. Bohemians won it on no fewer than 15 occasions in that period, but their victory in 1903 would prove to be a hollow one. As usual, the Big Two qualified for the final, but Shelbourne objected to the appointment of a local referee, Mr Greer, claiming that he was either a member of, or partial to, Bohemians FC. A Belfast referee was then chosen to take the whistle, but this was also unacceptable to Shelbourne, who protested that unless a cross-channel official was appointed, they would not turn up for the game in three days' time.

Negotiations on the stalemate continued until the eve of the match, at which stage a composite team made up of players from other clubs in the capital was put on stand-by, to play Bohemians in the event of Shelbourne failing to appear. The south city club remained unshaken in its belief, however, and fulfilled their threat on the morning of the game. Plan B was then put into operation, Shelbourne were suspended and Bohemians proceeded to win the hollow match and were awarded the trophy – the only occasion in the long history of the competition that the final had been decided by default.

Clearly upset by the tidings emanating from Dublin, Mr D.W. Foy, chairman of the Irish Football Association, travelled from Belfast to address a meeting of the LFA and promptly warned that no club could dictate to the Council in the appointment of referees for such games. Neither could they scratch from a final. Subsequently, the Council ruled that the club must pay all expenses for the aborted final and would stand suspended until the start of the following season unless they did so. A meeting the following month was told that no payment had been made by Shelbourne and as such, a decision was taken to award the trophy and

winners' medals to Bohemians. In the event, it was not until
27 September, three days before the original deadline expired, that the
sum of £10-14-0, the LFA's estimation of the expenses involved in the
aborted final, was handed over.

The Leinster Cup being the most important prize in football outside
Ulster, the competitive element in the competition was intense. A year
before the Shelbourne debacle, Bohemians had been ordered to hand
back the trophy, pending the outcome of a replay after Tritonville FC had
successfully protested that the replacement referee, the same Mr Greer, had
not played the full, regulation 90 minutes in the final. It mattered little,
however, for the Cup ended up at Dalymount Park yet again.

In the early, formative years of the IFA, protests and counter-protests
dominated the agenda in committee rooms, and it required strong
legislative measures to establish guidelines which would stand the test of
time. William Sheffield, first paid secretary of the LFA, was an important
if frequently controversial personality in the complex co-existence of north
and south, but in 1904 a new name began to emerge in Dublin which
would command even greater respect.

J.A. (Jack) Ryder was a man who, early in life, set himself the task of
promoting football in Leinster in any way he could, and relatively soon his
considerable talents were being channelled into the legislative side of the
game. After at least two letters of resignation, later withdrawn, Sheffield
finally took his leave of the LFA in 1907 and, from a list of more than forty
applicants for the vacancy, Ryder was appointed to a position which would
soon come to be regarded as second only in importance to the secretary of
the national Association.

Ryder would guide the LFA to a position whereby they replaced the
County Antrim Association as the largest constituent body of the IFA in
1912. That wasn't reflected in the composition of the Council in Belfast,
but thanks to Ryder's clarity of purpose and ability to get his message
across to the hierarchy in the IFA, his input into the changing priorities of
Irish football in the first quarter of the twentieth century was profound.
It was he who helped orchestrate the campaign which saw the LFA secede
from the parent body in 1921 and, following his appointment as the first
secretary of the infant Football Association of Ireland, his contribution to

the Association's accession to membership of FIFA in 1926 was equally crucial.

Meanwhile, Freebooters FC illustrated the expanding ambition of Dublin clubs to match the enterprise of longer-established units in Belfast, by obtaining permission for a three-match tour of Belgium; and the ready response of football to requests from charitable trusts in different areas of the country was demonstrated by the manner in which a range of interested parties came together to stage a fundraising game between a north Dublin selection and their counterparts on the other side of the river, in aid of the Marley Disaster Fund.

In spite of the financial difficulties the Leinster Association encountered in its early years, the expansion in numbers which would eventually enable it to overtake the County Antrim Association as the biggest constituent body in the IFA was quite spectacular. The progress achieved at legislative level was suitably complemented by the provision of more playing facilities in the capital. A recurring topic at the annual general meetings of the LFA in the late 1890s was the dearth of pitches in and around the city centre, and eventually it was decided to embark on a lobbying campaign, involving all the public representatives in the region.

The pressure paid off in 1901 when the Commissioners for the Board of Works ruled that a number of football pitches be laid in the area of the Phoenix Park known as the Fifteen Acres. At the time, the Phoenix Park was the largest enclosed public facility of its type in Europe, an oasis of green which brightened the lives of successive generations of Dubliners. The cynics attributed the development to the Commissioners' determination to limit the damage caused by the young people playing football in areas of the park adjoining cricket pitches. The official line was that the new facilities would obviate the risks presented by the erection of unauthorised temporary goalposts and the danger of the improvised structures injuring players and onlookers alike.

Whatever the reasoning behind the move, the new facilities proved an instant success and, a year later, the Commissioners were able to report that there were more than a thousand applications for their use. By 1903, that figure had doubled, and in the course of the 1903–04 season more than three thousand games were played on the grounds in the Fifteen Acres.

Changing rooms were constructed at the site in 1907, but while the LFA can only have been astounded at the growth in the number of fixtures played there, the GAA was significantly less impressed. The area had always been a focal point for the game in Dublin, and in 1896 Michael Cusack railed against "the spectacle of Orange Catholics and West Britons playing football in the Phoenix Park".

The GAA's concern was not without good reason. By the start of 1906, no fewer than 29 of the 31 pitches in the Park were being used for football, and the agitation of the rival Association was such that the Nationalist MP for Co Dublin raised the matter in the House of Commons, arguing that the discrepancy indicated a bias against "Irish Games". Undeterred by a cool response from the House and the concession of a single extra pitch for Gaelic Games at the venue, he tabled a second motion on the Fifteen Acres pitches just a couple of months later, only to be told that the allocation was "fully proportionate to the relative demand".

The GAA's campaign for a bigger share of the facilities in the Park didn't abate, however, and by 1925 the number of football pitches there had reduced to 25. Yet, the Fifteen Acres continued to be a hub of activity at weekends and on long summer evenings. At a time when few clubs had facilities of their own, their role in the development and promotion of the game at Junior and under-age level, was rightly regarded by the LFA as one of the Association's greatest assets.

Chapter Three

Belfast Celtic Arrive

One of the more significant events in the evolution of Irish football in the early years was the foundation of Belfast Celtic in 1891. Almost from the launch of the Irish Football Association some 11 years earlier, the spectre of sectarianism, and the scourge of sport being hijacked to enable religious and political issues to be vented in public, had occupied the attention of the more discerning observers in Dublin and Belfast.

Linfield, one of the enduring powers in Irish football, was quickly perceived as identifying a unionist ethos and a staunch upholder of the Protestant faiths. It was a charter shared by other, lesser clubs in the north-east of the country at a time when there was no discernible voice for Catholicism and the rising tide of nationalism in the young organisation.

The formation of Belfast Celtic at a meeting held in the Beehive public house on the Falls Road would change all that. The founders made it clear from the start that they wished to build a team on the Glasgow Celtic model, a decision which inevitably laid them open to charges of sectarianism. Of the professional players registered with the IFA at the start of the twentieth century, 14 gave their religion as Roman Catholic. Significantly, nine of them played for Celtic, a club predominantly nationalist in its philosophy and almost exclusively Catholic in terms of its general membership. Linfield, on the other hand, listed a wider spread of religions in the personal details of their investors and playing staff. Pointedly, however, they employed no Catholics, and from this base would emerge, as time went on, a religious and political divide to equate with the infamous Celtic–Rangers rivalry in Glasgow.

Within three years of their admission to the Irish League in 1896, Belfast Celtic were embroiled in a major controversy after rioting broke out during their Irish Cup semi-final replay against Glentoran. The trouble was interpreted by one local paper as "marking the entry of the curse of party bigotry into football, thus threatening not only the reputation of footballers but the peace of the community".

Those astute comments would find an echo during the 1900–01 season following rioting by rival supporters in a game between Belfast Celtic and Cliftonville, a club with no obvious political or religious leanings at that point. Just a year later, it was reported in a Belfast paper that fans of Linfield and Belfast Celtic were chased by police down the city's Donegall Road, after throwing stones at each other and exchanging "party tunes".

Political activists on both sides had, it seemed, already identified football as a convenient vehicle to score points in the propaganda war. In the ensuing years they would exploit it mercilessly to inflame the ideological rift which would soon bring about profound change, political and sporting, on the island of Ireland.

It would be unfair to suggest that thuggery on this scale was unique to Belfast. For example, stones were thrown and the pitch was invaded after Bohemians' win over Richmond Rovers in 1899, and six years later Cliftonville's visit to Dalymount Park also ended in scenes of violence. In general, however, it was the intrigue off the pitch rather than the action on it which characterised the period in football in the capital.

At a time when international games were a rarity in Dublin, inter-provincial fixtures involving Leinster and Ulster held unusual appeal. Thus, when four players withdrew from the Leinster team for one such match for what were regarded as spurious reasons, the LFA saw fit to suspend them. But when one of the quartet informed the IFA authorities in Belfast of this development, it led to a stern rebuke for the Leinster officials.

Belfast firmly took the Leinster Association to task for suspending the players without first sending on the relevant documentation to the IFA. Dublin was told, none too politely, that while they were empowered to adjudicate on disciplinary matters in games within their jurisdiction, they had no authority to rule on matters pertaining to inter-provincial games. Grudgingly, the Leinster body was forced into an embarrassing climb-down and it did nothing to improve the relationship between the two sets of officials.

That incident embodied much of the resentment and distrust which stained football on the island at the turn of the twentieth century. They were in evidence again when Leinster delegates, enraged and possibly embarrassed by the ease with which Ulster overpowered their weakened team in Belfast, revisited the matter at their Senior Council meeting on 9 April 1902. That day a Mr H. Duggan gave notice of a motion as follows: "In view of the fact that the Irish Football Association has allowed a sub-committee to interfere with the internal arrangements of the Leinster Football Association, contrary to the rules governing the IFA and also the LFA, we, as a protest, withdraw from membership of the IFA. That we also request the English Scottish and Welsh Associations to take our case before the International Board at its next meeting in June and that all competitions under the jurisdiction of the LFA should be continued as heretofore and further, that we call on all clubs connected with the LFA who are also connected with the IFA, to resign membership of the latter body at once."

An amendment in the name of Mr Larry Sheridan, already emerging as one of the more influential voices in Leinster, that the secretary of the IFA be written to, asking if he had read and studied the implications of Rule 4, governing the relationship between the parent body and its subsidiary organisations, was carried only on the casting vote of the chairman. For the moment at least, the dangers of a split had been headed off, but Belfast can scarcely have been unaware that Dublin's pressure for a realignment of the balance of control in Irish football was growing apace.

Another area of contention was the cut-off point between the professionalism of the game in Ulster and the manner in which it impacted on the amateur ethos of the Leinster FA. It came to a head in August 1902, when the IFA ruled that the LFA should delete the word "amateur" in the description of the Dublin-based organisation in Rule 3 of its handbook. In response to the allegation that Belfast was overstepping the mark in this matter, Mr Jack Reid, the IFA secretary, wrote: "I am directed to point out that the IFA delegated the power of dealing with players to the LFA and that your organisation should be prepared to deal with professional clubs if and when the necessity arises. That is all we require. The IFA has legalised professionalism in Irish football and only desire that all the affiliated Associations are brought into line."

As recorded earlier, part of the IFA's reason for embracing professionalism so quickly was the hope, forlorn at best, that if undercover payments to players were legalised, it would dissuade some of the more talented local players from moving to England or Scotland in pursuit of a livelihood from football. Eventually, clubs like Shelbourne would ensure that some of the better performers in the Dublin area were similarly facilitated, but it would take time for that transition to be reflected in results in the Irish Cup and Irish League competitions.

More obstinate, and certainly a lot more controversial, was the IFA's steadfast refusal to allow games to be played on the Sabbath. Despite some advances in workers' conditions, notably in Belfast and district, the vast majority of those fortunate enough to be part of the workforce at the turn of the twentieth century were required to turn up for duty six days a week. This did not affect the growth of the GAA, which had no such rule, and at that point most of its membership was drawn from the rural labouring class. Sunday games, without any counter-attractions offered by its major competitors, were perhaps the main reason for the spectacular increase in the GAA's activities in the first two years of its existence.

With its Scottish Presbyterian influence, the IFA felt perfectly justified in its stance of excluding even the remotest possibility of football following suit. And even as the northern officials continued to prevaricate, so Dublin's frustration grew to a point where it was already becoming clear that a crisis was imminent. In its stance on Sunday football, the Leinster body had a staunch ally in Belfast Celtic who, shortly after their formation, were rapped on the knuckles for permitting their ground to be used for a Sunday sports meeting.

By 1898, the Leinster FA was sufficiently agitated by the situation to table a proposal at the annual general meeting of the IFA in Belfast demanding that they sanction Sunday fixtures, only to see it rejected out of hand. To aggravate the situation, a counter-proposal, stressing that Sunday football was "very detrimental to the best interests of the game", was approved by a resounding majority.

One of the first moves of the Munster Football Association, on its foundation three years later, was to appeal to the parent body to look again at the prohibition, which was impacting adversely on the growth of the game in the southern part of the country. Even more, perhaps, than their counterparts in Leinster, Munster clubs were seriously disadvantaged by the implications of the six-day working week, which meant that relatively few were able to participate in games on Saturdays. And it handicapped them to a huge extent in their attempt to establish football in a province in which the rival GAA code was at its strongest. Imagine their frustration, then, to be told that while there was no specific rule to prevent Sunday matches, the IFA had invariably prohibited them.

Belfast Celtic's renewed attempt to redress what was seen in most of the country as an intensely naive stance by the parent body, was dismissed with equal contempt; and the anti-Sabbatarians knew for certain that theirs was a lost cause as far as the IFA was concerned when, in response to an enquiry from the Irish League authorities, the parent body ruled that it was unacceptable for clubs to play games on grounds that had been used for Sunday athletics meetings.

That kind of rationale from the decision makers of the IFA in Belfast did nothing to silence the GAA lobby who, in their persistent campaign to discredit football, were wont to describe it as a predominantly British and Protestant game. Whatever they felt about the British jibe, the second part of the smear was an undeniable affront to those of the Roman Catholic faith who embraced the Association game in such large numbers in the more densely populated areas on the island of Ireland. In this context, it is interesting to note that while the Catholic authorities in Belfast had no difficulty in countenancing the prospect of sporting events being held on the Sabbath, their counterparts in Derry inclined to the opposite view.

In spite of the limitations imposed by Saturday fixtures, the game in Leinster continued to flourish. Dalymount Park opened its gates to the public for the first time in 1901 with Timothy Harrington, the Nationalist MP for the Harbour Area in Dublin and a forthright speaker in the Land League movement, performing the ceremonial kick-off for the first game to be played there between Bohemians and Shelbourne. It was the practice at the time for well-known political figures to involve themselves in such ceremonies, and the football fraternity liked to chastise their GAA friends by reminding them that Michael Davitt, one of the original patrons of the GAA, had kicked off a Glasgow Celtic game at Parkhead in 1894. Likewise, Joe Devlin, who championed the interests of Belfast Nationalists, in particular, in the House of Commons, was actively involved in a GAA club in the city while playing a leading role in the affairs of Belfast Celtic at the same time.

With the opening of Dalymount, the Leinster Association could at last claim to have a reputable home for big games in the capital. A year earlier they had been quoted what were described as "exorbitant terms" when they sought to hire the Catholic University ground in Sandymount for the final of the Leinster Cup. Eventually, the match was played at the City and Suburban Ground at Jones Road, the site of what would later become Croke Park. And a crowd representing gate receipts of £44 saw Shelbourne lift the trophy after a 1–0 win over Freebooters.

The withdrawal of some of the British garrison forces in Ireland, to serve in the Boer War, had a negative impact on the development of Irish football in some areas. However, with Shelbourne emerging to provide credible opposition for Bohemians, the competitive element was finely honed in the Leinster Senior Cup, and this in turn helped bridge the gap in standards between them and the major Belfast clubs.

Shelbourne's insistence that a cross-channel referee be appointed to take charge of their Leinster Cup final date with Bohemians in April 1903 and their subsequent suspension after they refused to accept the LFA's ruling against the additional cost of doing so, testified to the intense rivalry between the Big Two in Dublin. And that rivalry was taken to a higher level later in the same year when Shelbourne followed their north city adversaries into the Irish League. Now these clubs had to juggle with their Leinster Cup and League commitments to fit in games against clubs like Linfield, Glentoran, Distillery and Cliftonville, and while the results were initially disappointing, it served the purpose of raising standards in the southern part of the country.

Differences between Dublin and Belfast officials still persisted, however, and they manifested themselves again early in 1903 when, at an IFA Council meeting at which Dublin was not represented, it was decided to cancel Ulster's annual inter-provincial games against Leinster. Given the importance of these matches in raising funds for the LFA, it was a serious setback, and while the decision was promptly reversed on appeal, it underlined the problems lying just beneath the surface.

We have seen how the development of football in Munster was hampered by the militant stance of the GAA in its efforts to prevent the code taking root in the province, a campaign which expanded to the point where local newspapers were pressurised into largely ignoring the game. A measure of the Munster FA's difficulties was that they were forced to apply for a loan of £7 to ensure that they were in a position to fulfil their scheduled game against Leinster in 1903. Statistically, the number of clubs in Munster didn't even begin to compare with the figures in Leinster or Ulster, but it has to be recorded that many unaffiliated teams are said to have existed in Cork and District at the time.

Ulster's lukewarm interest in preserving their annual meetings with Leinster continued to be a source of frustration in Dublin, but the decision to stage Ireland's meeting with Scotland at Dalymount Park in 1904 was generally interpreted as a genuine attempt by the IFA to keep their southern colleagues on-side. It was the first international match to be awarded to the capital since the 2–0 loss to England four years earlier, and Belfast officials were sufficiently impressed by the match-day arrangements – the game ended in a 1–1 draw – to invite the Leinster body to host the next two home fixtures against Scotland in 1906 and 1908. Significantly, however, the plum fixture with England, regarded as the highpoint of the Irish season, did not return to Dublin until 1912.

Chapter Four

Steady Growth

Within the first decade of the twentieth century, Dublin and Belfast were both able to report that participation in the sport, on and off the pitch, was gathering momentum. However, because of the game's origins in Ireland, northern officials still tended to regard Leinster, and to an even greater degree Munster, as junior partners, and this did nothing to alleviate growing doubts in the south about the validity of some of the figures being submitted as official by the Irish Football Association.

According to the IFA, the Co Antrim Association was still far and away its biggest constituent body, a statement which stoked fires of resentment down south. Leinster believed that, with the connivance of the IFA, the figures presented by the Co Antrim Association were being artificially boosted to tilt the balance of power towards the north. And to prove that distrust was mutual, northern delegates promptly accused Dublin of indulging in precisely the same practice.

Hurt by that statement, the LFA Council, at its meeting on 5 December 1906, adopted a resolution that "owing to the repeated insinuations being put forward, regarding bogus clubs in Leinster, the IFA be asked to form a Commission to enquire into the status of all clubs under its jurisdiction, the Commission to sit in Dublin to take evidence of the existence of clubs in the Leinster area". In the event, it was an invitation which was never accepted.

In terms of spectator interest, the Leinster Association claimed that the numbers watching senior games in the province had increased dramatically. In 1905, for example, they reported that some 9,000 fans, just a thousand short of the figure returned for the Irish Senior Cup final in the same year, had turned up for the Leinster Cup final in which Bohemians defeated Shelbourne

1–0. That was a reassuring statistic for Dublin officials who contended that the stubborn refusal of Belfast to countenance any suggestion of finding a way around the Irish Sunday Closing Act, introduced in 1878 and strengthened in 1906, by which pubs were required to shut on the Sabbath in rural areas and most large towns, was disadvantaging them in their efforts to compete with the GAA for the allegiance of the general public.

Sport was predominantly a male preserve in that era, although IFA and Leinster officials made a conscious effort to attract women to their games, at first offering to admit them free of charge to football grounds. This concession was subsequently dropped, possibly because the response was so positive. For example, on the occasion of the Irish Cup final in 1905, some 200 ladies, chosen from the crowd, were introduced to the President of the IFA, Lord Londonderry. Another attraction was the opportunity of enjoying afternoon tea with the Lord Mayor of Belfast.

International games, particularly the annual fixture against England, were a valuable showcase for the development of the game in Ireland. Even more importantly, they provided much of the IFA's early funding at a time when the finances of the Association were still pretty fragile. As noted earlier, results in the meetings with the English were rarely encouraging, but it still did not detract from the interest or, perhaps more accurately, the curiosity of local fans, on those occasions when England arrived in town. An interesting statistic shows that in March 1904, Belfast hosted two international fixtures on the same day. The football game against England at Cliftonville's ground attracted 16,000 spectators, whereas the visit of the Welsh rugby team to Balmoral enticed only 5,000 through the gates. It could be argued that meetings with England in any sporting discipline were always likely to be more marketable than those involving Wales or Scotland, but the steep discrepancy in the public response to those two games was still revealing.

At a lower level, Leinster's inter-provincial games against Ulster, together with Shelbourne's frequent Leinster Cup final meetings with Bohemians, continued to be the LFA's principal source of funding, with the occasional international fixture in Dublin a valuable if highly irregular bonus. The northern teams generally proved stronger in the inter-provincial series, but the home team's 1–1 draw at Dalymount Park in January 1907 was interpreted as encouraging. An interesting postscript was provided when the captain of the Leinster team, Mr H.A. Sloane, reported one of his players, Mr J. Whelan, for refusing to change positions when requested to do so during the game. The LFA Council found in Sloane's favour and Whelan was cautioned about his future conduct.

A more significant detail emerged later that year when the LFA's full-time secretary, William Sheffield, resigned after his failure to affiliate a number of local clubs to the IFA had raised some accountancy problems. Sheffield, who had earlier resigned of his own volition, only to change his mind just days later, would subsequently prove an additional divisive influence in the relationship between Dublin and Belfast.

Sheffield sought, unsuccessfully, to reclaim his old position before Jack Ryder was appointed to replace him in May 1907. If, at that point, the Leinster hierarchy felt that they had seen the last of their former secretary, they were wrong. When the LFA sought to secure a loan of £200 from the parent body, Belfast enraged their southern colleagues by insisting that Sheffield be appointed as one of the two southern trustees for any such deal. And they incensed them still further shortly afterwards in overruling a decision of the LFA and insisting that he be co-opted on to the Council in Dublin.

The discredited former secretary was seen by the IFA as somebody who could help them rein in the more militant members of the LFA, in the course of settling some old scores with those who had forced him from office. Jack Ryder was instructed to reply to Belfast in suitably indignant fashion and point out to them the reasons why he was not co-opted on to the Council in the first instance.

On 13 April 1909, a meeting of the LFA Council was informed of an IFA directive "that the LFA have until the following day to co-opt Mr Sheffield as a member of their Council and if they fail to do so, the said Council of the LFA will stand suspended". Faced with this ultimatum, the LFA capitulated in the matter. Ryder responded "that in accordance with the directive of the IFA, we hereby co-opt Mr Sheffield as a member of this Council but having regard to the statement of the Honorary Treasurer, we consider that it is against the best interests and purity of football". This was promptly followed by the resignations of six members of the LFA Council, but since that would have left only four members of the Council in their posts, the resignations were not accepted.

Sheffield failed only narrowly to be elected to the Council in his own right, at the annual general meeting of the LFA, held in the Molesworth Hall on 15 May 1909, but soon afterwards his support base in Belfast crumbled. After considering a letter from the IFA, stating that the saga was now at an end, the LFA Council passed the following resolution: "That having regard to the irregularities disclosed in Mr Sheffield's letters read at the annual general meeting, this Council suspends him from taking part in the management of football in Leinster." It represented the final humiliation of a man who had once been central to the development of the game in the greater Dublin area, at a time when the LFA was still only putting its administrative structures into place.

Billy Lacey from Co Wexford, regarded by many as the greatest Irish footballer of his generation, enjoyed an outstanding international career which started in 1909 and didn't end until some 21 years later. For all his talent on the pitch, however, he was regarded as something of a thorn in the flesh of officialdom on occasions, and in 1907, at a time when he was a registered professional player with Shelbourne, he was suspended after turning out without permission for another club, Herbert Park, in a friendly game against Worcester Regiment. In this instance, the IFA backed Dublin's stand, but it was something of an exception in the relationship of the two bodies at the time.

Soon afterwards, the IFA refused to accept what they perceived as an unduly short suspension imposed by the LFA on another Herbert Park player, Michael Nugent. They informed Dublin that because of the gravity of the offence allegedly committed by Nugent, they could not endorse a ban of less than three months. This stance drew a sharp response from the LFA, who stated that on the evidence presented to them, the action suggested by Belfast was both unhelpful and inappropriate.

By and large, however, it was finance and a perceived reluctance by the IFA to lend a helping hand to those in the southern part of the island, which occasioned the most bitterness between them. Leinster's controversial request for a loan of £200 proved fruitless when, after the row over the proposed trustees for the deal had subsided, the parent body cited reports that Bohemians and Shelbourne intended to withdraw from the Leinster Cup as another reason why the LFA might not be in a position to repay it. Games involving the two big clubs in Dublin provided the Association with the majority of its funding, and while the rumoured boycott of the competition didn't materialise, it did nothing to improve the chances of securing the loan. And it was followed soon afterwards by the IFA's refusal to reduce the affiliation fees paid by the LFA.

Away from the political manoeuvres and the posturing being adopted in Dublin and Belfast, football continued to make impressive progress in the new century. Windsor Park, the most modern football stadium in the country at that point, was officially opened as the new venue for international football in Belfast in 1905. Appropriately, Cliftonville, who had provided the facilities for most of Ireland's early international games, played Linfield in the first game at the new venue. It was at Cliftonville's ground in 1891 that some of the first floodlit football games anywhere in the world were played, with rows of lights, suspended in close proximity across the pitch, enabling winter fixtures against Distillery and the Black Watch to be played in late evening. A highly sceptical public was not impressed, however, complaining that the players in the centre of the ground "appeared to be having all the fun"; but in spite of a summary ending to the bold experiment, it fanned the imagination of those who, more than half a century later, would help revolutionise football with similar starting times.

We have seen how Billy Lacey was already embarked on his remarkable international career in 1909, joining his Shelbourne club-mate Val Harris in the Ireland team, but in Belfast other distinguished names were emerging. Billy McCracken, the man responsible for the offside rule being introduced, was among the most prominent of these, but it was without doubt the famous Scott family who were the game's main attraction in the northern capital. Tom Scott of Cliftonville, the eldest of three talented brothers, won 13 caps between 1894 and 1900; Billy Scott made 25 international appearances in spells with Linfield, Everton and Leeds City, while Elisha Scott, a third distinguished goalkeeper, took part in no fewer than 31 Ireland games.

In spite of suffering a shock defeat by Derry Celtic in an Irish Cup tie in 1905, Linfield remained the most successful club in the country, but in Dublin it was Bohemians and to a lesser extent Shelbourne who set the standards. Befitting their status as the longest-established club in Dublin,

Bohemians reached the Irish Cup final in 1895, 1900 and 1903, only to lose in turn to Linfield, Cliftonville and Distillery.

That was enough to tax the faith of even the most optimistic members of the club, and their sense of frustration was heightened when Shelbourne, after going down 3–0 to Distillery in the 1905 final, became the first Dublin team to lift the trophy, outplaying Belfast Celtic 2–0 the following year. The Irish Cup was the competition which defined the season for every club, and it is a measure of the interest generated by Shelbourne's progress to the final, that they were accompanied to Belfast by a train load of supporters. It helped boost the gate receipts to £427, a huge figure at the time, and the following day the *Evening Herald* reported that blazing tar barrels and bonfires greeted the winners as they paraded the trophy around Ringsend and Sandymount on their return from Belfast.

That marked a significant shift in the battle for control in Irish football, and the surge to the top by Leinster was confirmed in 1908 when, for the first time, Bohemians and Shelbourne met in an all-Dublin final. Shelbourne's 5–1 win over Distillery was adjudged the better of the two semi-final ties – Bohemians defeated Belfast Celtic in the other tie – but in spite of their rating as favourites, the south city team lost 3–1 in a replayed final. It provided some compensation for Bohemians' misfortune in their earlier appearances in the final, but for Shelbourne, revenge was close at hand.

After Bohemians had lost the 1909 final to Cliftonville, Dublin's Big Two met again in the final in 1911, and on this occasion it was Shelbourne who emerged victorious on a 2–1 scoreline. To compound southern joy, Chapelizod won the Irish Junior Cup in the same year, and for the first time the two major trophies in Irish football rested in the capital.

Quick to record the significance of this double, Jack Ryder noted in his report to the annual general meeting of the LFA in the Molesworth Hall: "It is with pride that we are able to commit to the record book another great season for our Association. Now our challenge is to use these victories to consolidate our position at the top of the game in Ireland." He wasn't to know it then, but within another ten years Shelbourne and Bohemians would be chasing a different trophy, the pristine Football Association of Ireland Challenge Cup.

Chapter Five

Clubs Revolt

The rising tide of nationalism that led to the Easter Rebellion in Dublin in 1916 would later also help bring about the most contentious split in Irish sport; and in hindsight increasing attention would be focused on the operations of the Irish Football Association in the pre-Rebellion period.

With society in the north-east of the island becoming increasingly polarised, football grounds quickly emerged as the arenas in which those differences found expression. With the occasional exception, the opening years of the twentieth century proved relatively trouble free, but as the campaign for Home Rule gathered momentum, so the interventions of police to separate the vociferous factions on big match days took on an element of inevitability.

Ever since its foundation in 1891, Belfast Celtic was identified as projecting the nationalist ethos in Belfast. Linfield, initially based in the Sandy Row area in the city, was likewise seen as the symbol of unionism, while at the same time embodying the best in Irish football. And, in their unique ways, the two clubs contributed much to enriching the lives of tens of thousands of people in the city and district.

In March 1910, for instance, the rivals met in a benefit match for injured and retired players with Joe Devlin, the Nationalist MP for West Belfast, performing the ceremonial kick-off. The same ritual had been observed two years earlier, when local police authorities were able to report that the fixture had occasioned little or no trouble. Soon, however, the mood would change. The progression of the Home Rule Bill in the House of Commons, and the loss of the House of Lords veto, inflamed unionists just as surely as it encouraged those on the other side of the sectarian divide to believe that long-cherished aspirations could soon be realised.

Chapter Five

By the start of 1912, life in some areas of Belfast was in turmoil, as illustrated by two incidents when Winston Churchill visited the city to speak in support of Home Rule. Even at that early stage of his political career, Churchill was a controversial personality, and with his stance on the third Home Rule Bill he obviously antagonised the unionist community. And that sense of outrage was heightened when he chose to deliver a keynote address at Celtic Park, home of Belfast Celtic.

Even as the Royal Irish Constabulary finalised their preparations for what was obviously going to be a vital test of law and order in the city, rumours spread that loyalist workers had been armed by some of the bigger Belfast employers, in anticipation of trouble at the political rally. In the event, Churchill narrowly escaped injury when the mob attempted to overturn his car outside Celtic Park; and later, when he was leaving his hotel at the start of his return journey to London, he was again left shaken and distressed after a hostile crowd converged on him. Unsurprisingly, that unsavoury conduct rang alarm bells for the police authorities in Belfast, and they eyed the start of the 1912–13 season, especially the games between Linfield and Belfast Celtic, with growing apprehension.

In the event, the Big Two clashed on the opening day of the new season and a volatile situation was worsened, undeniably, when Edward Carson, the Dublin-born leader of the Irish Unionist party, visited Belfast to address members of some unionist clubs, just 48 hours before the game. Carson, who spent much of his early life in Dublin at 80 Merrion Square – the building which, ironically, would later become the headquarters of the Football Association of Ireland – was reviled by Celtic fans as much as he was revered by those in the opposite camp and his intrusion, at that particular time, was designed to send out all the wrong signals.

As it transpired, the game attracted a huge crowd of close on 20,000, the biggest in the history of the Irish League to that point. It was, according to reports, a warm sunny day and at least some of the crowd were said to have been attracted to Celtic Park by the Air Show at the nearby Balmoral grounds. Others were almost certainly there to provoke trouble but, according to the match report of the English referee who was brought over to officiate at the game, the first half was largely mundane, in spite of Linfield taking a 1–0 lead.

Clubs Revolt

The trouble started with a number of fist fights on the terraces during the half-time break, and when police intervened, they too became targets for the rival factions. Thereafter, the violence spread on to the pitch and, while the teams were still locked in their dressing-rooms, gunfire was heard. With the violence ongoing, some fifty people were taken to hospital with injuries of varying gravity. In the direct aftermath of the riot, troops were dispatched to the nearby shipyards to contain any violence which might erupt there. Predictably, the unionist press portrayed Celtic fans as the culprits, while the nationalist *Irish News* accused those cheering for Linfield of fanning the flames of sectarian anger. Even by the lowest standards of the violence which stained the image of the game intermittently over the following years, that was a notorious day in the annals of Irish football and a presage of difficult times ahead for the police and civil authorities.

The RIC Commissioner for Belfast warned his superiors in Dublin Castle that all future games involving Belfast Celtic would warrant special policing, and he called for urgent discussions on crowd control at all games in the city. Within a week of the riot, the Irish League notified all clubs that in future no banners, flags or other emblems would be permitted at any football ground under their jurisdiction. A few months later, in December 1912, the League's Management Committee ruled that "in all future League and City Cup games where revolver firing is resorted to by spectators, such games are to be abandoned and the replays to take place behind closed gates".

Earlier in 1912, Derry had experienced its own moments of terror during a game in aid of charity in which Institute, drawn from the Presbyterian Working Men's Institute, opposed Derry Guilds, made up of members of the Derry Catholic Young Men's Society. The Protestant *Londonderry Sentinel* reported that following a foul on a Guilds player, a fight broke out between two players from each team, before eventually spreading to engulf the general body of spectators. Conceding that the trouble emanated from a fracas involving players, the Nationalist *Derry Journal* blamed the Institute team for refusing to continue the game and thus escalating the trouble. The *Journal* reporter at the match rejected the suggestion that the Institute players had been penned for two hours in their dressing-room by the home crowd, counter-charging that there was no violence until a Protestant mob arrived from the Fountain end of the city, interspersing bouts of stone throwing with shouts of "No Home Rule".

The sequel was that six months later, the Presbyterian clubs in Derry and District broke away from the existing administrative structures in the city to form their own Alliance competition, effectively ensuring that football in the region would be played on sectarian lines. Quick to seize the high moral ground, the *Derry Journal* was soon referring to the new tournament as the "City of Derry and District (Protestant) Alliance". It wasn't until early the following year that the IFA moved to resolve what was seen as an increasingly embarrassing situation for the Association. Far from improving matters, however, they merely compounded the problem by allowing the Alliance to remain in existence, on the somewhat naive condition "that it would cater for both sides".

One of the by-products of the saga was that it served to illustrate the religious as well as the political divide in the game in the northern part of the country. Two years earlier, at the annual general meeting of the IFA, attempts to have the AGM staged at different centres around the country or, more realistically, alternate the venue between Belfast and Dublin, were successfully resisted by the County Antrim Association lobby. Belfast Celtic interpreted that action as "an attempt by Protestant Belfast to prevent the Association's most important meeting of the year going to Roman Catholic Dublin".

Meanwhile the Leinster FA, monitoring the sectarian strife in the north from afar, had problems of its own. Owing to the General Strike of 1913 fewer games were being played in the capital and fewer people were turning up to watch them. Nor was football immune from the fallout from the strike: in the build-up to a game between Shelbourne and Bohemians, to mark the opening of a new ground in Sandymount, the *Irish Worker*, the official organ of the Irish Transport and General Workers Union, named two players, one from either side, as strike breakers.

Through the medium of their newspaper, ITGWU officials urged people to boycott the event. On the day of the game, trams conveying supporters to Sandymount were stoned, and people were attacked as they attempted to enter the ground. It was only after the sound of a revolver shot was heard that a semblance of order was restored, but this in turn led to further rioting in the city. With some justification, perhaps, Belfast was able to say that it was no longer safe to send either players or officials to the capital.

If anything, the competitive element in the tournaments organised by the Leinster FA was more pronounced than in the corresponding grades in the north, a point which was emphasised in a communiqué from the Referees Committee in Dublin. Ever since the formation of the IFA in 1880, the relationship between its Council and referees had been a difficult one, with match officials frequently complaining that they got little or no protection on match days. Eventually, they were forced to write to the Council requesting financial assistance in any legal action members of their Association might take against offenders, at a time when the number of assaults was showing a dramatic increase. The response when it came, however, was only mildly encouraging. While stressing that Council was always ready to assist match officials in the task of minimising attacks on them, it emphasised that before any legal action was contemplated by the Referees Committee, the full facts of any such incident should be forwarded to them.

Aside from politics and religion, other ominous clouds were looming on the horizon for the IFA at the time. And the most serious of them surfaced in 1912 in the aftermath of Linfield's refusal to agree a fee with the IFA for the rental of Windsor Park for big games. Whereas Linfield were insisting on getting 20 per cent of the gross receipts, the Association was prepared to pay only half that amount. A not dissimilar situation existed in Dublin, where Bohemians were occasionally trenchant in their dealings with the LFA on their terms for the hire of Dalymount Park. That was the core issue in the rising climate of discontent, but it also embraced other perceived grievances, such as direct representation for clubs on the Council of the IFA.

These disagreements hardened the perception of the professional clubs that the amateur officials who ran the game, north and south, were out of touch with reality; and to the thinly veiled astonishment of both the IFA and its constituent bodies, the professional clubs announced that they were seceding from the Association, to constitute a new governing body for the sport in Ireland.

Chapter Five

Although some in the inner circle of the IFA may, possibly, have anticipated the clubs' precipitous action, the news came as a bombshell to the authorities in Dublin, and their reaction was to convene a special Council meeting on 27 February 1912. The agenda consisted of just one item, a discussion on the following resolution passed by the IFA: "Having observed what the Committee believe to be an official report of the proceedings at a meeting held on Wednesday, 21st inst, at which the following clubs, Glentoran, Distillery, Belfast Celtic, Derry Celtic, Shelbourne, Glenavon and Cliftonville are reported to have been represented, and having further observed an advertisement published under the name of M.J.T. Gibbs as Secretary pro tem, that a new Association to govern Irish football was formed by the said clubs on that date and that the said clubs invited applications from clubs and referees, although at the time, the clubs represented at the said meeting, were members of the I.F.A. Ltd, the Committee has decided that the said clubs so represented, stand suspended as of this date, from taking part in Association football or football management under the jurisdiction of I.F.A. Ltd." As a gesture of support for the beleaguered parent body, the Leinster Council resolved as follows: "The Council of the L.F.A. desires to assure the I.F.A. Ltd of their continued support in the present crisis and, further, that the (Leinster) Association considers it its duty, to urge upon clubs and players under their jurisdiction, the necessity for remaining loyal to the I.F.A. Ltd."

Ironically, Linfield and Bohemians, who as owners of Windsor Park and Dalymount Park respectively were at the centre of the original grounds rental dispute, had earlier settled their differences with the authorities and were not among the rebel clubs suspended by the IFA. In consequence of Shelbourne's inclusion in the list, the LFA decided that the second semi-final of the Leinster Cup, in which Shelbourne were scheduled to meet Bohemians on 9 March, could not be played. As an alternative, it was agreed to play an exhibition game on that date between Bohemians and a Rest of Leinster selection but, for obvious reasons, this proved impractical. After several cross-channel clubs had decided against filling the vacant date, Bohemians were given permission to open negotiations for a fixture with Glasgow Rangers on a fifty-fifty split basis.

Clubs Revolt

The suspended clubs later decided to stage their own Irish Cup competition. A new trophy was purchased, a curtailed draw was made and, eventually, Belfast Celtic defeated Glentoran 2–0 in the final. As a mark of respect to those who had perished in the *Titanic* disaster just months earlier, the players wore black crepe armlets in this game. Within a matter of months, the clubs had won the right for direct representation on the IFA Council; it was agreed that a sub-committee of seven would manage the Irish Cup; the ground rental issue was resolved, and the suspensions were lifted in time for the start of the 1912–13 season. The replacement Irish Cup was not lost to football: it is now offered for competition in the Gold Cup tournament for Irish League clubs.

In the IFA's greatest hour of need, the Leinster Association had stood shoulder to shoulder with them in what turned out to be a futile effort to restrict the clubs' influence in the corridors of power. Soon, however, old animosities began to surface once more, with the LFA railing against the parent body's decision to exclude St James Gate from the draw for the Irish Cup. Dublin demanded an immediate apology for what they deemed a high-handed action in dismissing a club which had competed in the competition since the 1911–12 season; but, in the event, none was forthcoming. Later, the IFA suggested that the relevant rule be amended and entry to the Irish Cup be open to all Irish League and Leinster League clubs. Shortly afterwards, it was agreed that a qualifying competition be inaugurated to facilitate entry to the premier knockout competition.

Chapter Six

Wartime Problems

There were many who viewed the increasingly tense coalition of north and south in the Irish Football Association as a barometer of developments in conventional politics and they can have been left in little doubt of impending change after 15 March 1913, when the international game against Scotland at Dalymount Park descended into something of a shambles.

Three earlier meetings with the Scots at the same venue had gone off without any real problems, but the 1913 fixture, awarded to Dublin by the IFA to mark the 21st anniversary of the founding of the Leinster Football Association, did not fit into this category. The early signs were not encouraging: a local civilian band refused to perform what they termed the British National Anthem; and the low-key reception accorded the Lord Lieutenant in Ireland, the guest of honour at the game, struck a raw chord with the unionists in the crowd.

A newsman at the game noted: "The band of the West Ridings played the National Anthem, Ireland's own bands apparently having some difficulty about the inclusion of God Save the King in their programme. This is another example of that spirit which cannot allow even sport to be uncontaminated by hostility to everything dear to the King's loyal subjects." Enthusiasts hoping to witness Ireland's first win at Dalymount left disappointed after Scotland held on for a 2–1 success, and it would be another 48 years before the Scots' national team set foot in Dublin again.

Given that Ireland had won only two of their 26 earlier games against Scotland, supporters of the Ireland team were not unfamiliar with the experience of losing to the Dark Blues. What made this defeat a bitter one to swallow was the fact that just four weeks earlier at Belfast's Windsor

Park, the same Irish team had defeated England with two goals from Billy Gillespie of Sheffield United. The English had never been beaten in 31 earlier games against Ireland, but it was the goals for and against columns which conveyed the true discrepancy between the teams in that period. For all the fire and enthusiasm they took into the annual fixture against England, Ireland amassed the paltry total of 19 goals in that period while conceding the staggering tally of 149.

With just 14 victories in 90 fixtures overall by the end of the 1912–13 season, 11 of those wins coming against Wales, the lack of success at international level was a serious blight on the development of football in Ireland.

We have seen how the blinkered judgement of the national team selectors, exclusively from Belfast and District in the early years, enraged Dublin just as much as the refusal to alternate the venue for Council meetings between the two major cities on the island or the award of a mere handful of international fixtures to Dalymount Park. There is little doubt that the LFA and its players were short-changed in all three of those areas; just as surely, however, other divisional bodies like the North West and the Fermanagh and South Tyrone Football Associations also felt disadvantaged in their dealings with the parent body and its perceived fixation in preserving the primacy of the County Antrim Association.

Heading into the 1913–14 championship, the feeling was that notwithstanding the most recent disappointing Scottish result in Dublin, Ireland were poised for a big title charge. As ever, however, much would depend on how they handled an England team motivated by the desire to avenge that fall from grace at Windsor Park the year before.

The optimism pervading the Irish camp stemmed from the outstanding club form of key members of the team. Mickey Hamill, a match-winner in any company on his day, was running into form with Manchester United, and then there was the formidable partnership of Billy Gillespie and Billy Lacey up front. Gillespie, born in Derry, played with Leeds and Sheffield United, with whom he secured an FA Cup winners' medal in 1925 before returning to his roots to coach Derry City for nine years.

Of Lacey it can be said that he was one of the brightest talents in Irish and British football for the greater part of thirty years. From Wexford,

he moved to Dublin to join Shelbourne at the age of 16, and after
that he had spells with Everton and Liverpool, sojourns with Belfast
United and Linfield during the First World War, and then further stints
with Shelbourne and Liverpool before ending his playing career at
Cork Bohemians. Capped for the first time in 1909, he made his last
international appearance in 1930, and when his playing days were done, he
was employed as trainer/coach of the national team for a spell in the 1930s.

Val Harris, another revered name in the capital, was a prominent
member of Dublin's Gaelic football team before moving, like Lacey, to
Shelbourne. A member of the team which became the first from Dublin to
secure the Irish Cup in 1906, he won 20 caps before the outbreak of war in
1914 effectively ended his international career. His playing days were over
by the time the FAI came into being, but subsequently he too became a
member of Ireland's technical team.

And then there was Patrick O'Connell. A Dubliner from the north city
suburb of Drumcondra, he played in Junior club football with Strandville,
somehow managing to elude the attention of both Shelbourne and
Bohemians in his early days before moving up north to align himself with
Belfast Celtic. It was the start of an extraordinary career as a centre-half
which, long after his death, continues to fascinate football historians.

From Belfast he moved to England, winning two international caps with
Sheffield Wednesday before arriving at Manchester United via Hull City.
It is a measure of O'Connell's leadership qualities that, on his arrival there,
he was appointed club captain, and while the club only narrowly escaped
relegation at the end of the 1914–15 season, he might well have become
a household name there but for the suspension of club football for the
duration of the First World War.

In all, he spent just three seasons in English football, but it was his
post-war career in Spain which ensured his place among the more
significant personalities of the period. After a brief spell as player/manager
of Ashington FC, the local club of Jack and Bobby Charlton many years
later, he moved to Spain in 1922 to manage Racing Santander, replacing
Englishman Fred Pentland, and later Real Betis, whom he led to their first
and only success in the Spanish First Division championship.

It was on the back of that achievement that, in 1935, he succeeded to one of the top managerial posts in Spain, taking control of Barcelona FC at a time when the Spanish Civil War was already looming and the very survival of the club was under threat. O'Connell, known locally as Don Patricio, was credited with saving it from extinction by taking the club on an extended tour of Mexico and North America.

As it transpired, only a handful of Barcelona players returned home, the remainder choosing to stay in the United States rather than risk the wrath of Francoist forces. O'Connell was one of those who came back to Spain, and his role in the episode is acknowledged in the history of Barcelona FC and commemorated by a bronze bust in the club's museum in the Nou Camp stadium.

No less than Lacey, Gillespie and Hamill, O'Connell would figure prominently in Ireland's opening game of the championship in 1914. Fortunately, that first fixture was against Wales, traditionally the weakest of the teams on the British mainland, and while the Welsh benefited from home advantage, the Irishmen were up for the challenge. At a time when substitutions were still a long way off, the visitors were forced to play without Harris, the team captain, for the entire second half, but they still held on for a 2–1 win with the goals coming from Gillespie and Sam Young.

Next up was England at Ayresome Park, Middlesbrough, just four weeks later, and while Harris hadn't fully recovered from the injury sustained at Wrexham, the Irish travelled with more hope than usual. To beat England in Belfast was one thing, but to repeat that success in front of a partisan home crowd would require a lot of character and commitment. However, showing no nervousness they proceeded to dominate England in a manner which surpassed all expectations, with Lacey (2) and Gillespie supplying the goals in a 3–0 victory.

After years of recurring defeat, Ireland were now within sight of winning the championship for the first time, and the public response was such that Cliftonville FC, who had originally been selected to host the final game in the series against Scotland, graciously permitted the fixture to be switched to Windsor Park, where the ground capacity was considerably larger. Harris was sufficiently recovered from injury to take his place in the half-back line but, unfortunately, Gillespie was unavailable. As it transpired, his loss deprived the attack of its earlier cutting edge and it showed as the Irish struggled to convert their territorial supremacy into goals on a wet, wild afternoon.

In the end, Young's goal was sufficient to earn a 1–1 draw and secure the title which had had once looked so hopelessly out of reach. Had it not been for Gillespie's absence, they might well have taken the Triple Crown too. That disappointment didn't dampen the jubilation of the crowd, however, in the celebrations which greeted the final whistle, and as supporters made their way home in the rain, they were entitled to believe that Irish football had at last turned the corner. The IFA obviously thought so too, presenting every team member with a gold watch to mark the historic achievement.

On the face of it, there was good reason for that climate of optimism. The bulk of the successful national team was still on an upward curve and, with average luck, could expect to be competitive at the highest level for the next three or four years. At club level also, the signs were encouraging. Glentoran's win over Linfield in the Irish Cup final was acclaimed as one of the best in the history of the competition; Shelbourne and St James Gate likewise produced a Leinster Cup final of quality in 1914; and, generally, there was more money circulating in Irish football that at any time in the past.

How ironic it was, then, that at a time when Irish football authorities were at last able to contemplate the prospect of back-to-back title successes, the storm clouds of war were already beginning to darken Europe. Within months, the toxic relationship between the Central Powers had flamed into war and, for the next four years, sport and all forms of recreation would have little relevance in an increasingly disturbed world. In the opening weeks of the Great War, declared on 5 August 1914, hundreds of thousands of people were committing themselves, voluntarily or otherwise, to the Allied cause. And in that situation, the reaction of the major players in sport was revealing.

Rugby, which provided thousands of young men to the officer corps, acted quickly and decisively by suspending its programme indefinitely in September 1914, with the exception of schoolboy competitions. Football, by contrast, started the new season on schedule in the same month, unsure of the future but hoping that the conflict on mainland Europe would resolve itself sooner rather than later. As the events of the next three months would prove, optimism on that scale was at best naive, and in January 1915 the four British Associations met in urgent session to consider the consequences of a rapidly deteriorating situation. Two weeks earlier, a sub-committee of the FA of England had met with representatives of the British War Office, and those talks formed the agenda for a meeting of the British International Board in Blackpool.

Unlike their rugby counterparts, the football authorities decided that the season should run its course and, on its completion in April 1915, all competitions, ranging from club to international football, would be suspended. The IFA, alone of the four Associations, voted against a closedown of club tournaments, one of their points being that games at the weekend would help military recruitment. Following a meeting of British inter-league authorities, it was decided to suspend the Irish League for the 1915–16 season however, a ruling which would stay in place for the next four years.

Instead, it was agreed to regionalise Irish football, with the formation of a Belfast and District League in the north-east of the country, and Shelbourne and Bohemians restricting their operations to the Leinster League. A similar arrangement was put in place in Munster. At a time when the profile of the game in Ireland had never been higher, the outbreak of war had a shattering effect on that progress in all parts of the country as young men enlisted in their thousands, for service with the British Army. Bohemians, for example, were reported to have lost almost half their players, as many took the boat to join regiments such as the Dublin Fusiliers, the Irish Guards and the Royal Irish Rifles. At Junior level, too, the impact was severe, with many of the football pitches in the Phoenix Park going unused because of the inability of clubs to field teams.

In Belfast, the effects of war were even more dramatic. Apart from the loss of so many young men to the Army, those of more mature years were required to assist the war effort in industrialised areas of the city by working at weekends, with a corresponding drop in attendance figures for games on Saturdays. So severe was the effect on the professional clubs in the city that they were forced to rewrite the contracts of professional players in order to stay solvent. Although a proposal that the IFA ban all payments to players was defeated, a subsequent motion calling for a ceiling of £1 a week for professionals was passed, amid protests that players could not be expected to sustain families on this level of payment.

On the credit side, many of the Irish players involved in English club football, including Val Harris and Billy Lacey, returned home to help raise the level of the domestic game. And in the case of Lacey, who rejoined Shelbourne initially, that led to an unsuccessful protest by Shamrock Rovers after they had lost a Leinster Cup semi-final tie to their arch-rivals from Ringsend. Rovers claimed: "William (Billy) Lacey is a registered professional player for Liverpool. He has also played as a professional for Shelbourne and Belfast United, thus breaching the rules of the Leinster Cup competition." In response, Shelbourne produced a letter from Liverpool FC, stating that they had given Lacey permission to play as an amateur for the Dublin club. They also pointed out that all professional players in Britain had been reinstated as amateurs by the FA of England, since the outbreak of war.

The badge of Lacey's outstanding career was that he could slot seamlessly into almost any position. A singularly gifted inside-forward, he also played as a wing-half for Ireland, and on other occasions he locked their defence together as a centre-half whose reading of games invariably took him into the right place at the right time. Apart from winning two First Division championship medals with Liverpool, he was in the Linfield team which outplayed Glentoran in the Irish Cup final in 1919, thus compensating for his disappointment in losing out on a winners' medal with Shelbourne in 1908.

While the Great War invaded the lives, directly or indirectly, of most families in the country, the Easter Rebellion in Dublin in 1916 had only a minimal effect on sport in the capital. The exception was in the weeks immediately following the armed rising when many events had to be postponed for a short period. In the case of the Leinster Football Association, that meant applying to the IFA for an extension of the season, in order to conclude the various competitions, but in the end all of the Association's operations were finished by 10 June of that year.

In view of the deprivations which had been visited on them during the war, it was perhaps not surprising that one of the first decisions taken by the surviving professional players in the country when peace was eventually restored in 1918 was to align themselves with the trade union movement. Fifty-four players joined the Irish Football Players' Union, but their demand for a minimum weekly wage of £3 was rejected by the IFA, who set the figure at £2. When a similar application was rejected the following year, the majority of the IFPU's members were said to have abandoned the idea of collective bargaining.

Such was the enduring appeal of football that, for all the hardships of wartime living, many of those who had drifted away from the game in 1914 were back on the terraces again by the time the artillery eventually fell silent in Europe. The meeting of Belfast Celtic and Linfield in the Irish Cup final, which went to two replays, attracted gate receipts of more than £1,000; and in Dublin the Leinster Cup final was also provoking greater interest than usual.

For much of its 26-year history, this competition had been dominated by just two clubs, Shelbourne and Bohemians, but in 1917 a Dublin Junior club, Glasnevin FC, had made people sit up and take notice by reaching the semi-finals of the competition. It may have been that achievement which fired the imagination of another Junior team, Olympia FC from the south inner city, when they embarked on the glory trail some nine months later.

Olympia had won the Leinster Junior Cup and reached the final of the Irish Junior Cup before making their bid for the biggest prize of all in the province, but even that impressive progression can scarcely have prepared Shelbourne for the shock of losing out to the men from the Coombe in the final. A single goal was enough to win it for the no-hopers, giving birth to a famous rallying call for all football's underdogs – "Remember Olympia once beat the Shels."

In spite of the interest generated by the emergence of new names in the Leinster Cup, and although the Leinster FA were now the largest divisional organisation in the country, their financial state was parlous, and in 1918 they were forced to apply to the IFA for a subvention of £300, to enable them to act on a directive from Belfast "that they participate in a Commission to consider ways and means of fostering the spread of Association Football throughout Ireland".

The parent body had itself been embarrassed in having to apply to the

County Antrim Association for assistance a couple of years earlier, but even allowing for that circumstance, its response to the Leinster body was still startling. While prepared to make a loan of £100 available to the Lurgan club, Glenavon, they offered just £50 to the Leinster FA to participate in the Commission. The Munster FA, who had sought a subvention of £200, got nothing at all, and the effect was to deepen the conviction in Dublin that when the IFA's priorities were condensed, they cared only for those in close proximity to them in Belfast.

Chapter Seven

Trouble in Store

In many ways, the meeting of Leinster and Ulster in an inter-provincial game at Dalymount Park in October 1919 was fated to be influential in defining the deteriorating relationship between the Leinster Football Association and the County Antrim Association, the body it had replaced as the largest constituent member of the Irish Football Association.

Initially, the County Antrim Association rejected the suggestion of a belated fixture to mark the 25th anniversary of the Dublin body, on the grounds that the cost of sending a team south would be substantial and also that it would be difficult to accommodate the game in an already crowded programme. But at a meeting of the LFA at which Comrades of the Great War was one of 12 new clubs admitted to membership of the Association, it was agreed to increase the match guarantee to the northern authorities, and this apparently was enough to bring about a change of heart.

As it transpired, the discrepancy in standard between the teams was such that Ulster eased into a 5–0 lead without too much trouble, at an advanced stage of the second half. In spite of this, or perhaps because of it, a crowd representing gate receipts of £250 and made up predominantly of Leinster supporters invaded the pitch in ugly scenes which, not surprisingly, spread raw fear into some of the Ulster players. At a time when many were querying the feasibility of attempting to smooth over perceived differences in the cause of preserving the status quo in the hierarchy of Irish football, it was enough to cause consternation in both Dublin and Belfast – and it showed.

At a meeting held on 29 October 1919, the Leinster Council was handed a copy of the report sent to Belfast by the referee, Mr Kelly, in which he stated that seven minutes from full time, a section of the crowd came on to the field of play at the Ulster goalmouth, next to the pavilion. The play at the time was at the other end of the ground. On turning around, he observed a large crowd of spectators on the field and, also, that some of the Ulster players were jumping over the railings into the reserved section of the enclosure. He called on the Ulster players who were near him to do the same. Mr Kelly added that when he reached the pavilion, he enquired if any of the Ulster players had been seriously hurt and was informed that Reid had received a kick in the stomach.

Mr Kelly, who attended the meeting, said there was no rough play during the match and he didn't see any players being struck. After members of the Council who attended the match had offered their opinions, it was decided to "put the matter in the hands of a detective and enquire about the names of those spectators arrested by the police in attendance". The Secretary was instructed to write to the Chief Commissioner of Police, asking him to receive a deputation with a view to obtaining what assistance the authorities could give, in putting down such conduct in the future. He was also instructed to send a letter to the County Antrim Association, expressing regret for the crowd disturbances.

Three weeks later, the Leinster Association received a letter from the IFA, confirming that the following resolution had been passed at their Council meeting: "That the [IFA] Council, having gone into the referee's report on the Leinster–Ulster game and having heard reports from the Co Antrim Association and the statement of Mr Wigoder, President of the LFA, is glad to observe that the Leinster Association is taking steps to grapple with the disorderly conduct that has of late, crept into matches at Dalymount Park and wish to assure the LFA of their wholehearted support in this matter." A second letter was read from the County Antrim Association, stating that they believed the Leinster Association had done all in its power to deal with the problem.

It was a rare display of solidarity by the two main power brokers in Irish football, probably because it was felt that this was needed to counter the adverse publicity which accrued from the unsavoury scenes; but the reality was that northern officials were now more convinced than ever that it was unsafe for teams from their region to play in Dublin. And this underlying fear would be central to the dispute which eventually led to the partition of the game in Ireland in 1921.

The influence of referees in that strained relationship was eased somewhat after the Dublin-based Referees Union had reached an agreement with their Ulster counterparts in establishing a system in which Leinster officials could be appointed to take charge of games in Ulster and vice versa. Referees, and the matter of their rate of payment, had always been a thorn in the side of the administrators, but the issue was resolved to a large degree when the Leinster Association decreed that match officials in their area of jurisdiction would receive a standard fee of four shillings per game.

The other recurring theme of discord among referees revolved around the reluctance of the bigger clubs in Dublin and Belfast to accept local officials to take charge of derby games. Bohemians and Shelbourne, for example, invariably insisted on the appointment of English referees for their Leinster Cup games, while a similar prejudice existed in Belfast for Linfield's big fixtures against Glentoran and Belfast Celtic. At a meeting on 12 June 1918, Leinster officials confirmed that the decision to appoint a Belfast referee for the Leinster League play-off between Bohemians and Shelbourne had been taken by the clubs themselves. In accepting it, the League warned that in future they would make all such appointments. In addition to increasing match expenses, the implied insult to local officers caused a lot of discontent, but in spite of all the counter-arguments, the practice of bringing over cross-channel referees to officiate in big Cup ties endured for much of the next fifty years.

Mr Tom Coleton, one of the more prominent Dublin referees of the period, occasioned controversy and not a little exasperation on one occasion when, in response to an incident on which he was forced to adjudicate some time earlier, he sought a directive from the Leinster Association regarding his decision to allow a goal after a cross-kick had struck the branches of an overhanging tree, without being diverted from its original trajectory.

Coleton was embroiled in another controversy shortly after the Dalymount riot when he was appointed to a crucial Irish League game in Belfast, between Belfast Celtic and Distillery. His performance did

not endear him to IFA officials at the game, who later notified the LFA
of a motion which had been passed at a meeting of their Council: "That
in the opinion of Council, the referee was negligent in his duty in not
reporting the scenes which occurred at the conclusion of the game, he
being cognisant of the condition in which the linesman, Mr McClean,
returned to the pavilion, and that he be suspended from taking part in
football or in football management for the remainder of the season." It was
not immediately clear whether this amounted to an accusation of perceived
bias in favour of Belfast Celtic or a commentary on the general level of
refereeing in Leinster, but it did nothing to improve dialogue between
Dublin and Belfast.

Belfast Celtic were involved in another fracas later in 1919, when their
Irish Cup semi-final tie against Glentoran ended in chaos with the sound of
gunfire echoing across the stadium as the rival fans taunted each other with
flag waving and party songs. Crowd trouble was now associated with many
of Belfast Celtic's games, and this latest violence led to the suspension of
the club and then, days later, their temporary withdrawal from all grades of
football.

Nor could Dublin afford to be smug about the problems erupting at
regular intervals in the north. After players of Jacobs FC had been found
guilty of invading the dressing-room of their opponents, Olympia FC, at
the end of a Leinster Cup game, the turmoil was discussed at some length
by the Leinster Council. Two Jacobs players received lengthy suspensions,
as did J. Chadwick of Olympia after it was revealed that Jacobs had been
taunted about "playing soldiers" in their team.

The question of whether Belfast City Cup games took precedence over
Leinster Cup fixtures was posed by Shelbourne on at least two occasions,
with the LFA, as expected, ruling in the negative on both occasions.
Notwithstanding this, Shelbourne, who alone of the senior Dublin clubs
appeared to enjoy a reasonable rapport with the IFA, taxed the patience of
Leinster officials once too often when they opted out of their Leinster Cup
semi-final tie against St James Gate, in order to fulfil a fixture in the Belfast
City Cup. Later, they had a change of heart and agreed to play the Leinster
Cup match, only to be told that St James Gate were being awarded a walk-
over. Shelbourne's subsequent protest was dismissed on a 5–3 vote and the

"Gate" progressed to the final, in which they beat Bohemians in a second replay.

In 1920, with the reverberations of the 1916 Easter Rising still being felt around the country and the clamour for Home Rule growing apace, law and order were coming under increasing threat, and football was not exempt from the general chaos. The semi-finals of the Irish Senior Cup made the point in varying degrees of pain and anguish. After Glentoran and Belfast Celtic had drawn 1–1 in the first semi-final at Windsor Park, the replay was scheduled for Cliftonville's ground on St Patrick's Day. A highly charged game descended into anarchy in the second half when a section of the crowd invaded the pitch after Fred Barrett had been sent off. The other players were then instructed to make their way to the dressing-rooms as the stadium resounded to Celtic fans singing "The Soldier's Song" and "A Nation Once Again" and rival supporters responding with "God Save the King".

Belfast Celtic were suspended just three days later, only to protest that Hugh McIlveen's name was not included in the list of players submitted by Glentoran before the game. This protest was upheld and Glentoran were dismissed from the competition. Shelbourne, 3–1 winners over Glenavon in the other semi-final, were awarded the trophy, but only after their ground had been closed because of crowd trouble during the game. Irish football was in a shambolic state and, in the opinion of many, headed inevitably for even more squalls.

At the annual general meeting of the Leinster Association, held on 26 May 1920, the Secretary, Jack Ryder, was able to report that income for the season amounted to £1,275-4-10, thanks in some measure to a grant of £200 from the IFA, made "to help clubs which had been affected by the Great War and bring the standard of football back to pre-war levels". Ryder went on to say that the drop in the number of affiliated clubs experienced during the war had now been reversed and, from a low of 73, the LFA now had 120 clubs in its membership.

There was another significant development in December 1920, when the IFA reneged on a pledge to stage one of the Irish Intermediate Cup semi-finals in Dublin, ruling instead that Belfast should host both games. That incensed St James Gate, who were defending a trophy they had won the previous March, and on 15 December they tabled a motion at a meeting of the Leinster Council, urging them to contact the IFA with a view to having the original commitment honoured. This proposal had the unanimous support of the other Dublin clubs but the IFA, unmoved, stated that in 1921 the semi-finals of both the Irish Intermediate and Irish Junior Cup competitions would be played in Belfast.

St James Gate enjoyed a reputation as one of the strongest, most progressive clubs in the country, and that added another element of indignation to the high-handed action of the IFA in arriving at their ruling without the courtesy of consulting with the LFA. Later, officials in Belfast would claim that in making their decision, they were influenced by a letter from Shelbourne stating that, in the prevailing climate of unrest in Dublin, it would be unwise to stage any big games in the capital. This allegation was never subsequently confirmed by the club.

If people in Belfast considered themselves at risk in travelling to Dublin at that time, the converse was equally true. Reports in the Dublin newspapers of the increasingly serious crowd disturbances at Belfast Celtic's games were perceived in the south as symptomatic of the civil strife pervading society in the northern capital. The Irish League championship, suspended in 1915, had yet to resume in 1920, and having measured the risks in the light of the ugly scenes which marred the semi-finals of the Irish Senior Cup the previous March, the three Dublin clubs involved in the competition in the 1920–21 season, Shelbourne, Bohemians and St James Gate, can only have felt apprehensive as they embarked on the road to the final.

As things evolved, Shelbourne made it into the last four, which in a sense was only appropriate. As holders of the trophy, albeit by default, they coveted the chance of re-establishing themselves as the premier team in the country, and the fact that they were drawn against Glenavon, in a repeat of their semi-final tie 12 months earlier, gave the tie an added element of attraction. Ominously for Shelbourne, however, the draw ordained that they travel north and, given the violence which stained their 1920 game in Dublin, the prospect can only have filled them with alarm.

To make matters worse as they headed for Belfast, injury deprived them of the services of four key players, among them team captain Val

Harris, but in a resilient performance which delighted those who had accompanied them by train, they absorbed all the pressure that Glenavon exerted to escape with a goalless draw. Now, with the roles reversed and Glenavon faced with the prospect of making a daunting journey to Dublin for the replay, Shelbourne could look forward with some confidence to an appointment with Glentoran in the final.

To the consternation of the holders, however, they were ordered back to Belfast for the second game. The ruling, by the IFA's Senior Clubs Committee, flew in the face of justice and incensed those who held the opinion that the IFA was indeed an organisation which favoured its northern members. The Committee insisted that their decision was based on fears for the safety of Glenavon players who, mindful of their experience a year earlier, had expressed reservations about making the return trip to Dublin. Shelbourne, perplexed, sought in vain to have the ruling overturned by the more moderate element of the parent body, but the only joy they got was the IFA's agreement to pay their overnight expenses for the first game, a cost necessitated by the military curfew in operation in Belfast at the time. They refused to travel, and were given the unqualified support of the LFA.

Journalists in Dublin described the ruling as a decision which could fracture the entire structure of Irish football and persuade the Leinster Association to sever the link with the Belfast-based administration. Those sentiments would, in the end, prove prophetic.

Chapter Eight

Separate Ways

With Ireland moving inexorably towards political partition in the spring of 1921, Shelbourne's sense of grievance over their treatment by the Irish Football Association, an organisation perceived in Dublin as one more and more in thrall to the other British Football Associations, struck a raw nerve in the capital.

On the club's own admission, the problem of policing football grounds adequately in Dublin, at a time when the tide of anti-British feeling was running high through much of the country, was making it increasingly difficult to host big games against teams from the north-east. And for the Lurgan club, Glenavon, there were vivid memories of the hostile reception they received in their last Irish Cup game in Dublin in 1920.

It ought to be recorded that on 3 April 1921, just 24 hours before Dublin United were due to meet St James Gate in the Leinster Cup final, the Emergency Committee of the LFA was summoned to attend a meeting to postpone the game "because of the prevailing conditions in the city". Developments like that appeared to validate the judgement of the IFA that it was unsafe to arrange the Shelbourne–Glenavon replay for the capital.

The counter-argument was that the experience of Belfast Celtic and their nationalist supporters, in meetings with clubs like Linfield, Glentoran and Distillery, proved there was a significant section of the population in Belfast who also viewed football as a convenient means of making points on both sides of the political divide there. And convention decreed that having journeyed to Windsor Park for the drawn game, Shelbourne should have advantage of a local venue, almost certainly Dalymount Park, for the replay.

Against that background, a special meeting of the Leinster Council was convened on 14 March 1921 to review the growing crisis. Mr J. Walsh, who was present at the IFA Council meeting which considered the recommendation of the meeting of the Senior Clubs' Protest and Appeals Committee to order Shelbourne back to Belfast, reported on what had taken place. After a discussion, Mr L.C. Sheridan proposed and Mr P.J. McEvoy seconded the following resolution: "That the Council of the Leinster Football Association strongly condemns the unsporting action of a majority of the members of the Irish Senior Clubs' Protests and Appeals Committee in ordering Shelbourne to replay in Belfast their drawn Irish Cup tie with Glenavon FC. We regard the decision to be against the best interests of the game. We further deprecate the action of the Glenavon club in its refusal to come to Dublin, more especially since the votes and influence of Leinster delegates was always generously given in the past, to support the claims made by Glenavon FC to the IFA, when their existence as a football club was threatened." On the proposal of Mr J. McDonnell, the last sentence in reference to Glenavon was deleted. After the remainder of the resolution had been passed, Mr Sheridan proposed that the Leinster Football Association should determine its stance regarding the IFA, in connection with the foregoing. Consideration of this proposal was left over to the next meeting of the Council.

Three weeks later, a letter confirming the following resolution passed by the IFA Council was received in Dublin. It read: "The Emergency Committee is very sympathetic and in accord with the resolution passed by the Leinster Association but having regard to the fact that the Senior Clubs' Protest and Appeals Committee has Council powers, it is unable to take any action in the matter." After some discussion on the advisability of the LFA maintaining the status quo in Irish football, the following was proposed by Mr Sheridan, seconded by Mr R. Balbernie: "That the matter be referred to a small committee to report as to whether the LFA should continue its connection with the IFA." The following were appointed to act on the Committee together with the honorary officers: Messrs J.L. Brennan, J. McDonald, J.F. Harrison, H. Wigoder, R. McDonald and H.A. Wills. Messrs H. Wigoder, R.E.T. Richey and P.H. Stewart were subsequently nominated as Leinster's representatives on the IFA Council.

At the first meeting held in the Leinster Association's new offices at 45

Middle Abbey Street, Dublin, on 4 May 1921, Jack Ryder, Secretary of
the LFA, read the resolution passed by the Committee to consider whether
the Association should continue its connection with the IFA, as follows
– "It is the opinion of the Committee that the time has arrived when the
Association should stand on its own and, if the Council so approves of the
resolution, authorise the Council to circularise clubs as to their views on
the matter and that Council then submits a report for consideration by the
clubs at the annual general meeting."

Mr Richey, the chairman, said that under the Association's rules, he
could not accept any resolution which was contrary to those rules and,
if asked to do so, he would place his resignation before the Council.
A proposal that the action of the Committee be endorsed and that it
be empowered to ascertain the views of the clubs in reference to their
connection with the IFA, was passed – a decision which the chairman
refused to accept. It was then proposed that a special general meeting of
the LFA be called for the purpose of disbanding the LFA and putting into
operation a new Association next season. The chairman refused to accept
same and left the meeting. Mr Stewart was elected to take the chair and, on
the proposal of Mr Sheridan, it was agreed that: "The action of the Council
be endorsed and that they be empowered to take views of the clubs in
reference to their connection with the IFA and that the report be submitted
to the Council before being presented to the annual general meeting." Mr
Richey, being a member of Council by virtue of his office as chairman,
and he having asked to be relieved of this office, was then elected to the
Council on the proposition of Mr McDonald.

Richey, a man who had strong connections with Belfast, formally
resigned from his position at a Council meeting on 11 May and then
resisted pleas from colleagues to change his mind, repeating his earlier
assertion that the Council had acted in contravention of its own rules.
At that point, Mr H. Wigoder was appointed to act as chairman for the
remainder of the season.

At the annual general meeting of the LFA held in the Molesworth
Hall in Dublin, a copy of the following circular to clubs, signed by the
Secretary, Jack Ryder, was read: "I have been directed by my Council, to
bring before you the following matter and ask you to give it your careful

consideration viz. – Is it in the best interests of football that the Association should continue its connection with the IFA Ltd? This subject is purely for the clubs themselves. The Council wishes to draw your attention to the following points. Should you not wish to affiliate [to the IFA], other Associations would not immediately give recognition to a new one. Your club would not be eligible to compete in the Irish Senior Cup, Irish Intermediate Cup or Irish Junior Cup, according to your status. Your players would not be considered for international honours next season. During the present season, the principal rounds of the Irish Senior and Intermediate Cups were forbidden to be played in Dublin [by the IFA] and the Irish Junior Cup competition was not played. In fact, no matches with northern clubs took place, thus the IFA Ltd cut itself adrift from our organisation. It is considered that if the [Leinster] Association had a free hand, a lot could be done to develop and popularise the game, rules being drawn up on lines suitable to the clubs, without any restrictions. As stated before, the matter is one for the clubs and it is for them to decide. The Council would be glad if clubs placed the matter before their members for their consideration and I should be glad if you would communicate same to me at the earliest opportunity."

At the Leinster Council meeting held on 8 June 1921, Mr J.F. Harrison was elected chairman of the Leinster Association after Mr Richey had again declined an invitation to resume his old position. The following resolution, which had been passed at a meeting of the clubs, was read: "That the time has come when a new Association should be formed, independent of the IFA Ltd. That the newly elected Council of the LFA should constitute itself for the purpose of establishing the new body and report to a full meeting of the clubs when the draft constitution and rules have been considered. It is decided to call the new organisation 'The Football Association of Ireland' and that the LFA should affiliate to the new body. The following committee is appointed to draft the rules etc of the new organisation – Messrs J.F. Harrison, J.S. Smurthwaite, R.E.T. Richey, B.W. Mainey, J.L. Brennan, P.H. Stewart and L.C. Sheridan."

Ten days later, the draft rules of the Football Association of Ireland were approved, subject to some slight amendments. On the proposition of Mr Stewart, it was agreed to convene a special meeting of the clubs to place the rules before them for adoption. It was also decided that the Council and Honorary Officers place their resignations before the meeting and then offer themselves for re-election in the new organisation.

The final pieces in the plan to establish a new organisation in Dublin were now in place and two weeks later Jack Ryder informed the IFA in a terse communiqué: "At a meeting of the representatives of our clubs, it was decided to form a Association, independent of the IFA." The reply from Belfast was equally curt, warning that clubs affiliated to the Football Association of Ireland would be suspended from competition with those affiliated to the IFA or, indeed, any British Association. The new Association would also be blacklisted in terms of international competition in the British home championship.

Thus, after 41 years of uneasy co-existence, Dublin and Belfast were set on divergent paths in football. It would be many years before a working relationship was re-established and the affairs of sport were seen to concur with an increasing climate of ecumenism in conventional politics. In the immediate aftermath of the split, there is evidence of doubt surfacing in both camps as they pondered the consequences of that infamous Irish Cup tie involving Shelbourne and Glenavon. Deprived of the opportunity of playing against the leading northern clubs, Shelbourne, no less than Bohemians and St James Gate, worried about whether they would be able to maintain standards when restricted to the League of Ireland championship. The power players in the north-east, for their part, fretted about the Irish League dwindling into little more than a grandiose Belfast city competition with corresponding risks for standards.

After resisting demands for a more influential role for the LFA, the largest of its constituent bodies, so stubbornly for so long, the IFA now seemed to be prepared to compromise on key issues. Not only would Leinster's measly representation of three seats on a Council of 12 be increased, but the IFA was ready to talk about the possibility of rotating Council meetings between the two cities, as well as holding out the carrot of more international matches for Dublin. This latter point was important, for of the 42 home international fixtures since the meeting with England in 1882, only six were awarded to Dublin.

In the event, the gestures failed to impact on the growing militancy in

Leinster. True, they cherished the dream of England coming to play at Dalymount Park, but only if they were in sole control of the fixture and the team in the home dressing-room was selected by them. Giving in to demands like these, however, would have represented abject capitulation by Belfast, and for all their apprehension about the way ahead, they were not prepared to compromise on core issues which would, effectively, have meant Dublin wresting control of the game on the island.

The new Football League of Ireland championship kicked off on 7 September 1921, featuring eight Dublin clubs, St James Gate, Bohemians, Shelbourne, Olympia, Jacobs, Frankfort, Dublin University and YMCA – they finished in that order – and another landmark had been reached on the journey to fulfilment. The differences between Dublin and Belfast were now entrenched, and the students of Queen's University knew for certain that the old order was gone when they were made to apply for permission to journey south, to renew an old rivalry with Trinity College.

The Munster Football Association, if not yet an equal partner, supported Leinster in their breakaway, and while the administrative structure of football in Connacht was still only in its infancy, there was every indication of satisfaction about the removal of the old IFA structure, under which the province fell within the remit of the Fermanagh Association.

Nor was dissatisfaction with the parent body restricted to the southern and western parts of the island. West Belfast, a hotbed of Irish nationalism, suffered the dictates of unionism with increasing frustration, and for many in the community, the IFA was the very symbol of British imperialism. To the dismay of the ruling body, many Junior clubs left the organisation and affiliated to the FAI within weeks of its foundation. At one point, Dublin claimed to have received more than forty such applications, and while this figure may well have been inflated, there is no doubting that the Falls and District League claimed the allegiance of the majority of the nationalist population in the region. Belfast Celtic, as we have seen, was suspended in 1920 and didn't reappear until some three years later. In the intervening period, many of their players joined Alton United, and with this broad seam of experience, Alton lifted the FAI Cup in only its second year of competition in 1923.

Over the years, many conflicting reasons have been advanced for the football split. It is valid to suggest that the Shelbourne–Glenavon saga, and the refusal of the Lurgan club to play in Dublin because of the growing unrest in the city, had an impact. Some saw in Glenavon's action a betrayal of the trust built over years of cordial relations with the Leinster FA. But their refusal to travel ought to be seen in the light of the fact that just three days after the proposed date for the replay, six Republican volunteers were due to be executed in Dublin. Given the civil disturbances which followed similar sentences in Cork a short time previously, their fears were scarcely irrational. It should be noted too that the northern branch of the Irish Cricket Union advised against teams playing in the capital in the summer of 1921, and women's hockey was similarly affected.

There is no denying that on at least two earlier occasions, the Leinster FA was close to seceding from the parent organisation because of a perceived bias in preserving Belfast's primacy. On reflection, it was a working relationship which did well to survive for 40 years, but on the rising tide of nationalism and the campaign for Home Rule in the early years of the twentieth century, it could not reasonably be expected to endure indefinitely.

Alone of the major Irish sporting associations, football had its headquarters in Belfast, a product of the Scottish influence in the introduction of the game to Ireland. And unlike rugby, which began with separate administrations north and south before the foundation of the Irish Rugby Football Union in Dublin, there was never a realistic chance of the contrived unionist majority in the Irish Football Association following suit.

The concept of an all-Ireland organisation being administered from Belfast in the Ireland of the 1920s was simply unworkable, and it is valid to suggest that the great sunder was more a product of politics than a commentary on the differences at Council level, which characterised the IFA in its early years. Coming six months before the formal declaration of political independence, the FAI was seen in the north as a tool of those who wielded political power in Dublin.

Given the reaction of the GAA to the formation of the FAI, that was indeed ironic. To those in authority at Croke Park, the FAI was seen as a partitionist body which had sold out on the notion of a united Ireland. This, however, was to overlook the fact that it was a sense of patriotism, misguided or otherwise, in refusing to be subservient to an organisation perceived as British, which brought the new body into being in the first place.

As matters unfolded, no cultural or sporting movement did more to publicise the infant Irish Free State than the body dismissed by its critics as the mouthpiece of a garrison sport. For many thousands of people across Europe, the playing of the Irish national anthem and the tricolour on display at international games, was very often the first manifestation of the birth of a nation. Of all the major sports, football was uniquely placed to promulgate the message of a new Ireland, but it would be many years before the wearing of the green received due recognition from those disposed to overlooking the lessons of history.

Chapter Nine

Life After the Split

Sir James McIlmunn Wilton was a man who personified the dark intrigue of politics in the train of events leading up to the infamous split in Irish football. After he ascended to power in the IFA in 1914 and then, astutely, went against the grain in attempting to unravel the problems which resulted in Dublin's final disillusionment with the affairs of the Irish Football Association in June 1921, his was a name which commanded respect on either side of the border.

Wilton combined the posts of President and Chairman of the IFA, one of only three men to do so, and when he died, in 1945, he left a proud record of 31 years' unbroken service at the helm of the organisation, an achievement surpassed only by Sir Harry Cavan, a senior vice-president of FIFA, in post-war years. A skilful strategist, Wilton was perceived in the north-east of the country as a bulwark in preserving the region's primacy in Irish football, and by the Leinster Association as a person who chose to ignore, or misread, the warning signs of impending separation in the months and weeks preceding the foundation of the Football Association of Ireland.

Originally from Derry, Wilton was among the members of the city's Ulster Volunteer Force who enlisted for service in the Great War. He was seriously wounded in action on the first day of the Battle of the Somme, suffered a similar fate the following year and was subsequently awarded the Military Cross for bravery. An obdurate defender of the Union, he served two terms as Mayor of Derry before being knighted for services to Northern Ireland in 1937. On his death, even the nationalist press in Derry was moved to concede that in spite of his unswerving commitment to the Crown and all it stood for, he also had his admirers in the Bogside area of the city, testimony to his ability to surf the tidal waves of Irish politics.

More transparent by far were the hardline instincts of one of his trusted allies on the Council of the IFA, Thomas Moles. Once linked to the Loyalist gunrunning at Larne in 1914, Moles used his profession as a journalist to formulate and promulgate the strategy of Northern Ireland in the immediate aftermath of the Declaration of Independence in Dublin in December 1921, and in football he found a ready platform to articulate his preferences. Moles was among the most forthright in his denunciation of any sporting contact with the infant Irish Free State and, in tandem with Wilton, he represented a powerful voice at the time for the embattled IFA.

After the IFA's refusal to permit Queen's University to play Trinity, under the terms of their blanket suspension of every southern club, had provided the final, damning evidence of the breakdown in relations between Dublin and Belfast, there followed a period of relative calm in which the rival Associations reflected on the pluses and minuses of separatism. For the northern body, the first and most prized result was the immediate support of the other three British Associations. This, of course, was always in prospect, but the manner in which it was delivered was calculated to demoralise Dublin as much as uplift those in authority in the north-east of the island.

Britain may well have disenfranchised itself from the game on mainland Europe in the 1920s, a policy which would carry a heavy price in the context of playing standards, on their return to the FIFA fold in 1948, but in the context of Ireland it would be difficult to overstate the importance of the FA of England and, to a lesser extent, the Associations of Scotland and Wales in the immediate post-war years. To that extent, Northern Ireland was entitled to believe that it held most of the trump cards in its dealings with the new organisation.

They knew their British allies would support them in their claim to go on selecting players born in any part of Ireland for their international team, while at the same time denying the rival body a corresponding arrangement. Meanwhile the blanket suspension, imposed with indecent haste on the FAI, was designed to alert FIFA, the world governing body, to the advisability of giving Dublin a wide berth. In the event, that was never more than a forlorn hope for those who wished to see the new organisation founder. On the contrary, it merely served as a useful negotiating ploy when the FAI went in search of support for their application for membership of the parent body.

In one other aspect, the split could be said to have had a beneficial effect for the IFA. Given the location of their headquarters in Belfast, they were never really in a position to administer on a 32-county basis, as evidenced by their reluctance to restart the Irish Junior Cup competition after the war. Historically, this was always the most difficult event to organise, because of the geographical spread of the competing clubs, and having regard to the growth of the game on the island between the two World Wars, that inability to govern throughout the land might well have rendered it incapable of retaining control even had the rift not occurred when it did.

On the debit side, the effect of Dublin pulling the plug was to demote the IFA to a regional body, controlling the game in just one-sixth of the landmass on the island. One of the recurring criticisms levelled at the organisation in its early years was its failure to promote the game adequately outside the greater Belfast area. The Divisional Association in the North West of the province, as well as those in South Tyrone and Fermanagh, were all moved on occasions to lament the failure of those wielding power to have due consideration for the people struggling to nurture football in less densely populated areas. Now, the consequences of that systemic failure threatened to be even more expensive.

For the FAI, the challenge of going it alone carried the bonus of breathing new life into areas which had previously suffered from the mistaken perception that football was inherently a garrison sport. Adopting a convenient party line, critics had earlier contended that football in Ireland was administered directly or indirectly by London, a notion that sat easily with a significant section of the public, at a stage when the campaign for Home Rule was becoming more vociferous by the week. In the first year of the FAI's existence, membership of the Leinster Association was said to have increased by almost 25 per cent, and if the GAA's crusade to drive the Munster Association to extinction continued to restrict the development of the game in the south, there was a steady if not spectacular rise in the number of affiliated clubs in that province.

There was also the bonus of having an experienced administrative structure in place in Dublin when the parting of the ways eventually came. Because of the suspension of cross-border competition during the Great War – a suspension which, in the case of the Irish League championship, stayed in place in the years immediately after the guns had fallen silent – the Leinster Football Association had been, in effect, an autonomous body for much of the previous seven years. Now, on the formation of the Football Association of Ireland, the same personnel were entrusted with the task of steering it through those difficult early years when it took on the British football establishment in their pursuit of international recognition.

The notable exception was Robert Richey, the erstwhile LFA Chairman, who was so passionate in his opposition to the Council's decision to go it alone, that he resigned. He was later persuaded, under some duress, to rejoin the Council, but then within a matter of months he again cut adrift from the organisation, citing pressure of business in Belfast as the reason. John F. Harrison, who along with Larry Sheridan, Jim Brennan and the Secretary, Jack Ryder, had been highly influential in ending the link with Belfast, promptly resigned his position as LFA Chairman to fill a similar role in the FAI.

The downside was that there was little or no money available to fund the new body. Much of the revenue accrued by the LFA over the previous 29 years had been siphoned off to the IFA, and compared to the resources available to the County Antrim Association, Leinster was in a parlous financial state in 1921. To that extent, the timing of the break could scarcely have been more inopportune, but it testified to the depth of the disillusionment which had developed in Dublin's relationship with the parent body at that point.

No less than their northern counterparts, senior clubs like Shelbourne, Bohemians and St James Gate fretted that they would now be competing in a regional league championship. And the prompt suspension of the FAI by the British Board ensured that international matches, and the special buzz at Dalymount Park on big match days, would not be back any time soon. Against that, however, local players were entitled to believe that when the good times returned, they would have a more realistic chance of representing their country. That was an expectation which simply didn't exist for the majority of senior players in the capital in the pre-split era when, as we have seen, northern clubs monopolised the distribution of international honours. The reasoning behind that, Belfast would claim, was that playing standards in the north were that much better, and looking through the roll of honour in club competitions, it would be difficult to demur. It is true that Shelbourne, on three occasions, and Bohemians both won the Irish Cup, but that represented only a small percentage in terms of success rate. And, significantly, no Leinster club ever won the Irish League championship.

Taken in conjunction with what was interpreted in the south as prejudiced team selection, it meant that international status was no more than a distant aspiration for the majority of Leinster players as long as Belfast stayed in charge. As it transpired, it would be another five years before the FAI was involved in a senior international fixture, but when the upturn came, the national team was indeed comprised exclusively of locally based players. Encouraged by that turnaround, players suddenly discovered an added sense of purpose in the Free State championship and subsidiary competitions, and it showed in the intensity of local rivalries.

From a financial perspective, the dearth of international fixtures deprived the FAI of urgently needed revenue. An appearance by the England team, for example, was guaranteed to command a full house anywhere they played, and Dublin desperately needed to tap into that reservoir. London, however, motivated by the requirement of being seen to support the IFA, was unresponsive to their entreaties, and the consequences were such that there may have been occasions when the FAI pondered the wisdom of their audacious move. So acute was the shortage of money that, at one point, it was proposed to scrap the established practice of awarding medals to the winners of the Leinster Cup.

The newly donated FAI Challenge Cup hadn't yet displaced the Leinster Cup in terms of prestige in the capital, and with the majority of the eight clubs involved in the League of Ireland, operating on an amateur basis, the notion of withdrawing the winners' medals from the Cup competition was treated with contempt. Eventually, player power won out and the winners got their medals, but not before they were made to agree to senior clubs joining others from lower divisions in preliminary qualifying rounds of the competition. The primary purpose of the move, initially resisted, was to generate the additional funding which would enable the organisation to survive, and in that the Leinster Cup was still hugely important in the province.

It has to be said that the funds of the IFA were not significantly better at that point. But, with its superior industrial base, Belfast was still better equipped to finance its football programme in the 1920s when, quite apart from international fixtures, Linfield's games against Glentoran and Belfast Celtic, after they returned to the Irish League, invariably attracted big attendances at Windsor Park. Before long, they were able to survive comfortably without the money which once flowed northwards from Dublin.

The glamour team in the FAI's first full season was undeniably St James Gate, a club which would later nurture the emerging talent of Jack Carey, one of the enduring greats of Irish football. Funded by the Guinness Brewery, the "Gate" enjoyed better facilities than most at the Iveagh Grounds in Crumlin and duly won the inaugural League of Ireland championship by a margin of two points from Bohemians before completing the big double by defeating Shamrock Rovers 1–0 in the FAI Cup final. In the north, Linfield likewise achieved dual success, but the absence of Shelbourne, Bohemians and St James Gate, allied to the suspension of Belfast Celtic, somewhat diminished the satisfaction of victory.

The completion of the first season in the new format of Irish football had, perhaps, gone better than Dublin dared hope or Belfast feared; but behind the scenes, the growing problems of a partitioned island, in football as well as politics, were exercising the attention of those who longed for a return of the old order. After the IFA's stonewalling of all attempts for change in earlier years, the realisation began to dawn on James Wilton and his advisers that there was little prospect of Dublin changing tack in the immediate future and a different approach was now needed. To his credit, the IFA President was not found wanting in either courage or initiative in the new circumstances in which he now found himself.

Acknowledging the merit of at least some of the grievances which the LFA had expressed at regular intervals, he promised reform on a grand scale if they would now return to the negotiating table and talk their differences through. The location of the IFA headquarters remained a huge stumbling block in any conciliatory moves towards a settlement, but with Wilton ready to compromise on almost every other issue, there was a growing sense of optimism in Belfast that they could yet convince their old colleagues in the south of the folly of the course on which they were now set.

The FAI, for its part, expressed tentative interest in the proposed talks but, far from moving closer to Belfast, Dublin was probably motivated in this action by the thought that it could be a useful bargaining ploy in getting the British International Board to lift its suspension on the newly created Association and opening the way to those coveted fixtures against England at Dalymount Park. And it was this line of thinking which saw them make a surprising appointment in the summer of 1922.

Apart from the odd time when he had made representations on behalf of the Irish Red Cross in the campaign to maximise that body's fundraising activities, the name of Sir Henry McLaughlin KBE had never surfaced at meetings of the Leinster Association. A native of Belfast, he played for a time with Cliftonville before moving south with the long-established family firm which, in addition to Belfast and Dublin, had offices in London. Aside from his service to the Red Cross, McLaughlin also acted as a recruiting agent for the British Army during the Great War, and it was in recognition of this work that he was later awarded a knighthood.

In spite of his brief flirtation with Cliftonville, he was never active in football in Dublin until the FAI invited him to become the first President of the Association, an invitation which was accepted with some alacrity. At the time, his nomination was said to have come as a shock to the rank and file members of the Association. Others interpreted it as a shrewd move to help in the process of developing a good working relationship with Belfast while ensuring that the short-term future of the organisation was protected.

Chapter Ten

Looking to Europe

At the start of 1922, the men who had turned their back on the concept of Irish football unity and brought the Football Association of Ireland into being some seven months earlier, were faced with a difficult balancing act in their attempt to convince international opinion of the legitimacy of the decision which had invited the wrath of the British International Board.

On the one hand they wished to have the blanket ban imposed on them by London lifted, in the hope that they would be allowed to compete in the British championship, a move which would enable the fledgling organisation to survive financially. The problem was that they were not prepared to accept English advice to rejoin the Irish Football Association, at least not in its old format. If the IFA were willing to shift their headquarters to Dublin, they might at a push agree to it, but the word from Belfast was that the IFA viewed this core issue as non-negotiable.

Confronted by this dilemma, the FAI decided to turn to Europe. The British Associations had walked away from FIFA in high dudgeon because of that body's refusal to blacklist the "Central Powers" who had waged war on the rest of Europe in 1914 and who were now desperately trying to rehabilitate themselves in the world of international sport. The consensus in Dublin was that if they succeeded in their application for membership of FIFA, they would then be better positioned to bring pressure to bear on London without having to bend the knee to Belfast.

The first step was to notify all member countries of FIFA of the new order in Irish football. Because Britain still controlled much of the communications industry in the opening half of the twentieth century, it was suspected that news of the decision to secede from the IFA, and the implied snub to the British Board, might not have been circulated widely. Thus, it was agreed to write to every country in Europe, as well as those in North and South America, informing them of the birth of the FAI, enclosing a copy of the rules and regulations of the new Association and canvassing their support for membership of FIFA.

The circular, signed by Jack Ryder, stated: "The FAI derives its authority from the will of its affiliated clubs, numbering upwards of two hundred. These clubs are comprised within the following bodies – (1) The Leinster Football Association. (2) The Belfast and District Football Association. (3) The Athlone and District Football Association and (4) The Munster Football Association. The FAI assumed control of the game outside the greater part of the Belfast and Co Antrim areas last year with the object of giving Ireland a full, free and unfettered opportunity of asserting itself in the international football tournaments of the world. Ireland never had that opportunity as the country declined to co-operate with the Irish Football Association Ltd."

Predictably, the initial response from the world governing body was cautious. In a letter dated 16 February 1922, they stated that provisional membership could be awarded to any national body providing they met the required criteria and their claims could be authenticated. Confirming that the rules of the Federation specified that only one national federation could be recognised in any one country, they asked the FAI to make their case as to why they, rather than the IFA in Belfast, should be so recognised. Replying to the FAI, FIFA's Secretary/Treasurer C.A.W. Hirschman wrote: "In order to take a well-based decision in such a serious question as the recognition of a national federation in your country, it is necessary that our committee is able to overlook [analyse] the situation. With regard to the confused conditions in Ireland, you will understand that we are presented with a difficult question which we cannot solve at the moment. At any time when you consider the situation has become clearer, we shall be pleased to reconsider your application." He also enquired how many clubs were affiliated to each body and if a "fusion" was possible. The format of that response strengthened Dublin's suspicions that the FA of England was utilising some of its former contacts in Europe to build a case against the FAI.

Looking to Europe

In a separate letter to the French Football Federation inviting them to play an international game "in the capital of Ireland" before the end of the season and by extension granting formal recognition to the newly established body, Jack Ryder wrote: "The body of which I am Secretary is in sole control of the game in the Irish Free State and in addition, possesses a large membership in that part of Ireland known as Northern Ireland. My Council is therefore justified in submitting that we alone are really qualified to enter into negotiations on behalf of Irish association footballers and we trust that your Council may find it possible to make the necessary arrangements. It is felt here that the moment in which the Irish Free State is about to take its place among the nations of the world, is an opportune one for an endeavour to establish a sporting alliance among two countries, so closely united by ties, extending far back in the annals of history."

The French response, stating that they were unable to countenance the proposal for a game against Ireland until such time as the world governing body had ruled on their application for membership of FIFA, could scarcely have been unexpected. The consolation came in the form of letters of support from not only the French, limited as it was, but also Hungary, Turkey, Sweden and the US. The Austrian FA was not among the early respondents, but on 10 April the FAI received a letter from the First Vienna club, exploring the possibility of games against Irish teams. The Austrians were informed that of the five clubs mentioned in their dispatch as possible opposition, Bohemians, Glentoran, Belfast Celtic, Linfield and Glenavon, only one was affiliated to the new body; and, mischievously, the FAI added that their understanding was that because of the newly created split in Irish football, the Irish Football Association was discouraging its clubs from competing with those in Europe.

Then, in December 1922, came the first real hint of a breakthrough, in the form of a copy of a letter received from Bob Murphy, a prominent name in football in the Dublin region. Murphy, who was involved with the Pioneers club, had earlier written to the French club Cercle Athlétique de Paris (CAP) exploring the possibility of their coming to play in Dublin. He now suggested that because of the favourable tone of the French reply, Bohemians, as well as the League of Ireland, should make further enquiries. Negotiations were duly opened, and on 28 December 1922,

CAP confirmed that they had received permission from FIFA to undertake a two-match Irish tour at Easter 1923.

It was the first formal acknowledgement by FIFA of the new organisation in Dublin, and for a guarantee of £400 – or £350 if the gate receipts did not exceed £600 – CAP agreed to travel to Ireland. Faced with that kind of financial risk, the match organisers saw fit to raise the admission charge to Dalymount Park to one shilling. Although many football enthusiasts found themselves priced out of the game, organising officials were still able to report a profit on a historic fixture.

At that point FIFA had not ruled on whether to grant provisional membership to the Football Association of Ireland, but there was a straw in the wind in May of that year. C.A.W. Hirschman, FIFA's secretary/treasurer, sent them a copy of his report to its upcoming Congress in Geneva, the first since the outbreak of war nine years earlier, in which he stated: "The outrage of war reminds us of the great social side of our international work, to assure peace by fostering friendships and better understanding between the nations." He added that because FIFA's funds had been deposited in a neutral country (Switzerland), they had not depreciated greatly during the war.

On his return from the FIFA Congress, Bob Murphy, one of the delegates who had presented the Irish case to an international audience, sent a personal letter to the Minister for External Affairs, seeking the active support of the Government in protecting Dublin's sporting rights. Reporting on his submissions to the meeting, Murphy said that while France and Belgium were not favourably disposed to their application initially, the FAI's cause received instant support from Italy and Switzerland and there were strong indications that Norway, Finland and Sweden would also fall into line before FIFA's Emergency Committee arrived at a decision in the matter. Murphy stressed that the FAI had no desire to interfere in the affairs of the Belfast-based Irish Football Association but disputed the right of that body to represent itself as "Ireland" in games against England, Scotland and Wales. He concluded by stating it was intolerable that inhabitants of the Irish Free State should have to submit to foreign control and said that as a matter of urgency, the Government should take steps to prevent unwarrantable interference.

Responding positively to that request, Oliver Grattan Esmonde, acting on behalf of the Minister for External Affairs, sent an official Government letter to be read at the next meeting of FIFA's Executive Committee. In it, he reaffirmed that "The FAI, established two years earlier, is acting with the consent of the Government of Saorstat Eireann [the Irish Free State] in controlling and regulating Association Football within all the territories of Saorstat Eireann and in that capacity, is entitled to all the rights and privileges appertaining to and enjoyed by, each and every separate National Association in accordance with Rule I of the articles of FIFA." In a covering letter to Jack Ryder, Grattan Esmonde, who was later knighted before becoming President of the Football Association of the Irish Free State, stated: "The Minister sincerely hopes that Ireland will be enabled to take her proper place in the world of international football, a game which is today such a powerful means of renewing and strengthening international friendships."

Some two months later, on 10 July 1923, Jack Ryder cabled FIFA, using the new title of the association for the first time: "The Football Association of the Irish Free State, formerly the Football Association of Ireland, desires information if an enquiry has yet been made to the British Foreign Office, regarding status of (the Irish Free State) being a distinct nation." Hirschman replied that the British authorities hadn't yet responded on the point. He said that FIFA had just received a letter from the Irish Football Association in which it recognised the status of the Irish Free State but defended the view that it didn't necessarily follow that football in Ireland should be administered by two separate organisations. Hirschman added: "They [the IFA] also allege that a number of clubs within the Free State, with full regard for the fact that the Irish Free State has separate political status, are still desirous of remaining members of the IFA."

In a letter to FIFA dated 20 July 1923, Ryder reiterated that the Irish Free State, as a national political entity, was entitled to its own football association and could not be expected to bend the knee to Belfast or any place outside the Irish Free State. Referring to the credentials handed to FIFA at their Congress in Geneva in May, Ryder stressed that "My Association is the competent governing body for football within the Irish Free State." He went on: "As stated at Congress, my Association for a long time possessed membership outside the Free State but in order to comply with the expressed wishes of the Federation, my Council surrendered this membership and thus gave practical evidence of their desire to avoid any interference with the rights of the Irish Football Association Ltd, Belfast. With the objective of defining still more clearly the limits of my Association's control, its name was changed from the Football Association of Ireland to the Football Association of the Irish Free State."

Refuting the IFA statement that clubs in the Free State wished to rejoin the Belfast body in order to play in the Irish League and Irish Cup competitions, Ryder described it as "an impudent effort to confuse the issue". He pointed out that the IFA's expressed desire to acquire membership within the Irish Free State was in direct contravention of the principle laid down at the Geneva Congress by the representative of Belgium and endorsed by the Federation, that "with the independence of the Irish Free State defined, the Federation would allow neither the FAIFS to hold membership within the area controlled by the Belfast Parliament nor permit the IFA to interfere with the affairs of the Irish Free State".

The fact that the four British Associations were not involved in FIFA's decision-making process boosted Dublin's hopes of a favourable outcome, although English FA officials were still thought to be making contact with old friends in Europe in the hope of blocking any move which would be seen to endorse the legitimacy of the Free State organisation. If they succeeded in that aim for any length of time, it might well precipitate divisions in Dublin between those who wanted international football and others who believed that this attraction, however admirable, should be secondary to the fundamental issue of total independence for the FAIFS in the territory they aspired to control.

Fittingly, the good news that the FAIFS had been admitted to provisional membership of the world governing body came in a tip-off from the Cercle Athlétique de Paris, the club which had set the train of events in motion by agreeing to travel to Ireland for that meeting with Bohemians. After informing Bob Murphy of FIFA's decision, Monsieur Achille Diecenne, secretary of the Parisian club, advised him that the Association should now commence preparations to send a team to the Olympic football championship in the French capital the following summer. Two days later, on 10 August 1923, came official confirmation that the infant organisation had been cleared to join the world's biggest sporting organisation, when Hirschman said the application had been approved by their Emergency Committee.

Full membership was still some way off, but with a foot in the door to the corridor of power, Jack Ryder and friends knew that just two years after that momentous decision to leave the IFA and embark on the journey to fulfilment, a major advance had been made. Now they could hope to convince mainland Europe to share their view that the dismissal of their claims for equality by the British Associations, acting in concert with the Irish Football Association in Belfast, had been high-handed and unjust.

Chapter Eleven

False Dawn

Confirmed as provisional members of FIFA and already building a reputation as a young, progressive organisation with an eye on the latest legislative and technical innovations in the global family of football, the Football Association of the Irish Free State had good reason to feel satisfied with their rate of development in the first half of 1923.

Thanks in the main to the astute leadership of Jack Ryder and the European connections of Bob Murphy, the FAIFS had succeeded in cultivating a significant relationship with FIFA in the space of less than two years. In that respect, progress was being made at a faster rate in football than it was with many of the other international aspirations of the infant State.

The importance of this cannot be overstated at a time when London was not overly keen to promote the image of a new nation. Delegates who attended FIFA's Congress in Geneva in May 1923 recalled the surprise of many of the European and South American delegates on learning of the foundation of the Irish Free State and the sense of pride felt by Irish people at the spectacle of the national flag fluttering alongside those of other, longer-established countries on the streets of the city.

On one front, however, ambition remained unrequited. Relations with the IFA had now become more estranged than ever after Belfast realised that, far from their original perception of the split as a temporary demonstration of petulance, the division was now hardening into a permanent one. And this, in turn, led to a more confrontational stance by the other British Associations in their attempt to bring the new organisation to heel. Already at loggerheads with the rest of the football world, they did not relish the prospect of further turbulence on their doorstep.

For Dublin there was also the dilemma of how to handle the problem of the northern clubs who had opted out of the Irish Football Association. Initially, the decision of the clubs competing in the Falls and District League in Belfast and others in Co Armagh to affiliate to the southern body was seen as something of a coup. But soon the practicalities of managing the situation convinced the FAIFS authorities that, in this instance, they would be better advised to adhere to the political partition of the island.

For example, they were not impressed when Alton United of the Falls League upset all predictions by reaching the Free State Cup final against Shelbourne at Dalymount Park on St Patrick's Day, 1923. At the time, the much longer-established Irish League ridiculed the playing standards south of the border as being little better than Junior level. And they were apparently vindicated in that viewpoint when, against all the odds, Alton defeated Fordsons in the semi-final, to set up a novel date with Shelbourne. It is true that they included members of the suspended Belfast Celtic team in their ranks, but essentially they were a Junior team taking on a talented Shelbourne side which included senior international players like Val Harris and Mick "Boxer" Foley. To all but the most optimistic Alton supporters, it appeared to be a massive mis-match, but to the dismay of local officials and the thinly veiled delight of those in the north, the visitors won by the only goal of the game from Andy McSherry.

To make matters worse, the build-up to the game attracted a lot of adverse publicity when it was revealed that on arrival at Amiens St (Connolly) railway station, the Alton players and supporters had been given an armed escort by the IRA. The reasons for that were not immediately clear, but with the turmoil occasioned by the Civil War still lingering and clubs from the Falls League attracting a large nationalist following, the threat was sufficiently real to move the security authorities in Dublin to put the north city area on special alert. And there was a revealing postscript when, before FAIFS officials would allow the trophy to be taken across the border, they insisted on Alton producing established people from the local community who were prepared to write personal guarantees concerning its safe return the following year.

That didn't sit easily with everybody on the Falls Road in Belfast, particularly in view of a conference which had been held at short notice, at the request of northern clubs, in Dublin the previous month. Representatives of 42 clubs met with the officers of the FAIFS, hoping to bring pressure on them to regularise the relationship between the two Associations in the context of their membership of the body. Alas, the meeting broke down in some disarray, and Jack Ryder's handwritten notes of the talks disclose that Dublin felt the time wasn't opportune for the rival Associations to face each other across the table.

Conceivably, that was because discussions were already in train for a special meeting of the British International Board in Liverpool, convened by the FA of England with a view to resolving the Irish crisis. This Conference had come about largely through the persistence of Ryder and his determination to persuade the Government to take a more active role in what was clearly an extension of the political settlement of 1921. Eventually the Department for External Affairs was sufficiently exercised to invoke the assistance of Tim Healy, the Governor-General in Ireland, in putting pressure on the British Government to get involved. This, in turn, led to British parliamentarians, with an eye on the vote of the Irish diaspora, persuading Lancaster Gate to intervene. Both the Irish Associations were invited to hold a watching brief at the Conference, and the Dublin body, seeking to build a credible case for a seat on the Board, was anxious to be seen to remove any obvious roadblocks in pursuit of that objective. One of them was the need to conform to a directive of FIFA to restrict their activities to the boundaries of the Irish Free State. To this end, having changed the title of the organisation and by distancing themselves from the Falls and District League, they could claim, with some justification, to be doing all in their power to meet the requirements of both FIFA and the British Board.

The Conference, chaired by Mr J.C. Clegg, President of the FA of England, took place at the Lime Street Station Hotel in Liverpool on 18 October 1923, and the FAIFS was represented by Messrs J.F. Harrison, H.F. Murphy, L.C. Sheridan, J.S. Smurthwaite and J.A. Ryder. The IFA delegation was headed by Captain J.M. Wilton, with Messrs A. McAughey, J.M. Small and J. MacBride also in attendance. In addressing the delegates, the Chairman said he had called the Conference to see if anything could be done to straighten out matters relating to football in Ireland and promptly called on the representatives of the FAIFS to state their case. They made the following five points:

1. The Free State Football Association recognises the Northern Ireland Football Association as the sole governing body of football in that portion of Ireland which is outside the Irish Free State and, in exchange, expects to be recognised as the sole governing body of football in the Irish Free State.

2. The Free State Football Association will, on reciprocal terms, recognise and enforce within the Irish Free State all suspensions, etc in the territory under control of the Northern Association.

3. In order that the whole of Ireland may be represented in international matches with England, Scotland and Wales, the Free State Football Association is prepared to join with the Northern Association in setting up a selection committee with equal representation from the two Irish Associations to control such matches. As regards Ireland's home international matches with the countries of Great Britain, it will also agree that they should be played alternately, in Northern Ireland and the Irish Free State.

4. The Free State Football Association will facilitate intercourse between its clubs and those of the Northern Association and it is prepared, should any desire for competitive games between the two sets of clubs manifest itself, to confer with the Northern Association with the object of fixing regulations to govern such competitions.

5. The Free State Football Association, having altered its original title of the Football Association of Ireland in order to define precisely the limits of its jurisdiction, expects that the Irish Football Association Ltd. will in turn substitute for its present name some title which will indicate, in similar fashion, the extent of its control. In the opinion of the Free State Football Association, the title, Irish Football Association, is not appropriate in existing circumstances.

Chapter Eleven

According to the official minutes of the meeting, the Chairman commented that having heard the submissions and the demands made by the Irish Free State Football Association, the Conference should retire to consider them. They then reported as follows: No objection was made (1) to the Football Association of Ireland changing its name to the Football Association of the Irish Free State; (2) to the Irish Football Association and the Football Association of the Irish Free State exercising full jurisdiction within their own area; and (3) to the mutual recognition of suspensions. The Conference recommends (1) That the Football Association of the Irish Free State be recognised as an Association with Dominion status, that the Associations, clubs and players of the Football Association (of England), the Scottish Football Association and the Football Association of Wales be eligible to play matches with the Football Association of the Irish Free State, its clubs and its players. (2) That the present suspensions by the Irish Football Association be removed.

Weighed against the high hopes which Dublin took into the Liverpool Conference, those recommendations were vastly disappointing. The first three points of Clegg's findings were fatuous to the point of being wholly cynical. Refusing to acknowledge it for what it was, the FAI's action in changing the title of the organisation smacked of a degree of disdain which suggested that the FA of England was not interested in brokering a compromise deal, and it reinforced the views of at least some of the southern officials that the hand of England could be detected in the early reluctance of some European countries to admit the FAIFS to membership of FIFA. To their credit, however, the next generation of legislators at the FA of England was markedly more sensitive about the grievances felt by the newly created body.

The primary purpose of the Conference, as Dublin saw it, was the opportunity it could provide to facilitate their rehabilitation in the British championship, as part of an all-Ireland team. And this was driven by the parlous state of their finances since seceding from the IFA. Gate receipts from a game against England in Dublin would almost certainly fund their operations for an entire season in addition to providing a stimulus for the development of the sport throughout southern Ireland. And while Scotland lacked that kind of charisma, they too had a role to play in the grand plan of the FAIFS.

All this, it was hoped, could be achieved without sacrificing their new independence, and with a sense of optimism which bordered on naivety, they believed that Belfast would buy into it in the belief that it could herald a return to the old order. James Wilton, for one, was unlikely to be hoodwinked in this manner, however, and he had, almost certainly, discussed all possible scenarios with Clegg, in the approach to the Conference.

Yet the formula of words, when it emerged, was still designed to shock the Dublin contingent. Ignoring unashamedly the reference to all-Ireland teams playing home games on a rotational basis in Belfast and Dublin, the recommendations focused instead on an arrangement which amounted to nothing less than blanket support for the Irish Football Association. Fearing the worst but anxious to put their apprehension to the test, the FAIFS contacted the Welsh Association just six weeks later, with a view to their national team playing in Dublin. They responded, after another six weeks, on 10 January 1924, stating that they were unable to accept the invitation because they were already committed to playing an international game against Ireland in Belfast in March. That reply confirmed the suspicion that, stripped of the verbosity, the Conference in Liverpool had indeed been nothing more than an exercise in cynicism.

It is probable that the Dublin delegation did not fully comprehend the consequences of the term "Dominion status" in England's acceptance of the FAIFS until they returned home, by which time it was too late to seek quick redress. With the insertion of those two words, the English had handed the IFA carte blanche in the blatantly unfair practice of selecting players born outside Northern Ireland for their team while at the same time denying the FAIFS a reciprocal arrangement. Moreover, it encouraged the Northern Ireland body in their belief that they were entitled to the exclusive right to play under the title of Ireland in British championship games – apart from three non-competitive fixtures against France (twice) and Norway, these were the only international matches they played for the next 27 years. On these two basic issues centred the bitter discord and mutual contempt felt by the rival organisations for at least another five decades.

The findings of the Liverpool Conference were sugar-coated by the inclusion of the paragraph stating that the Football Association (of England), like those of Scotland and Wales, would now be eligible to play against the Irish Free State. That, however, was shown to be no more than a wicked deception, for the events of the next 40 years proved that there was little or no intention in Britain to engage the southern Irish in competition. England eventually broke the ice in 1946, and Wales followed 14 years later, but it required the lottery of the draw for the preliminaries of the 1962 World Cup to force Scotland to Dublin in 1961. In a very real sense, those omissions invalidated all the conclusions of the Conference, but in spite of Dublin's protestations, the IFA, with the active support of the other British Associations, continued to select players from the south, based on the Liverpool talks, until eventually FIFA brought a semblance of rationality to the whole sorry affair in 1950 by decreeing that Northern Ireland could no longer lay claim to players born outside their jurisdiction.

The effect of that Liverpool rejection was to convince the FAIFS of the fact that now, more than ever, their future was tied up with Europe rather than Britain, and while subsequent attempts were made by the British Board to rationalise the structure of Irish football, all were predicated on Dublin abandoning "the folly of its ways" and realigning with Belfast.

Within months of the failed Lime St talks, another attempt to find a viable working relationship between the rival Irish Associations was up and running. Through it all, however, a broad seam of distrust permeated every attempt to reconcile differences on the core issues which had driven them apart four years earlier. Deep down, the pragmatists on either side sensed that, unlike the problems experienced by rugby union almost fifty years earlier, this dispute would not be solved by negotiation any time soon.

Wholly disillusioned by what they had seen and heard in Liverpool, the southern delegation set about nurturing fledgling relationships in Europe, with a view to securing full membership of FIFA. Foremost among these was the partnership with Italy, who had been quick to respond to the call when erstwhile officers of the Leinster Association went in search of friendly voices in the summer of 1921. Little surprise, then, that when

Dublin needed a formal proposer to back their application for full status, it was to Rome that they turned. The possibility of doing business with the British Board would, of course, be revisited in future years, but only as an adjunct to their European connections.

Chapter Twelve

Olympic Odyssey

When Monsieur Achille Diecenne, Secretary of the Cercle Athlétique de Paris club, tipped off Bob Murphy, one of the FAI's power brokers in its formative years, that FIFA's Emergency Committee had just admitted the Association to provisional membership of the world governing body in August 1923, he included a rider that they should now start preparations to enter immediately a football team for the Olympic Games in Paris the following summer.

The Olympic Council of Ireland had only just been formed, and it is quite possible that the officers of the FAIFS had been unaware of the football championship and, more importantly, that Ireland was now in a position to join the elite of amateur sport on a major international stage. The time frame was such that they had little more than 10 months to put things in order before the big kick-off but, undaunted, they set about ensuring that for the first time Ireland would be represented in the Olympic football competition.

The victory of Alton United, a Junior club with just a sprinkling of players with senior experience, over Shelbourne in the final of the FAI Cup proved that the standard in the new League of Ireland championship was far from exalted. That was an ominous reminder of the amount of work to be done if Ireland were to become competitive at a high level of international football, but in this instance the problem was aggravated, of course, by the fact that none of the professional players involved in the championship would be eligible for selection in Paris.

The Olympic movement in the 1920s was a long way removed from the sophistication of the modern era, with all the organisational work being undertaken by a local committee. Thus it was, that a group of expatriate

Irishmen living in Paris came to learn of the preliminary arrangements being put in place, and one of them, Charles McDevitt, offered to represent the FAIFS. Because of the Association's acute shortage of money, it was an offer that was gladly accepted, and within weeks they had reason to be glad they made the appointment.

J.J. Keane, a modest track runner whose only other sporting interest lay in the GAA, had emerged at the head of the Olympic movement in Ireland, and pretty soon he made it clear that he was opposed to the notion of the FAIFS sending a team to the Games in Paris. This was because the Olympic Council of Ireland was constituted on a 32-county basis and football was now, effectively, partitioned in the country. With the type of rationale which would inform GAA opinion for much of the next fifty years, Keane believed that football in Ireland did not deserve to be represented at the Games because of Dublin's decision to secede from the Irish Football Association in Belfast. Fortunately, McDevitt came to learn of his objections and informed the FAIFS of the urgent need to find a Northern Ireland player of reasonable proficiency who had the means to sustain himself in Paris for up to four weeks. This was duly done and the path cleared to a new chapter of Irish sporting history.

With the exception of the handful of international games which were played in Dublin, starting with the visit of England to Lansdowne Road in March 1900, Leinster officials had little experience of the routine involved in planning for big events and preparing teams to participate in them. To that extent, they were heading into largely unknown territory on this Olympian escapade, and it showed in some quaint decisions which would be ridiculed in the modern world. One of them, made at Council level, was to insert an advertisement in several newspapers seeking out players interested in taking part in the Olympic championship.

Players were requested to submit their CVs to the Association, stating their age, experience and preferred positions. They were reminded that their sojourn in France could be a long one, with the championship due to start on 24 May and the final taking place on 10 June. It was also made clear that the earliest return date would be 2 June and, most importantly, no expenses would be paid for loss of earnings in that period. The number of responses received is not recorded, but the likelihood is that only those employed in the professions were able to meet the requirements. In the event, the team did reasonably well, beating Bulgaria before losing to the Netherlands in extra time in the quarter-finals of the competition. A third game, against Estonia, was played before the team returned home, and the public verdict on the first overseas assignment undertaken by the FAIFS was not unfavourable. The following month, the first home international fixture for the amateur team was staged at Dalymount, against the US Olympic side on its way back from Paris. Only a small crowd, representing gate receipts of £259-9-0 – FIFA's percentage takings amounted to £1-18-6 – turned up to watch the match, but in a historical sense it was a significant occasion.

A sharp postscript to that ground-breaking expedition to Paris was provided by Larry Sheridan the following year when he drafted a letter to FIFA enquiring if they could assist in enabling the Association to circumvent the influence of Keane in any future involvement in the Olympic Games. Sheridan wrote: "I am desirous of availing of this opportunity to draw attention to the many difficulties which were placed in the way of my Association last year in connection with the entry of its national team for the Olympiad at Paris. As a result of the correspondence which passed at the time between my Association and the Executive Olympic Council, you are doubtless aware of the fact that Ireland's representative on that Council, Mr J.J. Keane, apparently from lack of sympathy with Association football and a desire that the Irish Free State should not be represented in that sport in the Olympic Games, withheld material official information as regards the rules and regulations governing the competition, and I may say that it was only at the last moment and on pressure from Paris, that he consented to confirm the official entry of the Irish football team. In the circumstances and in the hope of preventing a recurrence of the deadlock which almost shut the Irish football team out of the Games last year, I am to ask respectfully, whether the Board can suggest any means by which the entry can be made a mere matter of application by the recognised body of that sport, instead of being as it is in Ireland, conditional upon the sanction of an avowed opponent." The response was in the negative.

Less than five months after the failed Liverpool Conference, another

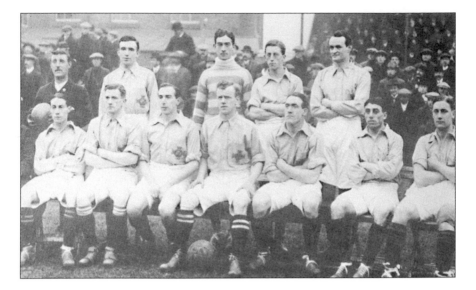

Above: The Ireland team which won the British championship for the first time in the 1913–14 season. Back row (from left to right): Val Harris, Fred McKee, Davy Rollo, Pat O'Connell. Front row: E.H. Seymour, Sam Young, Billy Gillespie, Alex Craig, Billy Lacey, Louis Bookman, Billy McConnell. O'Connell went on to enjoy a fine managerial career, including a spell in charge of Barcelona.

Above: The Irish Free State's first competitive game resulted in victory over Bulgaria in a first round tie in the Olympic football championship in 1924. They were eventually beaten by the Netherlands in extra time in the quarter-finals of the competition.

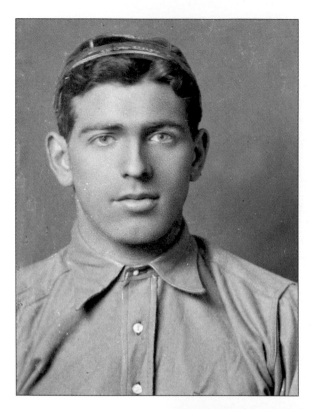

Left: Bill McCracken, a superb defender, won the first of his 15 caps against England in 1902 and his last in the meeting with Scotland in 1923. He demanded a fee of £10, five times the going rate for the match with England in 1907 and didn't reappear in the international team until 1922.

Right: Elisha Scott the youngest member of a famous goalkeeping family. His older brothers, Tom and Billy, also played for Ireland and in an era of relatively few international games, the trio won 69 caps between them.

Above: The Irish Free State team which staged a remarkable recovery to blast Belgium 3–1 in Brussels in 1930. From the left: John Joe Flood, Joe Goulding, Billy Lacey, Tom Farquharson, Frank McLoughlin, Jimmy Dunne, Freddie Horlacher, William "Sacky" Glen, Mick O'Brien, Harry Duggan, Jack McCarthy. It marked the last international appearance of Lacey who won his first cap against England 21 years earlier.

Above: The Ireland (FAI) team which defeated Switzerland 1–0 in Berne in 1937. Back row (from left to right): Johnny Feehan, Mick McCarthy (reserve goalkeeper), Joe O'Reilly, Charlie Turner, Tommy Breen, Con Moulson. Front row: Johnny Brown, Davy Jordan, Jimmy Dunne, William O'Neill, Paddy Farrell, Willie Fallon.

Right: Peter Doherty was acknowledged as one of the outstanding inside-forwards of all time before going on to become Northern Ireland's first manager. He led the team to the World Cup finals in Sweden in 1958.

Left: A youthful Jack Carey in only his fourth appearance against Switzerland at Dalymount Park in 1938. Carey captained Europe against Great Britain at Hampden Park in 1947 before ending his playing career in 1953. He later became manager/coach of the Republic of Ireland team.

Left: Jack Carey, captain of the Ireland team which played England at Dalymount Park in 1946, introduces the Irish President, Sean T. O'Kelly, to Paddy Coad in a pre-match ceremony. Alex Stevenson, the only Glasgow Rangers player to represent the southern Irish team, is on Coad's left.

Above: Ronnie Nolan makes a sliding tackle to deny Johnny Haynes in a memorable 1–1 draw in the return World Cup game against England at Dalymount Park in May 1957. Nolan's recall was described by Jack Carey as the catalyst in the team beaten 5–1 in the first leg of the tie at Wembley eleven days earlier.

Above: The celebrated Blanchflower brothers, Jackie (left) and Danny, an integral part of Northern Ireland teams in the 1950s. Injuries sustained in the Manchester United air disaster at Munich in February 1958 ended Jackie's playing career but Danny captained the northern team in the World Cup finals later that year before succeeding Peter Doherty as manager.

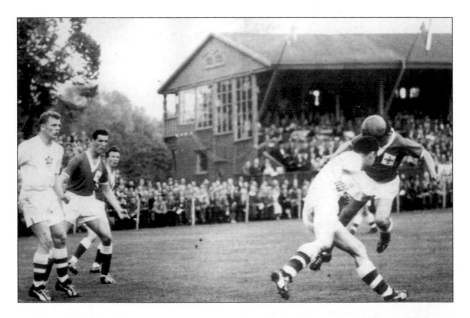

Above: Bertie Peacock, the skilful Glasgow Celtic player, wins a rare heading duel as Northern Ireland overcome Czechoslovakia 2–1 in a play-off at Malmo to reach the quarter-finals of the 1958 World Cup.

Above: Harry Gregg, a hero amid the carnage of the Munich disaster, pictured with the Northern Ireland team in 1957. Gregg, in the centre of the back row, has three of the province's most talented players, Jimmy McIlroy, Danny Blanchflower and Billy Bingham immediately in front of him.

Left: Danny Blanchflower, in a familiar pose, calls the shots as Northern Ireland take on England on their return from Sweden.

Above: Noel Cantwell, one of the great utility players in consecutive Republic of Ireland teams, has a scoring attempt smothered by the Spanish defence in the home team's 1–0 win in the opening leg of their World Cup tie at Dalymount Park in May 1965.

Above: Noel Cantwell, by now deployed at centre-half, can only watch in anguish as a shot from Antonio Ufarte leaves Pat Dunne stranded for Spain's winner in their World Cup play-off at Paris in November 1965.

round of talks, aimed at breaking the impasse between the FAIFS and IFA, was up and running. Having regard to the depth of disillusionment which set in at the end of the Merseyside negotiations, this was – to say the least surprising – and, in a perverse way, it served to emphasise yet again how committed the Associations were to achieving their ambitions without realistic regard for the aspirations of those in the opposite camp.

While grimly determined to retain their newly acquired independence, southern officials still clung to the hope that an arrangement could be made whereby they would join with Belfast in fielding a team in the British championship and share in the financial benefits flowing from such an accommodation. The IFA's line of logic was if they could bring Dublin back on board with the incentive of playing in the championship, they would then be closer to restoring the structure which obtained in Irish football prior to 1921.

On 19 November 1924, a letter was received in Dublin from the FA of England stating that they had considered the correspondence from both the FAIFS and IFA on the matter of fielding an all-Ireland team and were of the opinion that the only outstanding issue was that of agreeing an alternative chairman. If there were other points, they asked to be informed of them. By way of a reply, a draft letter was then approved in relation to the other issues which might arise on the proposed International Team Selection Committee: (1) the playing of Ireland's home games alternately in the Irish Free State and Northern Ireland, and (2) the financial arrangements for such games.

Some six weeks later, London replied that they had no desire to involve themselves in the internal affairs of either the FAIFS or the IFA. Regarding international affiliation, they would not arrange games with two Irish Associations but would continue to play against Ireland teams, providing the two Irish Associations agreed to act as one body in this instance. It was their opinion that the FAIFS should agree (1) to alternate chairmanship, and (2) to play international games alternately in Dublin and Belfast. No opinion was expressed as to the financial arrangements, in spite of the southern body's allegations that the IFA was seeking to take financial control of all Ireland's home games, in Dublin as well as Belfast.

On 8 March 1925, the FAIFS met to formulate their strategy, ahead of a meeting between representatives of the England, Scotland and Wales Associations in Liverpool the following month. It was decided to write a letter to the English FA asking if they would receive a deputation before the talks, with a view to an all-Ireland team playing in the British championship on the lines they had suggested the previous year. If this request was refused, they resolved to put their point of view in writing for consideration at the Conference. The FAIFS meeting was adjourned at that point, only to be reconvened the following evening, on receipt of a letter from the IFA.

It transpired that Belfast had agreed to accept two suggestions contained in a communiqué from the FA of England, i.e. (1) to rotate the chairmanship of match arrangements for fixtures involving an all-Ireland team, and (2) to stage international matches alternately in Dublin and Belfast, but only on the basis of the agreement unanimously arrived at by representatives of the FAIFS and IFA at the conference held in Belfast on 8 March 1924. This was a reference not just to the financial arrangements, but to the vexed question of the chairmanship of the committee which would select the Ireland team. In any such arrangement, the Associations would nominate an equal number of selectors with the chairman of the committee holding a casting vote. And crucially, the IFA was insisting that they retain the right to appoint a chairman, a point which was rejected by Dublin.

Not unexpectedly, perhaps, the outcome of the Conference held in Liverpool on 14 March 1925, between officers of the English, Scottish and Welsh Associations, held little joy for the FAIFS. A letter signed by the Secretary of the FA of England, F.J. Wall, stated, "It was with much regret we learned that the two Irish Associations have not come to a mutual agreement for united action in respect of international matches." It went on to say that no consideration would be given to any suggestion to play more than one international game in Ireland and that, in the meantime, the status quo would continue. Effectively, it confirmed the primacy of the IFA in British eyes.

Another potential flashpoint in north–south relations was averted after Jack Ryder, the FAIFS Secretary, notified his opposite number in Belfast of reports that representatives of a body styling itself "the National Football

Association" had sought affiliation to the IFA and been received by officials in Belfast. If this were true, he said, it would seem to be a breach of the terms agreed at the 1923 Conference, which stipulated that neither of the rival Associations would interfere in the domestic affairs of the other. No mention was made of the names of the people or clubs involved, but at different times both Shelbourne and Bohemians were thought to be unhappy with the ongoing strife in the two power bases of Irish football.

In this instance, at least, the IFA was quick to be seen to back the hierarchy in Dublin, stating that two gentlemen, purporting to represent the National Football Association, had indeed been present in Belfast and met with the President of the Association in relation to possible affiliation. They said that the Association had acted in accordance with the agreement reached at the Liverpool Conference and that the people in question had been told that in no circumstances could their application for affiliation be considered. That was mildly reassuring for the FAIFS, even if the incident served to remind them that not everybody was happy about the stalemate developing between the protagonists. Later, the IFA again wrote to Dublin stating that J.J. Kelly, a member of the FAIFS's Consultative Committee, had applied for membership of their Association and asking if he was in good standing with them. It was decided to reply in the affirmative.

With the experience of the Olympic football championship in Paris to guide them, the FAIFS was soon redoubling its efforts to organise a senior international fixture. Only then could they feel justified in their claim that they had completed the transition from junior partner in a contentious all-Ireland coalition to a fully fledged international entity in their own right. At a time when the IFA was restricted to playing games in the British championship, Dublin coveted the chance of competing against a top-class European country and the prestige which would accrue from it. The lessons of the Olympic odyssey had been sufficiently encouraging to expand their horizons, but the initial response to their enquiries for a game in 1926 was vaguely disquieting.

Given that it was a French club, Cercle Athlétique de Paris, who became the first overseas side to play in Dublin after the split, thereby setting in train the sequence of events which led to the FAIFS being admitted to membership of FIFA, it was reasonable that Jack Ryder should commence his search for European opposition for Ireland's senior team with a phone call to the French Federation. In a handwritten note to his French counterpart, Henri Delaunay, Ryder suggested an Easter date for the game, in the hope that he would be able to line up a second fixture later in the year. The response, when it came, was not quite what he had anticipated. Stating that it would not be feasible to accept the fixture, Delaunay attributed the high rate of exchange in what he termed "the British countries" as one of the reasons for declining the invitation.

The Italian Federation likewise turned down the suggestion of travelling to Dublin the following Easter, but undertook to visit the city in 1927 if Ireland agreed to play Italy in Milan, later changed to Turin, on 21 March 1926. That was an offer the Irish could not refuse and, five years after breaking with the IFA, the FAIFS was at last ready to test the water in senior international competition. As a means of raising money to fund the Turin engagement, the Association contacted both Glasgow Celtic and Rangers in the hope that they would be available to play at Dalymount Park, but like Manchester United, Everton and Aston Villa, they said they had no vacant dates.

In a stark reversal of the norm, the FAIFS later spurned an invitation for a game against Germany. Declining the offer, Larry Sheridan, Honorary Secretary of the FAIFS, wrote: "We are quite willing to have sporting intercourse with your Federation, but we regret to inform you that our international programme for the next two years is already made." That was a blatant distortion of the truth, and it could be attributed to the fixation to keep open the lines of communication with London.

For all the indications to the contrary, Dublin was still hoping against hope that the Football Association of England would change tack and, further down the line, put pressure on Belfast to co-operate with the FAIFS. That was never likely to happen, but it is a measure of the Association's desperation to access the big money available from games against England that they were prepared to turn down another offer on the basis of that slim possibility. And what better way of ingratiating themselves with England than in rejecting Germany, just a couple of years after the British had called for a blanket ban on all sporting contact with the Germans, in the immediate aftermath of the Great War.

Some 25 years on, Dublin was still playing a political game with Germany, but this time the roles were changed. With Hitler's Nazi movement becoming more menacing with each passing day, the Germans had few friends in Europe in the first half of 1939. Dublin was one of the exceptions. Germany's quest for international competition, in preparation for the Olympic Games planned for London in 1940, was now more difficult than ever but with all hope of cosying up to England long since abandoned, the FAIFS had no difficulty in agreeing to take on the German national team in Bremen in May 1939, the last western European team to do so, before the outbreak of the Second World War.

Chapter Thirteen

Italian Adventure

One of the consequences of the suspension of international football for the four-year duration of the First World War was that it left the game at this level in a state of flux. Promising young careers were abandoned, never to flower, while older footballers, approaching the end of their playing days, discovered that the sport had left them behind by the time that Ireland ran out for their first post-war game against England at Windsor Park on 25 October 1919.

In essence, it meant the loss of the majority of the talented Irish squad which had won the British championship for the first time just months before Europe was engulfed in flames and the deprivations of war were visited on every section of society. And that, in turn, impacted on the fortunes of the teams the IFA sent out on the resumption of the British championship. Among those lost to the team selectors were Val Harris, an inspirational team captain from the football heartland of Ringsend in Dublin, and Pat O'Connell, who by now was into his late thirties.

Even as Harris and O'Connell departed the scene, however, another father figure of Irish football in the pre-war era, Billy McCracken, was making a dramatic return. The redoubtable Belfast man was regarded as a master of the dubious art of exploiting the offside trap and is remembered in folklore as the man responsible for having the relevant rule amended in 1925. A rebel who found himself in constant conflict with authority, he was suspended indefinitely by the IFA after demanding a match fee of £10, five times the normal rate, for playing in the game against England at Liverpool in 1907. It is a long road that has no ending, however, and in 1922 McCracken finally made his peace with the football authorities and went on to make five more international appearances for Northern Ireland.

And then there was Mickey Hamill, a name which would invoke respect on both sides of the Irish Sea long after the sap had run dry and he had departed into the shadows. At just 5 ft 8 ins, Hamill didn't appear to meet the physical requirements of a top-class centre-half, but the measure of his power was that for all his lack of height, the man from the Falls Road still managed to dominate all the big-name centre-forwards of his time, in productive spells at Manchester United and Manchester City.

Unfortunately, he would make just two post-war international appearances before time ran out on him, but the selectors could still count on the front-line skills of Billy Gillespie, another of the father figures of their successful championship team in 1914. And it was Gillespie who came up with the precious goal which enabled Ireland to salvage a 1–1 draw with England in Belfast in 1921, a rare escape from the disappointment of having to settle for second best in meetings with the bluebloods of the British game.

At a time when the signs of fissure were already beginning to manifest themselves in the structure of the domestic game, two players born in the territory which would shortly become the Irish Free State, Billy Lacey and Patsy Gallagher, lined up in the Ireland team which opposed England in the game which marked the return of international competition in the post-war era. Lacey, as we have seen, was a much-travelled player at a time when the financial inducements of club transfers hadn't yet become extravagant, but the most authentic epitaph to his international career is that it spanned an astonishing 21 years, from 1909, when he won his first cap against England at Bradford, to 1930, when he played against Belgium at the age of 41.

Gallagher, a frail, slightly stooped man, was born in Milford, Co Donegal, but was taken by his family to Scotland as a boy. There he became a folk hero with Celtic, sharing in six League championship and four Scottish Cup triumphs between 1911 and 1926, and his winner against Dundee in the 1925 final is still regarded as one of the most remarkable Cup final goals on record. Although he played 11 times for Northern Ireland, he made just one appearance for the Irish Free State, against Spain at Dalymount Park in 1931, at a stage when his playing career was winding down at Falkirk.

For the next twenty years, Northern Ireland would continue to play southern players at their discretion, and while there were some notable exceptions, these individuals mostly welcomed the opportunity of additional international football, not to mention the match fees. Officials in Dublin continued to campaign against the system which allowed them to do so, but for all the protestations, the reality was that the majority of players were loath to surrender these extra perks until they were eventually forced to in 1950.

Ironically, Patsy Gallagher was in the Northern Ireland team beaten by Scotland some three weeks before the Irish Free State set out on their historic journey to Italy for the first senior international fixture undertaken by the fledgling organisation, in Turin on 21 March 1926. Because of the protracted nature of the trip, Glasgow Celtic refused to release their inside-forward for the historic game, a decision which put a strain on the exceptional rapport the club had with supporters based in Ireland. Likewise, Hull City declined to make Mick O'Brien, their towering centre-half, available for the Italian fixture, despite clearing him to play for Northern Ireland in the 3–0 defeat of Wales in Belfast the previous month.

Assembling a team capable of doing justice to the occasion wasn't the only problem on the horizon for harassed FAIFS officials. Two years earlier, the task of organising the participation of their amateur team in the Olympic Games in Paris had gone off without a hitch, but then the welfare of the players and travelling officials had been, to a large extent, the responsibility of the local organising committee in Paris. This was a more complex operation, and it didn't help that with just eight days to go, the Italian Federation moved the game from Milan to the Motovelodromo in Turin.

The switch was attributed to a serious but unspecified change of circumstances, and it did nothing to ease the job of those entrusted with making arrangements for the overland journey. So perturbed was the FAIFS about the possibility of taking a big financial hit on the fixture, that they had specifically requested that it be staged in the north of Italy to reduce the costs of travel. Earlier indications were that the hosts favoured Rome as the location, but after they were made aware of the Irish concerns, it was determined that it be played in either Milan or Turin. The Italians, meanwhile, had to consult Dublin, first on the colour or colours of the national flag, and then on the colour of the jerseys to be worn by the Irish team. The birth of a nation and the arrival of a new national football team would lead to more such enquiries as time went on.

It is a measure of the improvised nature of the assignment that less than three weeks before the international game, a second fixture was added. It was agreed that the Irish team would play Cercle Athlétique de Paris in an exhibition game in the French capital on the return journey to Dublin, on condition that the French club would make an Irish tour at the end of the season. On 9 March 1926, Larry Sheridan wrote to Henri Delaunay, the French Federation Secretary, confirming that the FAIFS had granted permission for a team styled as the Irish Nomads and including many of the players chosen to face Italy, to play CAP – on the express understanding that similar permission would be forthcoming from the authorities in France.

The effect of this was to lengthen the duration of the tour and, as a consequence, discourage English clubs from releasing players to join the Irish squad. It meant that Jimmy Dunne, later to mature into one of the most talented Irish players of his generation, was not released by Sheffield United, while Leeds United likewise refused to clear Harry Duggan who, in tandem with Dunne, might have been expected to bring an added touch of class to the forward line. Given that, in the context of football, Dublin had few friends in London in the immediate aftermath of independence, there was little point in appealing to the English FA to put pressure on the clubs to co-operate.

Originally, the fond hope was to select a team of sufficient talent to exploit any complacency the Italians might have, but with so many withdrawals, the selection committee was eventually forced to rely on a squad of home-based players. To this end, a trial game was arranged for Dalymount Park on 28 February, and three days later, when the team was announced, it was revealed that in addition to local part-time professional players, two amateurs from Bohemians, Harry Cannon and Jack McCarthy, were included in the side. John O'Sullivan, an amateur with Fordsons, was one of three reserves named to travel, but he promptly wrote to the FAIFS stating "that unless the Association makes arrangements for me as they have done for other players, I cannot afford to take time off work to make the trip".

Inevitably, the team announcement didn't meet with the approval of everyone, the biggest surprise being the omission of Billy "Juicy" Farrell. The colourful Shamrock Rovers forward was one of the bigger personalities playing in the new Free State League, but back in 1926, after suffering a sharp loss of form, he wasn't deemed worthy of a place in the national team. Instead, the job of leading the attack went to Ned Brookes of Athlone Town who, after winning an Irish Senior Cup medal with Shelbourne in 1920, went on to play for Northern Ireland against Scotland in Glasgow. Now, six years later, Brookes was summoned for a return to the big stage. Sadly, however, he never made it to Turin, as his seven-year-old son died in a motoring accident just days before the squad was due to leave. After that he never had an opportunity of playing international football again. Much to the disappointment of Rovers supporters, Farrell was again overlooked when the selectors met later to name a replacement, the position going to Fran Watters of Shelbourne.

Mick Foley, the veteran Shelbourne defender, was named as first captain of the national team and, like other members of the squad, he was informed by letter of his selection and the travel arrangements being put in place for the players. It stated that the official party would leave Dublin on Wednesday, 17 March for the Sunday game and, travelling overland, would arrive back on either Wednesday or Thursday of the following week. Foley was advised to obtain a passport by calling at the office of the Civic Guard authorities at Lower Castle Yard in Dublin and reminded that it should be endorsed for France, Switzerland and Italy. Like the other professional players selected, he would be paid a match fee of six pounds. Amateur players would be given a suitably inscribed gold medal.

It is a measure of the unknown quantity of the Irish team that Bruno Conevali, a journalist with the Italian newspaper *Gazzetta Dello Sport*, saw fit to write to the FAIFS, enquiring whether the team was amateur or professional. He also asked "if this is the same side which recently played Galles and Scotland". Perhaps it was Conevali's scepticism about the quality of the visiting team, rather than the heavy rain which swept Turin on the day of the match, which reduced the attendance to just over 12,000, but whatever the reason, it said little for the Italians' perception of the latest arrival on the international football stage.

Often playing at a different pace to Ireland, the home team were a goal up after 13 minutes, doubled the lead 20 minutes later and, figuratively, were home and hosed when Bernardini scored a third goal two minutes before half-time. Thereafter, Italy played conservatively to protect their advantage, but the Italian sporting press was somewhat less than complimentary to the visiting team in their post-match analyses. The Irishmen had battled well without ever threatening to disturb the Italian net, and a 3–0 defeat was sufficiently comprehensive to warn of further squalls ahead for the men in green, unless standards were improved sharply.

The Irish squad left Turin the following morning for that second engagement with Cercle Athlétique de Paris 24 hours later. They showed that they had learned something from their bitter experience the previous Sunday when Bob Fullam, wholly anonymous in the international match, at last hit the target to earn his team a 1–1 draw. The overall cost to the Irish Association was just under £700, but in terms of an introduction to the hard edge of international sport, it would prove money well spent.

The result apart, it had been an enlightening journey for the Irish party, thanks in part to the co-operation of British Consulate officials in smoothing the occasional problems which arose. If the British Foreign office was harbouring resentment following the declaration of independence five years earlier, it didn't show on the ground, with personnel at the Consulate in Turin doing everything possible to ensure that they were not disadvantaged. So impressed were the visitors that on their return to Dublin, Association officials made presentations of a gold cigarette case to a Mr Nosworth and a gold Tara broach to a Mrs Garbutt as tokens of their appreciation.

A postscript to the Turin game was provided three months later when the Italian Federation informed their Irish counterparts that Saturday, 23 April 1927 was their only available date for the return match in Dublin. They pointed out that they already had another international fixture, against France, arranged for the following day, but sought to minimise Irish disappointment on this count with the remark that they were capable of fielding two teams of equal strength. Was this a valid assessment of their resources, Dublin wondered, or was it a commentary on the visitors' poor performance in Turin? The bottom line, however, was that the Irish were not in a position to demur, and even if the Italians sent a weakened team to Dublin, the consensus was that they would still attract a large crowd.

In the meantime, there was the upcoming tour of Cercle Athlétique de Paris to warrant the full attention of the Leinster Association. Dublin enthusiasts had seen the French club in action in the capital in 1923 and could be counted on to turn out in large numbers when the Parisians showed up at Dalymount Park for a second time. The Leinster decision makers obviously thought so, for with scant regard for the deprivations of the day, they increased their admission prices for the match. This prompted Bob Murphy, a member of Council who had been primarily responsible for the Parisians' earlier visit, to return his tickets, stating that an admission charge of one shilling was too high and adding that neither team was capable of providing sixpence worth of entertainment.

The Parisians' second tour game was scheduled for Cork, representing the biggest attraction so far in the domain of the Munster FA. Dublin was particularly anxious that their southern colleagues should be seen to do their guests proud, and in requesting that they attend to every detail to make the occasion memorable, they reminded them that "this is the club whose visit to Dublin some years ago to play an Irish Free State XI, at a time when the Association was denied recognition by the English FA, was largely responsible for the position our Association now occupies in international football".

A second letter sent by the FAIFS to the Munster Association on 11 May 1926 stated that in spite of the prevailing coal strike in England and the disruptive effect it was having on transport, the visit of the CAP club to play a Munster XI would still proceed as planned. They requested that the Munster FA organise a trip to Killarney for the tourists and to ensure that the appropriate flags were flown at Victoria Cross and the Metropole Hotel. The teams were to tog out at the nearby Turkish baths and return there after the game. In the event, Munster officials delivered on cue and the French players were quick to confirm that theirs had been another gratifying trip.

Chapter Fourteen

Eligibility Issue

Belfast's stubborn refusal to abandon their policy of selecting southern-born players for international games, a practice which threatened the very core of the FAIFS's philosophy in upholding their right to be regarded as a wholly independent national federation, continued to agitate Dublin as the dawn of a new year heralded further attempts to regularise the position in 1927.

Motivated as much by the intransigence of some of their erstwhile colleagues in denying them a fair hearing on the grievances felt south of the newly created border, as the desirability of broadening their international team base, the Free State body began to formulate a new strategy based on the need to involve the International Federation to a larger degree, a plan of campaign first outlined at a meeting of the FAIFS's Advisory Committee in January of that year.

Tabling a proposal that the anomalies inherent in the situation were in urgent need of redress, Jim Mulligan said that the issue of the Association's jurisdiction would be called into question, if they couldn't access those of their players attached to cross-channel clubs for the purpose of international matches. The possibility of such players being included in international teams selected by the IFA was a serious matter, as the laws of FIFA prohibited any player from taking part in international matches for more than one country and the policy being adopted by Belfast would, if unchallenged, preclude these players from taking part in international fixtures for the Free State.

After a long discussion, it was unanimously decided to address a communication to FIFA on this point, and to inform them also that the rules of the IFA, as at present constituted, were outside the terms of the agreement entered into by the Associations of England, Scotland and Wales, as well as the FAIFS and IFA, at Liverpool in October 1923. It was agreed that before the matter was referred to FIFA, a further opportunity would be given to the IFA to amend its constitution and remove all anomalies. The response, when it came, was not encouraging. Instead of addressing the matter raised, the IFA pointed out that the letter had been signed by J.L. (Jim) Brennan, Chairman of the FAIFS, rather than Jack Ryder, the Secretary, thereby bringing its authenticity into question. It served to remind Dublin, yet again, that there would be no easy resolution of a problem which was now at the top of their agenda.

Brennan was seen by Belfast as one of the more obstinate of their adversaries, and the intervention of some IFA supporters was seen in an article in the sporting newspaper *Athletic News* containing several disparaging references to the Council of the FAIFS and what were said to be "their claims for full international recognition". Particular objection was taken by Dublin to certain members being referred to as "diehard". This was seen as an oblique criticism of Brennan, and a further source of irritation was a statement that information for the article had been provided by a Council insider.

At another meeting of the Advisory Committee in March 1927, it was agreed to submit a letter to FIFA on the issue of full international recognition, calling the attention of the International Federation to the fact that the IFA was not entitled to use the name "Ireland" in international competition and consequently, proposing an alteration to Statute 1, Article 1 of FIFA, which would change the title "Ireland" to "Northern Ireland". The Committee decided that in order to make the deadline for the receipt of proposals for debate at the Annual Congress in Helsinki two months later, the proposal be forwarded directly to FIFA, providing either Italy or Switzerland was prepared to second it. In the event, the Italian Federation was the first to reply in the affirmative.

Two weeks before the FIFA congress, FAIFS officers met again to formulate strategy, and a broad-ranging discussion ensued on how the three Irish delegates could best illustrate the reasons for the football split in Ireland and the problems faced by the new organisation south of the border. It was considered advisable to procure a number of small maps, illustrating Free State and Northern Ireland territory, to help delegates follow the arguments put forward by the FAIFS for the right to have their representative teams designated as "Ireland". This paid off in Helsinki, where the thrust of Dublin's case was again articulated precisely by Jim Brennan. Mainland Europe was convinced of its merits and in the absence of opposition from the Associations of England and Scotland, the proposal carried with unexpected ease. But if the FAIFS thought that was the end of the matter, they were wrong. Despite the stance of the English and Scottish Associations in Finland, they continued to recognise teams chosen by the IFA in the British championship as Ireland, and it would be some time yet before the IFA was compelled to designate its teams as Northern Ireland.

Aside from issues relating to Northern Ireland, the FAIFS agreed to recommend FIFA's proposal to stage a new international championship (World Cup) for acceptance, on condition that the financial terms were viable and that the competition was open to professional and amateur players alike. The championship, they were informed, would be held every four years and would not interfere with the workings of the International Olympic Committee. On the subject of the Olympics, J.L. Brennan reported that at the invitation of J.J. Keane, he had recently met with the President of the Olympic Council of Ireland with a view to becoming involved in fundraising for the 1928 Games in Amsterdam. Back in 1924, Keane had raised strenuous objections to the FAIFS being represented in the Paris Games on the basis that it was not an all-Ireland organisation. Ryder and Brennan had not apparently forgotten that rebuff and informed Keane that they would not be represented at any meetings to help the Olympic Council progress its fundraising activities.

It is interesting to reflect on the progress of the IFA's international teams after the two Irish Associations had split and gone their separate ways. In normal circumstances, victory in the British championship in 1914 ought to have provided the springboard for a relatively stable period in Irish football, with the experience born of that successful campaign dispelling the remnants of the self-doubt which had bedevilled so many Ireland teams in the early, formative years of the Association. But football was not exempted from the deprivations of the First World War, and by the time a semblance of normality was restored on the cessation of the conflict in

1918, the impetus of that ground-breaking achievement had been lost.

Allied to the problems being visited on the hierarchy of the IFA in the wake of the split with Dublin, that was vastly disappointing and at least some of their legislators were beginning to question the way ahead. With players of the quality of Billy Gillespie, Andy McCluggage, Billy and Bob McCracken in their team, it was also surprising, the more so since it coincided with an era when Linfield were producing some great teams. The club was the barometer by which many people measured the standard of football in the north, and in 1922 Linfield swept the board by winning no fewer than seven trophies. Meanwhile Belfast Celtic and Distillery were embarked on major ground development programmes, but the progress in club football was not being evidenced in the results of international games.

Southern players capped by the IFA in this period included Billy Lacey, Patsy Gallagher, Mick O'Brien and the flamboyant if occasionally controversial Cardiff City goalkeeper, Tom Farquharson, who competed with Elisha Scott for the keeper's sweater in the northern team for much of the 1920s. Of this quartet, however, only Lacey and O'Brien were available for selection when the Free State selectors took stock of their resources for the first international game to be staged in Dublin since the notorious split, against Italy in Dublin on Saturday, 23 April 1927. Farquharson, who would in time emerge as a revered name in the history of the FAIFS, was required to play for Cardiff City in the English FA Cup final against Arsenal on the day of the international game, a decision which Cardiff were quick to acknowledge as crucial, in their storied 1–0 victory over Arsenal at Wembley. Gallagher, who had ended his great romance with Celtic by signing for Falkirk some months earlier, was injured, and it would be another four years before he made his oft-postponed debut for the Free State against Spain.

Italy, as agreed, were returning the visit of the Irish team to Turin the previous year. For Ireland, the availability of their better players gave hope of exacting a measure of compensation for the heavy defeat sustained on that occasion. Gallagher's absence was readily disguised by the return of the redoubtable Lacey. The Wexford man, a specialist inside-forward who on two occasions in 1920 had played at centre-half against England and Scotland, was 37 and very much at the veteran stage, but his experience of international football, stretching back to 1909, was seen as crucial if Ireland were to be competitive in the Italian fixture.

O'Brien, a splendidly proportioned centre-half who did not take up football until late into his teens, had figured at left-half in the Northern Ireland team which drew 2–2 with Wales a fortnight before facing Italy, one of 10 appearances he made for Northern Ireland. Given his Kildare background, it is vaguely surprising that he won only four caps with the Free State, but like so many others, he was a victim of the politics of Irish football and the absence of southern teams from international football until 1926. Now his inclusion was an indication of the selectors' anxiety as they reflected on the comprehensive defeat inflicted on an all-local team in Turin. That painful exercise emphasised the need for a broader seam of experience in the side, and in addition to O'Brien, this was provided by the inclusion of Harry Duggan (Leeds United), Tommy Muldoon (Aston Villa) and Joe Kendrick of Everton. Additionally, Christy Martin was summoned from the Scottish club Bo'ness to lead the attack.

On the first occasion that Dublin staged an international game, against England in 1900, it was seen fit to hire the rugby union stadium at Lansdowne Road for the occasion. Now, given the role the Italian Federation had played in bringing the Irish Free State into the mainstream of international football, the expectation was that the visit of the Italians would attract an attendance in the region of 30,000, and it was deemed prudent to return there. In the event, circumstances, not least the weather, contrived to show that this forecast was overly optimistic, but in every other respect it was, indeed, an auspicious occasion. At one point, the FAIFS gave serious consideration to granting permission to 2RN, the national broadcasting station, to carry a live commentary on the game, a first for a football fixture in Dublin. Eventually, it was deemed inadvisable to do so, and among the reasons listed for this decision was "the difficulty in finding a suitable broadcaster [commentator]".

In agreeing to accept the Dublin game, just 24 hours before fulfilling a game against France, the Italian Federation had notified the FAIFS that their team on duty would be no less competitive than that chosen to confront the French. In fact it contained just three of the players who had outclassed their Irish opposition in Turin and was officially designated as a

"B" side. However, the FAIFS regarded it as a full international fixture, and caps were awarded to the Irish players selected.

William "Sacky" Glen, a name which would be synonymous with Irish football for the next 13 years, was in the team for the first time, but it was his Shamrock Rovers colleague Bob Fullam who captured the imagination of the crowd on the day. Fullam, who could strike the ball harder than any of his Irish contemporaries, was one of the riveting attractions of the Free State League in its early years, but in common with his team-mates, he had undeniably suffered in the total eclipse of the Irish team in Turin. Now, afforded the opportunity of playing international football for the first time in front of a home crowd, he aimed to atone for that flawed performance, and within six minutes of the kick-off he delivered on his pledge.

He had already tested the reflexes of the Italian goalkeeper, Marco Gianni, when he delighted his supporters by pouncing on a mistake by the keeper to open the scoring. It was the first international goal for the Free State and, for a spell, it threatened to avenge the indignities visited on the Irishmen in the first meeting of the countries. After the Italian full-back Marco Zanelli attempted to block Fullam's free-kick from just outside the penalty area, he had to be carried off on a stretcher, and folklore has it that when the home team was awarded another free-kick shortly afterwards, the Italians pleaded with the opposition not to allow Fullam to take it. Sadly, the wheels came off for the Irish in the second half following an injury to Tommy Muldoon, and two goals from Fernando Munerati, the second of them just nine minutes from the end, consigned the men in green to the losers' dressing-room. The consensus was that it had been a brave stand against the odds but before long, the clouds would roll away to reveal a triumphant Irish side.

In the meantime, the Free State League's representative team, containing many of the players who had taken part in the international game in Turin, struck a resounding blow for the standard of the game south of the border by outplaying the Irish League 2–1 at Dalymount Park, the goals coming from Charlie Dowdall and Billy Farrell. It would be another four years before the northern team ventured to Dublin again, but this time the outcome was vastly different, with the visitors recording a crushing 6–1 success. The bragging rights now resided in Belfast, and for this they could thank the deadly finishing skills of Linfield's Joe Bambrick, one of the most accomplished of all Irish strikers. Earlier in 1930, Bambrick had made the whole of international football sit up and take notice by scoring six times in the 7–0 rout of Wales in Belfast, a proud record which has stood the test of time. In the course of that tumultuous season, Bambrick accumulated a massive total of 94 goals, only to see his record eclipsed the following season by Fred Roberts of Glentoran, who scored 96 times.

In domestic competition in 1927, Drumcondra emerged from the relative obscurity of the Leinster Senior League to lift the Free State Cup by virtue of a 1–0 win over Brideville. It was a performance which would soon elevate them to senior status and establish their base at Tolka Park on Dublin's north side as one of the focal points of Irish football, until their controversial demise in 1972 when they were replaced by the predominantly Junior club, Home Farm.

Chapter Fifteen

FIFA Disappoints Dublin

Charles Liddy, a member of the FAIFS Council who would go on to make a significant contribution to Irish football at administrative level for much of the next fifty years, reactivated the campaign for a resolution of the north–south split when, on 12 May 1929, he made Jack Ryder aware of his intention to propose the following motion: "That this Council instructs its Advisory Committee to re-open negotiations with the Northern Ireland Association with a view to arriving at an amicable settlement."

Although still a minority viewpoint, Liddy's action reflected a sense of disquiet among some Leinster officials that not enough was being done to bring Belfast into line with European opinion and treat Dublin as an equal partner in the development of the game throughout the island. It transpired that the proposal was reluctantly withdrawn "for the present", but the effect was to convince the FAIFS to intensify its efforts to force a solution through the aegis of the world governing body for the sport. In his role of Secretary of the FAIFS, Ryder realised more than most that for all their vocal support, FIFA were powerless to impose any form of sanctions on the British Associations who, 10 years earlier, had cut adrift from the organisation.

Thus he can scarcely have been surprised when, in responding to his enquiry in June 1929, FIFA informed him that they had met with no joy in their most recent contact with the British International Board after querying, at Dublin's request, the practice of the IFA in continuing to field teams under the title of Ireland instead of Northern Ireland. FIFA noted, however, that not all members of the British Board agreed with the IFA's insistence in maintaining their right to select players born in the Irish Free State, raising hope that "your wishes may be fulfilled in the future".

This was interpreted as a reference to England's ambivalence in informal discussions during the previous 18 months. While continuing to offer IFA officials their steadfast support, English FA authorities had vacillated on at least two occasions before yielding to pressure from Belfast to support the prevailing order.

By February 1930, Ryder was back on the campaign trail once more, this time in contact with the Minister for External Affairs, canvassing Government support for action to end the "increasingly anomalous situation of the six north-eastern counties taking unto themselves the exclusive right to be described as Ireland in international games". Ryder contended that it was the intervention of the FA of England which thwarted their hopes of early election to full membership of FIFA. He also insisted that it was only after diplomatic pressure had been applied, that the FA of England grudgingly recognised the formation of the new football organisation in Dublin, and he was adamant that it would again require the intervention of Government to eliminate the "absurdity of the north-east team masquerading as Ireland".

Urging the Minister to take a more hands-on approach in supporting the FAIFS's campaign to achieve equality of status with the IFA in the workings of the British International Board, Ryder reminded him of the important responsibility the Association was discharging in raising the profile of the Irish Free State abroad. In doing so, he admitted for the first time that there had been a problem in their opening international game against Italy in Turin in 1926. "Despite some reluctance on the part of the Italian authorities," he wrote, "we insisted on the Irish tricolour being hoisted in the stadium and met the objection that none was available, by producing one we had (in accordance with our custom) brought with us. With similar precaution, we had brought with us the band parts of 'The Soldiers' Song', but in this instance, had to submit to a refusal as the band consisted of schoolboys and we were told that they could not play the music at first sight. On our next journey abroad, for the game against Belgium in Liège in 1928, no such difficulty was encountered. The Irish tricolour was everywhere and our National Anthem was played, not alone before the game but at its conclusion – in acknowledgement of our victory."

Then, in a sideswipe at the IFA, Ryder referred to Northern Ireland's game against France in Paris in 1928: "We are aware that when the Northern Ireland Football Association was last involved in a game against a Continental nation (France) at Paris in March 1928, in a match described as France versus Ireland, the flag flown in honour of the 'Ireland' team was the Union Jack, the anthem played was 'God Save the King' and at the banquet following the game, the man introduced as the 'President of the Association of Ireland' intimated that 'Ireland' intended to follow the lead of the 'other British nations' in seceding from membership of the International Federation of Association Football."

Minutes of the FIFA Congress held in Budapest in June of that year reveal that Austria, supported by Italy and the United States, empathised with the stance of the FAIFS on the Ireland issue, but they were of the opinion that FIFA's delegates to the British International Board should restrict themselves to technical matters, such as rule changes.

Following Jack Ryder's appeal for the Government to involve itself in the campaign to resolve the impasse with the Northern Ireland Association, the office of the Irish High Commissioner in London wrote to the FA of England, insisting that the two Irish football organisations should enjoy equal status and control of the game in Ireland. It restated the case that teams representing the entire island should alternate their home games between Dublin and Belfast and that the profits accruing from such fixtures should be divided between the two Associations. Some weeks later, a letter was handed to Mr Sean Murphy, Secretary at the Department for External Affairs, stating that an article in the London sporting newspaper, *Athletic News*, long regarded as a semi-official publication of the Football Association of England, indicated that there was no change of policy by that body in contriving to support Belfast in its usurpation of the rights of the FAIFS. Murphy later officially notified Ryder that the High Commissioner's letter, urging the British International Board to change tack on the Ireland issue, had been rejected on the basis that it was not empowered to effect such a change. He expressed the opinion that the FAIFS would itself have to make direct representation to member countries of the Board, to alter the status quo.

In further correspondence with the Department for External Affairs, Ryder stated that the indiscretion of the FA of England in allowing the letter which the High Commissioner had sent them to be published subsequently, had alerted the Belfast Association to the fact that the Irish Government was now involving itself in the matter and, as a consequence, merely strengthened their opposition to change. Perhaps it was this rider which prompted the FAIFS to take a different route to London through the person of Alex McCabe. McCabe, a respected sympathiser of the FAIFS cause, was a personal friend of Tim Healy, the former Governor-General in Ireland, and the hope was that Healy could utilise his contacts in the corridors of power at Westminster to persuade the British Government to take a more positive lead in resolving a dispute which was putting still more strain on the political dialogue between London and Dublin. Coincidentally or otherwise, the FA of England appeared to have had yet another change of direction in its evaluation of the "Irish problem" in the ensuing months, and an excerpt from a meeting of its Council, early in 1931, tended to support the point. In a section of the minutes dealing with the football situation in Ireland and the failure of the British International Board, at its meeting in Gleneagles, to back an English proposal to amend the agreement of June 1895 "that the basis of eligibility for international football shall be birth, with the addition of the words 'within the area of the National Association'", it revealed that the Scottish, Welsh and Irish (Northern) Associations voted against the proposal, while the Football Association (of England) and the International Federation (FIFA) voted in favour. It was the most revealing illustration so far of England's desire for an equitable solution to a highly complex problem and appeared to support FIFA's earlier prediction that fresh hope would shortly appear on the horizon. As in so much else in Anglo-Irish relations, however, it was never going to be quite as simple or straightforward as England's volte-face at Gleneagles had suggested, and there would be more twists and turns ahead, on the road to acceptable co-existence.

In a letter to Sir Frederick Wall of the FA of England, which was replicated for the Scottish and Welsh Associations in June 1931, Jack Ryder again emphasised the justice of their campaign to secure equality in the management and control of football in Ireland. "In soliciting the support of your members to decide this matter," he wrote, "I am to point out that under the terms of the Treaty of Ireland, the whole of Ireland became the

Irish Free State with the proviso that the six north-eastern counties should have the option of contracting out, a right which they duly exercised."

At a time when the IFA was still showing little sign of yielding to arbitration over their highly provocative policy of selecting for their teams players born in any part of Ireland, another difficulty now surfaced – and this time from an unlikely source. Bohemians, who epitomised the amateur ethos of football in the jurisdiction controlled by the Leinster Football Association in its early years, attracted many members from the professions. And it was largely due to their influence that football acquired an image as a sport for the middle class in the early years of the twentieth century. As a rule, people of that ilk weren't slow to voice opinions, and so it was that three Bohemians players, Jimmy Bermingham, Freddie Horlacher and Alex Morton – the first two had been capped by the Free State at senior level – chose to make themselves available for selection for the Northern Ireland amateur team which played England in Belfast on 15 November 1930.

In doing so, they contended that as amateurs they were not bound by rules which might be applied to professional players and, as such, they were perfectly entitled to take part in the game against England. Officials of the FAIFS were incensed by that apparent insensitivity. It was bad enough that the IFA should thumb their nose at Dublin in selecting professional players born in the south, but now living abroad, for their representative teams. The notion of players involved in the Free State League following suit was absolutely unacceptable to them, and they reacted accordingly by imposing indefinite suspensions on all three of the Bohemians members involved.

The players promptly sought redress in the courts and in one of the high-profile litigation cases of the period in the High Court, Mr Justice Meredith ruled in favour of the Association. The IFA was furious at the findings but Ryder was equally emphatic in rejecting Belfast's allegation that they did not have the authority to suspend the trio. "I am directed to inform you that my Council resents the discourteous and hostile tone of your communiqué," he wrote. "It contravenes the terms of the Liverpool agreement of 1923. The suspensions were declared valid and the action of my Council vindicated, in the case brought by the players against the Association in the High Court." There was a measure of solace for the northern body, however, when FIFA subsequently decreed that they were not empowered to enforce the recognition of the suspensions on the Associations of England, Scotland, Wales and Northern Ireland.

Soon afterwards, the IFA again contacted their southern colleagues to enquire, perhaps mischievously, if they would permit any player born in Ireland and under the jurisdiction of the FAIFS, to take part in the upcoming senior international game against England in Belfast on 19 October 1931. In its response, Dublin reaffirmed that it was "unable to acquiesce in any way" in the selection by the IFA of any player born in the area covered by the Irish Free State. Ironically, Dubliner Jimmy Dunne, a highly rated member of Sheffield United's team in the English First Division, was one of Northern Ireland's scorers in a comprehensive 6–2 defeat.

The attitude of players remained the Achilles heel of Dublin's campaign to prevent Northern Ireland selecting those born in the jurisdiction of the FAIFS. The opportunity of competing at the highest level of the game was prized by every player, and so were the monetary rewards which came with it. And at a time when club wages were distinctly modest, the extra money to be earned in international football was very important.

There were players, however, who put principle before professionalism, and one of those who endeared himself to the authorities in Dublin was the Cardiff City goalkeeper, Tom Farquharson, who was capped seven times by the IFA between 1923 and 1925. Farquharson had strong Republican tendencies, and in his student days he was arrested along with Sean Lemass, later to succeed Eamon de Valera as Taoiseach, for pulling down British Army posters in St Stephen's Green in Dublin. He subsequently settled in Wales and, before winning acclaim as one of the outstanding goalkeepers in Britain, had played rugby in the Welsh valleys. More than most, he appreciated the injustice of the IFA's high-handed dismissal of their southern counterparts, to the extent that he saw fit to go public with his decision never to play for Northern Ireland after Dublin had attained membership of FIFA. The southern body was so impressed by that show of loyalty that they offered to set up a fund for him, with one official suggesting that his portrait be hung in the offices of the Association.

Jimmy Dunne was another player who made a firm commitment.

Dunne ended his relationship with Northern Ireland in 1933 and went on to make 15 appearances for the southern international team, captaining the side on five occasions.

Farquharson, whose successful tactic of advancing off his line before the ball was struck resulted in the revision of the rules governing the taking of penalty kicks, made his first appearance for the Free State against Belgium at Dalymount Park in April 1929. Belgium, one of the weaker teams in Europe, had been outplayed 4–2 in Liège the previous year, and their eclipse in Dublin would prove even more comprehensive with the celebrated Shamrock Rovers player John Joe Flood hitting three goals in a 4–0 win. A third successive victory over Belgium followed in Brussels in 1930, and on this occasion Jimmy Dunne was the show-stopper on his international debut for the FAIFS. The Sheffield United forward, then among the leading scorers in Britain, twice hit the target to complement Flood's goal in a 3–1 win.

Three victories in a row, after the indignities visited on the Irish in two meetings with Italy, testified to the growing self-belief of Irish teams, but even the most upbeat supporters of the team can only have been apprehensive as they looked ahead to two games against Spain, home and away, in 1931. Then, as now, Spaniards were passionate about their football, with newspaper reports telling of huge attendances for international fixtures as well as the more important club games. Even that, however, could not have prepared the Irish for the scenes which marked their visit to Barcelona in high summer. After a tiring overland journey, the visiting party eventually made it to the Catalan capital to be confronted by dense crowds of Spanish supporters on the approach roads to the Mont Juic stadium which, some sixty years later, would be the site of the main arena for the 1992 Olympic Games in the city.

One report put the attendance at not less than 100,000 and possibly as high as 120,000. No Irish team had ever performed in front of a crowd of that magnitude, and it served to remind observers, north as well as south, that international football on mainland Europe carried big financial rewards for successful teams. Only two English-based players were cleared to join the Irish party, Farquharson and Celtic winger Peter Kavanagh. In order to make the trip, they, unlike Jimmy Dunne and Harry Duggan, turned down the chance of playing for Northern Ireland against Wales six days earlier. Dolphin, soon to be defunct, supplied three of the nine locally based players, but it was Shamrock Rovers who provided the most talked-about member of the side, Paddy Moore.

Moore, the first of the tragic heroes of Irish sport, would shine only briefly in football's firmament, but his reputation as a brilliant player of brittle character still endures almost sixty years after his death. He stood out among the teeming thousands who played the game on Dublin's north side, his ability as a skilled finisher quickly establishing him as an exceptional player in the making, but it was only after he returned to Shamrock Rovers from a frustrating season with Cardiff City that his talent really flowered. His international career spanned just five years but in 10 international appearances, including one for Northern Ireland, he scored seven times, quite the highest percentage of any striker for the southern team.

The first of those goals materialised in Barcelona, where 10 minutes before half-time, undeterred by the regular explosions of noise in the vast stadium, he linked with his club-mate John Joe Flood to arc the ball over Zamora, the Spanish goalkeeper. That was the stuff of fantasy for any 21-year-old and confirmed Paddy Moore as a player who prospered on the big occasion. The advantage lasted just a matter of minutes before Arocha equalised but, helped by Farquharson's penalty save late in the game, the Irish held on for a 1–1 draw. The match yielded a handsome profit of £1,243 for the visitors, and the FAIFS Council members were so impressed that for the first time in their short international history, they rewarded the players with a bonus of three pounds a man. Sean Byrne of Bohemians, the only amateur player in the team, was given a voucher for the purchase of a piece of jewellery to the value of £5. He asked for the voucher to be made out instead for the purchase of a suit, but his request was turned down flatly by the Finance Committee.

Moore had to miss the return game at Dalymount Park eight months later, and not even the first and only appearance of the veteran Patsy Gallagher in the Free State team could be expected to compensate for his absence. Breaking with tradition, the FAIFS decided to play the game on a Sunday – a decision which resulted in Jimmy Dunne (Sheffield United) and Jimmy

Kelly (Derry City) being withdrawn by their clubs. The game attracted an attendance of 30,000, the biggest so far in Dublin, but alas there was little joy on this occasion for the team in green. Farquharson, on his farewell international appearance, was forced to retrieve the ball from his net on no fewer than five occasions on a nightmare afternoon for the Irish – which, given the fact that the Spaniards had been routed 7–0 by England on their journey to Dublin, took much of the sheen from the earlier heroics in Barcelona.

Chapter Sixteen

Peace Talks Crux

After years of claims and counter-claims in apportioning blame for the impasse in relationships between the two rival Irish football Associations, Dublin knew for certain that the ground rules were starting to change when, on 27 January 1932, the IFA announced that, with the approval of the FA of England, they had appointed a delegation to meet the FAIFS in Dublin, in the first of two Conferences.

A month earlier, Shelbourne had called for a Conference involving all clubs to discuss the international status issue and with a corresponding campaign gaining momentum among the more prominent Belfast clubs, even the most intransigent of those on opposite sides realised that the blame game had to stop and an element of rationality be restored to football, north and south. More importantly still, there were increasing signs that London was becoming impatient with an apparent lack of urgency to redress the situation. Even allowing for a sharp increase in attendance figures south of the border, clubs still yearned for the competitive edge of north–south matches; and on the international front, it seemed that the FA of England was beginning to question the anomaly of players representing two separate administrations in international football.

That growing sense of agitation was lost on neither Dublin nor Belfast, and both organisations named their most skilful negotiators in ten-strong delegations. Pointedly, Larry Sheridan, chairman of the FAIFS and long regarded as one of their more erudite speakers, was relegated to a lesser role than might have been anticipated in the Dublin talks. This followed a meeting of the FAIFS Council to discuss strategy, in the course of which Mr T.J. Murray suggested that Sheridan's role should be restricted largely to opening and closing the meeting – a commentary, perhaps, on Dublin's determination to placate those in the north who regarded Sheridan as one of their more strident adversaries. Instead, Jim Brennan, Myles Murphy and Joe Wickham took the lead roles in presenting the southern case, with Captain James Wilton, Austin Donnelly and J.H. Smyth fronting the northern delegation.

That neither side trusted the other fully was shown when both asked for an official stenographer to be employed to produce a transcript of proceedings; and, at the request of the IFA, no representatives of the press were admitted. Further, it was agreed that if either party wished to issue a press release after the meeting, it would be released simultaneously with one from the other side. The meeting, at Jury's Hotel on Dame St, was originally scheduled for Saturday, 13 February but was put back a week; and, as a gesture of goodwill, northern delegates were invited to watch the championship game between Bohemians and Shelbourne at Dalymount Park, on the afternoon of the talks. Messrs A. Byrne, E.J. McDonnell, J. O'Toole, J. Younger, S.R. Prole and J.A. Ryder completed the southern delegation, while on the visiting side, Messrs M. McBride, J.M. Small, J. Ferguson, T. Cordnere, H. Mehaffy, E.R. Best and C. Watson provided the support for Wilton, Donnelly and Smyth.

Against that background, Sheridan was profuse to a fault in welcoming the northern delegation, speaking for almost 15 minutes before broaching the subject matter, in an obvious attempt to assure the visiting delegates that his was not a hostile agenda. Wilton, for his part, was both courteous and constructive, pointing out that while his fellow delegates had not been invested with Council powers, he coveted the opportunity of bringing hopeful tidings back to Belfast. Emphasising that it was the FAIFS who asked for the Conference, he said, "You suggested that we should meet to discuss the international question and deal with any points in dispute between the two Associations. But this is more or less in the nature of an abstract suggestion. That is why Council decided not to give our delegation Council powers."

Responding, Brennan said: "I will come to the point. We think that in view of the geographical division of the country and the success which has attended our efforts in the south of the country, a solution can be reached on the basis of equal control of international football, in other words on a fifty-fifty basis. We believe an arrangement can be arrived at, whereby international matches are controlled by a committee representative of the two Associations with an alternating chairmanship. This is our idea of a workable agreement." On the question of joint financial control of such matches, Wilton asked: "Do you mean to include all international matches played? Let us say we play England, Scotland or Wales and you play Spain. Do you also mean to include matches played against Continental [FIFA] nations?"

When Brennan replied in the affirmative, Austin Donnelly intervened: "Do you not think that this is an awkward proposition for us to put before our Council? The suggestion is that the two Associations should form a Joint Control Board in regard to international matches but it would only refer to matches against England Scotland and Wales." Chairman: "In so far as Continental matches are concerned, that is a question you could consider afterwards." Wilton: "I have no doubt that there are many of us who feel it is absolutely necessary that we field the strongest team available when we play as Ireland in an international match. Is that not the idea? Your Association may decide to play Continental matches and we play other British teams. Is it not essential that we field our strongest team in every instance?"

After the chairman had said that the matter of accommodating northern interests in Continental matches would not be an insuperable problem for the FAIFS, Wilton replied: "I am very glad to hear that – now we have a basis for discussion. Our idea is that we should have a fully representative team for all international fixtures. A joint Control Board has been suggested, consisting of an equal number of representatives from each of the Associations. That Board is to have complete control, financial and otherwise, and will deal with the selection arrangements in regard to what we call home international games. If that principle is accepted by the IFA and if they desire that it should go further and include all international fixtures, continental or otherwise, your Association would, in all probability, be prepared to include them. Is that the situation as of now?" Chairman: "Yes." Wilton: "We all know where we stand now."

Under questioning later, Joe Wickham admitted that, in his opinion, one Association governing football on the whole of the island was not a practical solution "at the present time", but he believed that the concept of fielding international teams worthy of the name Ireland was one deserving of unanimous support. He contended that, in the past, it was a travesty to have international teams fielded by both Associations, which were absolutely unrepresentative of all Ireland. He was of the opinion that the matter of "foreign" international fixtures had been unduly stressed by other speakers. "We did not conceive that you would be attracted to the prospect of matches with Continental teams after your decision to secede from membership of FIFA," he said.

In terms of what the IFA set out to achieve in the talks, their visit had been worthwhile. For 11 years, they wondered about the true agenda of the FAIFS and were now reassured in the knowledge that the new organisation had no plans to aspire to a 32-county structure administered from Dublin. They may even have felt that by opening up the prospect of Dublin's involvement in the home international championship as part of an all-Ireland team, they had raised the possibility of a return to the system which existed up to 1921.

Almost certainly, however, it was Dublin who sensed that they had done better in the first round of talks. After failing repeatedly in their attempt to benefit from the financial rewards which accrued from long-established games against England, Scotland and Wales, they were now being treated as an equal partner with the IFA in Ireland's involvement in the British home international championship. For the first time, they would fill an influential role in the selection of the team to participate in the championship; and with the chairmanship of the selection board to alternate between the Associations, the long-perceived bias against Dublin in the composition of Ireland's teams would at last be at an end. All in all, it had been a good day's work for Larry Sheridan and his team, and the level of confidence was such that a draft agreement was drawn up, for insertion in the rule books of both Associations, pending the outcome of a second Conference to be held in Belfast three weeks later.

For the Belfast session, held in the Imperial Hotel on 12 March 1932, Captain Wilton was in the chair and opened the meeting by summarising the first round of talks: "On the last occasion we met in Dublin, I think we came to a decision on what I might term the principles of the agreement.

It was an agreement by which there should be a joint committee appointed for the purpose of selecting international teams and for the purpose of arranging international matches. I think we are agreed on that. There were other matters discussed on that occasion, for instance the question of an all-Ireland Cup competition and the question in regard to Continental matches, but my recollection is that we agreed to only one thing and that was that we appoint a committee to deal with the selection of international teams and the arrangements for international matches, in so far as they pertain to those with England, Scotland and Wales. Someone introduced the question of Continental matches but there seemed to be some difficulty in regard to that. It was not pressed much and in the same way, we did not press the question of the all-Ireland Cup. I think we were agreed in regard to international matches, that there should be a joint committee of equal numbers from each Association and with alternate chairmen, to arrange these matches and select these teams. After the Dublin meeting, the report of the proceedings was laid before the IFA and a resolution was passed which Charles Watson will now read."

Watson read out the prepared draft agreement: "The undersigned, for and on behalf of the Irish Football Association and the Football Association of the Irish Free State respectively, having Council powers from their Associations, hereby agree as follows. (1) A joint Committee shall be appointed, consisting of members of the Council of the Irish Football Association and the Football Association of the Irish Free State, to select players for international matches and to make all arrangements for such matters, the President of each Association to act as chairman of the Committee in alternate years and to have a deliberative vote as well as a casting vote in case of a tie. (2) All profits accruing from international matches in each year shall be shared equally by and between the two Associations and all losses arising from such matches shall be borne equally by and between the two Associations. (3) This agreement, together with any details agreed on as necessary to carry it into effect, shall be inserted in the rule books of each of the Associations." Wilton said that the IFA Council had voted unanimously in favour of this recommendation and that there was now little more to do other than consider the matter of details.

Chapter Sixteen

Larry Sheridan agreed that little remained to be done and enquired if
the IFA was actively interested in pursuing the suggestion of extending the
Joint Control Board to cover FIFA international games. Wilton replied that
the northern delegation was not unanimous on that issue. While he himself
favoured the possibility of playing Federation matches, others had not
reached a decision on the point and he considered it wiser to concentrate
for the present on home international fixtures. John Ferguson, the veteran
IFA legislator, said that the question of Continental games was not put
to the IFA Council. After the Dublin talks, they were left with just one
matter to consider, equality of control in the home international fixtures.
Everything else was contingent on that.

Wilton was chairing the meeting with consummate skill and was
considerate to the visiting delegation to the point where at a crucial
juncture he even seemed to rebuke one of his fellow delegates. He appeared
to be winding down proceedings when, unfortunately, he allowed the talks
to deviate into the single minutia which would ultimately ruin hopes of a
settlement. Whether by accident or design, Larry Sheridan waited until late
in the meeting before mentioning the British International Board and his
presumption that the FAIFS would be awarded one of the IFA's two seats
on that Board. The subject had never been broached at the Dublin talks,
and Wilton wondered aloud why it was only being raised now. Bewildered
and frustrated in equal degrees, he said that a meeting of the International
Board was, in reality, nothing more than a "picnic party" and that the real
work in terms of match arrangements was done by the Board's Committee.
Sheridan agreed that no mention of the International Board had been
made in the Dublin talks, but said this was because they understood they
were entering into a partnership of equality in which everything would be
done on a fifty-fifty basis, and as such they believed that one of the seats on
the International Board would be automatically awarded to them.

Wilton replied this couldn't be so, because FIFA, of which the FAIFS
was a member, already held two seats on the British International Board,
which dealt primarily with technical matters such as rule changes, and
to give Dublin direct access to the Board would, in effect, mean that
they had a double representation on it. This was immediately countered
by the statement that before the IFA, in common with the other British

Associations, seceded from FIFA, they too held what was now being termed double representation.

In a short time the issue had driven a wedge between the two sides, who had been tantalisingly close to agreement. With the attainment of the primary objective of securing access to the British home championship in a partnership of equality with Belfast, as well as a guarantee in fielding a fully representative Ireland team, the southern delegation appeared to have achieved all they set out to do. And now it was being put in jeopardy by the suspicion that the IFA was pursuing a hidden agenda in denying them a seat on the International Board. The IFA, for its part, protested that with a settlement in sight, Dublin wasn't really interested in a solution to the problems of the previous 11 years; and matters weren't helped by the allegation that since the Free State Association held only colonial or dominion status, they were not qualified to join the British Associations on the Board.

Jim Brennan was infuriated by this. "It has been stated that we merely have colonial or dominion status, but that is merely an expression of opinion which, from time to time, has been given a deal of prominence in the press," he said. "We hold that we have more than dominion status but we will go no further on that point." Replying, Mr McBride said: "You were given dominion status at the 1923 Liverpool Conference at your request and then it was no longer a matter for the International Board. To put it in a different way, you cannot alter the rules of the Board in order to give representation to the Irish Free State Association." To which Brennan replied: "Do you seriously contend that the Irish Football Association, which controls six counties, is entitled to sit on that Board as Ireland?"

Asked by Sam Prole to explain his statement that equal representation on the Board was only a matter of detail, and why he was so obstinate in denying the FAIFS that entitlement, Wilton said: "I can give you the reason without the slightest trouble. We have heard talk about dominion status. It must be known to all the gentlemen here, how much you have tried to point out to other nations the fact that you are Ireland. Now you are not content to be represented through the Federation [FIFA] which deals with continental internationals. You want to be doubly represented on the International Board. You cannot have it both ways."

Myles Murphy interjected – "We never tried to inform anybody that we were Ireland, but I tell you that we are a big part of Ireland and we claim some rights for the part of Ireland we represent." To which Wilton replied: "Nobody is more anxious to admit that you are part of Ireland than Wilton. I have had some trouble in getting my delegation to agree to what I have signed my name to. I think if you were anxious for a settlement, you would agree to that and not baulk at what Mr Sheridan says is a small thing." At Wilton's suggestion, the FAIFS delegation then retired for about half an hour to consider their position. On returning, Sheridan said, "We have considered the matter very carefully and we have agreed to all you have put to us with the exception of the one point which has been stressed here tonight – representation on the International Control Board."

Responding, John Ferguson said: "I think it a great pity that we have got in to a position where we cannot agree. I do not think good will come from further discussion, for one or two things have been said which, perhaps, were better left unsaid." Then, in reference to southern suggestions that the FA of England was now changing direction and supporting Dublin's case in relation to the contentious policy of the IFA of selecting southern players in their teams, Ferguson commented: "The English Football Association did not attempt to pin us to Northern Ireland. What they did attempt was to say that we could not take players from within the jurisdiction of the Football Association of the Irish Free State. The International Board said we were Ireland as far as international football was concerned and that we could take players [from] where we liked. Is not that a fact?"

Clearly infuriated by the loss of a rare opportunity to heal the split after a marathon five-hour session, Wilton said: "As far as I am concerned, I don't give a damn if you are not on the International Board. You never put yourselves in a position to be on any International Board. Shall I tell you why? Because you insisted on being either a dominion or a republic." Later, the chairman apologised for introducing this remark. It was a sad ending to negotiations which promised so much, with the final minutes of the Conference descending into a series of recriminations on both sides. At one point, Myles Murphy alleged that an influential columnist in the *Belfast Telegraph* had predicted long in advance that the talks would fail, not on the perceived problem of finance but on the matter of representation on the International Board, hardening the suspicion that some in the northern camp had established this as a core issue.

On his return to Dublin Jack Ryder, the FAIFS secretary, wrote to his northern counterpart, Charles Watson, as follows: "It is regretted that the high hopes of a satisfactory arrangement have been dimmed by the failure to agree on a basis for settlement at the Conference in Belfast. In endorsing unanimously their delegates' action in declining to accept a proposal which would have deprived the Football Association of the Irish Free State of representation on the International Football Association Board, my Council direct me to re-affirm their willingness to sign, in conjunction with the IFA, an agreement which will establish the absolute equality of their Associations, in all matters in which the name 'Ireland' is used in relation to association football."

In expressing the hope that the IFA Council would agree to resume discussions, Ryder added: "Negotiations having progressed so far in the direction of agreement, it would be regrettable if any effort was now left undone to conclude an amicable arrangement, before asking the Football Associations of Great Britain to express an opinion on the justice of our claims. My Council, agreeing with the opinion expressed in your resolution to the Football Association of England, a copy of which was forwarded to my Council by that body, feel that the two Irish Associations should make another effort to arrive at an understanding."

Ryder didn't have to wait long for the response he feared. Just 10 days later, on 14 April 1932, Watson contacted him to say that no good purpose could be served by another Conference on the same subject. And three weeks later, Watson underlined that decision when he flatly contradicted the following sentence in a letter which the FAIFS had recently sent to London – "If we could induce the Associations of Great Britain to agree to our request, the Council of the IFA would have no objection [to a settlement]." Watson added: "It is inconceivable that the FAIFS could make such a claim just 12 days after the receipt of our emphatic refusal to agree to the Free State's representation on the International Board." It would be many years before the rival Irish Associations met again to discuss their differences – and then it was only in informal session.

Chapter Seventeen

Tension with GAA

Addressing delegates at the annual general meeting of the FAIFS in Dublin in June 1932, the Secretary, Jack Ryder, reported with some enthusiasm that the number of clubs in membership of the Association had expanded to 471, an impressive increase of 48 on the record established just 12 months earlier.

Inevitably, Leinster provided the bulk of that total with 369 affiliated clubs; Munster, still restricted by the aggressive opposition of the GAA in the province, accounted for 85; and Connacht, as yet at the infant stage of a promotional drive west of the Shannon, was credited with just 15 affiliations. Monaghan United and Clones Celtic affiliated directly from Ulster, but in view of the fact that the Association was just 11 years in existence, Ryder's optimism was not without a solid foundation. And yet, for all the growth in numbers, there were still some dark areas of contention.

At the top of that list, of course, was the breakdown in the negotiations designed to rationalise the relationship with former colleagues in the Irish Football Association in Belfast. The mood of the last hour of the talks in the northern capital was undeniably hostile, and from a situation in which the FAIFS delegation travelled north with justifiable expectation of an involvement in the British championship, the lines of communication were now seriously damaged. Within five years of the split in 1921, the representative teams of the Free State League and Irish League were meeting in regular competition and in April 1932, just weeks after the failed Conference, Shamrock Rovers were cleared to play Linfield in a benefit game at Windsor Park with Dundalk similarly facilitated for a fixture against Glentoran. In the latter two instances, however, permission was given only grudgingly, and by the time of the FAIFS's annual general meeting, there was no skirting the fact that the football authorities in Dublin and Belfast were now in open conflict.

Delegates making their way to the annual general meeting in the AOH Hall in Dublin's Parnell Square were keenly aware that one of the motions to be tabled would almost certainly reopen old wounds. It read: "That until such time as the FAIFS receives its just share in the use of the name 'Ireland' in international matches and in all matters in which the name is used or until such time as the IFA play representative matches under the proper title 'Northern Ireland', the Council of this Association is hereby directed to withhold permission for any games to be played between members or bodies of this Association and those of the IFA." Not every club was enthused about the prospect of having to cancel long-standing arrangements with those on the other side of the border, but in the event, there were no dissenting voices when the motion was put to a vote. At a time when there was little activity on the international front, the loss of the inter-league fixture with the North was serious and it would be another three years before it was restored. Bohemians reacted to the ban with an announcement that instead of an exhibition game against Northern Ireland opposition, they would now play Stade Française at Dalymount Park on Easter Monday.

The northern rift, however, was just one of the issues which exercised the minds of those at the meeting. Equally serious was the imposition of an entertainment tax imposed in the budget of 1932, a move which convinced many delegates that the new Government, led by Eamon de Valera, had an agenda against the Association. Events would prove that de Valera valued the showcase which international football provided for the emerging nation but, at a time of extreme austerity, the introduction of the entertainment tax was one of several expedient measures adopted by his administration in the hope of alleviating even greater hardship elsewhere.

That didn't appease the football fraternity, who contended that far from being rewarded for the public relations work they were undertaking for the new Free State on their missions abroad, they were actively victimised in being treated as a professional sports organisation. The reality was that apart from a tiny band of part-time professional players who made up less than .05 per cent of those involved in the sport, the FAIFS was a wholly amateur body which depended almost totally on the voluntary element to administer its operations. In that, their members were not far removed from those in the GAA who, some four years earlier, had received grant aid of £10,000 to build a stand in Croke Park for the Tailteann Games. That merely served to heighten the anger of delegates, who, before the meeting was adjourned, voted unanimously for the motion: "That we regret the action of the Minister for Finance in imposing a tax on Association football and thus discriminating between the various forms of sport."

When the annual general meeting was resumed two weeks later, it had before it a letter from the Minister for Finance, hinting at some relief for the Association from the entertainment tax. It was not sufficient, however, to head off the annoyance of many delegates who considered that Association football, or soccer, was being treated unfairly and it showed in the passing of the following proposal: "The Association deplores the recent legislation in the matter of taxation, whereby discrimination has been made between one code of football and another. Association football provides health giving exercise for all classes among the youth of our country and open air entertainment for the poorest of our people. Of all team games, it is best entitled to be described as the people's game, particularly in the cities and large centres of population. Apart from the hardship of the tax which must impact most severely on the humble patrons of the game and its players, this Association regards all preferential treatment in sport, as tending to create and perpetuate schism and antagonism among our fellow countrymen who deserve and require unity for so many sporting purposes."

The financial problems being encountered by some of the smaller clubs were illustrated in a letter from Dundalk FC, who said that the imposition of the controversial entertainment tax had compounded the difficulties occasioned by disappointing gate receipts. Because of their geographical location, they claimed they were being unfairly disadvantaged in their efforts to arrange exhibition fixtures as part of their fundraising programme. As a means of addressing this problem, it was suggested that they be allowed to organise games against clubs affiliated to the Irish Football Association, but this was dismissed by Council.

Clubs in the north claimed that they, too, were experiencing the draught caused by a restricted programme, but even if the parent body in Belfast empathised with them in that predicament, it still wasn't enough to force them back to the table to revisit the lessons of the failed Conference.

By April 1933, the financial plight of more clubs in the south had been brought into focus, and Joe Wickham, gradually emerging as one of the more articulate of the power brokers in Dublin, urged that moves be put in train to help club officials deal more effectively with their pressing problems. Among the measures suggested was a cap on the wages being paid by clubs, a limit on the number of cross-channel players being signed, the adoption of a percentage scheme in the distribution of gate receipts, and the arrangement of games against cross-channel teams to improve cash flow.

In that context, the entertainment tax was viewed as increasingly unjustifiable, but at the annual general meeting in 1933, Oliver Grattan Esmonde TD, who had succeeded Joe Cunningham as President of the Association three years earlier, reported that there had been no change of policy by the Government. In response to a letter from the Council, the Minister for Finance said that in the prevailing financial climate, it would be impossible to grant a concession in the tax on outdoor sport and that no useful purpose could be served in receiving a deputation on the matter. Just a year later, however, the tax on football was repealed, and in expressing gratitude to the Minister, Jim Brennan, deputising for the Secretary, Jack Ryder, acknowledged the assistance of local politicians in an extensive lobbying campaign.

At a time of upheaval in the relationship between the two Associations governing football on the island, the international fixtures programme produced only marginal relief. Ireland lost all three of their games in the British championship in 1932, an emphatic 4–0 home defeat at the hands of Scotland being followed by a 1–0 reversal against England at Blackpool and a much more surprising 4–1 loss to Wales at Wrexham. That did little to burnish the image of the game in Ireland, but there was a measure of compensation in the form of a 2–0 win for the Free State in their game against the Netherlands in Amsterdam in May of that year.

It was the first meeting of the countries since the Olympic tie during the 1924 Games in Paris, and it was finalised only after a protracted wrangle over the financial aspects of the fixture. Initially, the Irish Association held out for half of the gross gate receipts, only to be told that it was an impossible demand because under the terms of the hire of the De Meer Stadium in Amsterdam, the Dutch Federation was committed to paying the owners of the arena 50 per cent of the gross "gate". Instead, the Netherlands offered to follow the match with a return game in Dublin in 1934, with the home Association in each instance retaining the entire receipts. Because of their parlous cash flow situation, the FAIFS could not accept this, but eventually accepted a minimum match guarantee of £500. They also had to agree to support the Dutch Federation's campaign to have C.A.W. Hirschman re-appointed as the new secretary/treasurer of FIFA.

In the approach to the game, Sheffield United informed the Association that they would be unable to release Jimmy Dunne to play against the Dutch. That was a significant blow, but it was cushioned to a large degree by a belated clearance for Mick O'Brien, who had been named in the team for the first time since the win over Belgium in Brussels three years earlier. At the behest of his club, Watford, O'Brien personally contacted Jack Ryder regarding the delay in informing them of the amount of insurance cover being taken out for the players on duty in Amsterdam. After a satisfactory response on this count, the big Kildare man was cleared to play, and he celebrated his appointment as captain with an imposing performance in the middle of the Irish defence.

Among the more unusual requests from the Dutch Federation was one for a replica of the crest of the FAIFS for publicity purposes. They indicated they would also appreciate the receipt of a block of the crest of the Irish Free State, and enquired if the crest on the Association's notepaper was that of the new State. Whatever the obscurities which may have existed on the political front, the Dutch were left in no doubt about the quality of the Irish team after the visitors, against all the odds, had triumphed 2–0. Joe O'Reilly, revelling in the improbability of it all, secured the first goal before the irrepressible Paddy Moore, recalled to the team for the first time since the draw in Barcelona, fired in a spectacular shot from 20 yards to consign the Dutch to a wholly unexpected defeat. It was a characteristic flash of inspiration from Moore, who later in the year made his solitary appearance for Northern Ireland in the 1–0 defeat by England. On his return from Amsterdam, he was transferred to Aberdeen with his Ireland team-mates Joe O'Reilly and Jimmy Daly in a package which cost the Scottish club just £1,000.

FAIFS officials were not to know it then, but it would be almost another two years before their national team played again. A combination of adverse publicity, a product of the ongoing strife with the IFA, and the financial problems which made Dublin an unattractive port of call for visiting teams, contrived to bring the shutters down on international football in the capital, for what seemed an interminable spell in the wilderness.

In a carefully crafted letter to FIFA in December 1933, Jack Ryder chided the parent organisation for not doing enough to encourage member countries to accept invitations to play the Irish Free State, either home or away. After pointing out that they (the FAIFS) were the sole advocates of the merits of British and Irish football on the European mainland, at a time when the British International Board was wholly dismissive of it, Ryder bemoaned the fact that FIFA members, such as France and Austria, had no difficulty sending teams to England while at the same time citing crowded domestic programmes and adverse currency exchange rates as excuses for turning down invitations to play in Dublin. It was now two years since the last international game in the city, and in requesting FIFA to discharge its obligations to promote football in all member countries, he requested that the matter be put on the agenda for their annual Congress in 1934. The reply, when it arrived some three months later, was not encouraging. Dr J. Schicker, General Secretary of FIFA, said they were not in a position to coerce countries to play in Ireland. He suggested that future attempts to arrange fixtures should be directed primarily at northern European countries.

When international competition eventually returned in February 1934, it was in the format of the preliminaries of the World Cup, the finals of which were scheduled to be played in Italy later in the year. The Free State Association had accepted an invitation the previous year to enter a team for the first time in the championship. And when they were eventually drawn alongside Belgium and Holland in Group 11 of the qualifying process, FIFA suggested that to reduce costs, the three teams should meet in qualifying games in Holland, immediately before the finals in the summer. They informed the FAIFS that the other countries in the group feared they would not recover their travel costs if forced to play in Dublin. This, of course, was unacceptable to the Free State Association, and their alternative suggestion that they play one game at home and one away was eventually accepted by the championship organisers. Having beaten both Belgium and Holland on their home patch, the Irish were not deterred by the prospect of taking on the Dutch team in Amsterdam after hosting Belgium at Dalymount Park.

So it was that some four years after the competition was launched, World Cup football finally came to Dublin on 24 February 1934. Three times in the preceding six years, Belgium's national team had been met and mastered, a record which raised hopes of a relatively easy afternoon for the home side. Nothing could have been farther from the truth. Despite the indignities they had been made to endure in those games, or perhaps because of them, the Belgians were a revelation in opening up a 2–0 lead before the Irish got a chance to draw breath. In the end, the home team was reprieved only by Paddy Moore's uncanny finishing instincts. Four times the Aberdeen player put the ball in the net – the first time in the competition's brief history that the feat had been achieved – but Belgium were still able to reflect on a thrilling 4–4 draw as they set off on their return journey to Brussels.

Despite the Free State's 2–0 win in Amsterdam two years earlier, it was already apparent that the Dutch would provide a huge test of the Irishmen's character in the second of the qualifying games in the same city on 8 April 1934 – and so it proved. With the wounds of that embarrassing Dutch eclipse still not fully healed, the return was labelled a revenge mission by Dutch supporters, so much so that tickets for the match sold out within hours of going on sale. Thanks to the installation of 5,000 temporary seats in the stadium which had hosted the Olympic Games six years earlier, the capacity was raised to 38,000, but it still wasn't enough to satisfy the unprecedented demand. It meant that the FAIFS's headquarters were inundated with applications from Holland for Ireland's share of the match tickets, and the effect was to convince the Irish players of the enormity of the task they faced if they were to qualify for the World Cup finals.

Almost inevitably, the Irish selectors ran into difficulties in securing the release of their English club players. Jim Brennan wrote to the English League, seeking their co-operation in having Tom Farquharson (Cardiff City) and Willie Fallon (Notts County) cleared after the clubs indicated that they were prepared to facilitate the FAIFS if the League authorities approved it. In the case of Farquharson, Brennan also contacted the FA of Wales, but the reply, when it came, was negative. While the Association had no objections to the goalkeeper joining the Irish squad, they said that Cardiff City were in such a sorry state in the league table that they couldn't afford to do without him. Farquharson, of course, had earlier been embroiled in a political controversy because of his refusal to play for Northern Ireland.

In the end, neither Farquharson nor Fallon was permitted to play in the World Cup game, and in the case of the tall goalkeeper it would prove a sad ending to a career which, in its prime, held so much promise. Never slow to put his thoughts in writing, he provided a graphic epitaph to the controversy after the club had reversed its decision to allow him to travel to Amsterdam. "I feel my club has failed me at a time when we could have put the [English] Football League in its place," he wrote. "This was due to the fact that they will have to depend on the League for re-election at the end of the season."

As it transpired, Ireland's worst fears were to be realised in a game in which the Dutch team's technical superiority was everywhere in evidence. Moore again got his name on the scoresheet, but with word of his heroics in the Belgian match preceding him, he got little space to indulge his trademark skills in and around the six-yard area. Johnny Squires, on his debut, also hit the target, but in the end the Netherlands emerged as impressive 5–2 winners. Not for the last time, the visitors had been caught out by the intensity and sharp competitive edge of World Cup football.

Chapter Eighteen

Shelbourne Banned

Ever since their formation in 1895, Shelbourne had been central to the evolving story of Irish football. The first club in Dublin to embrace professionalism, the first from the capital to lift the Irish Cup in 1906, and the first in the south to form themselves into a limited liability public company six years later, they believed with a passion that theirs was a missionary role in fostering the development of the game throughout the length and breadth of the country.

Sadly, the Shelbourne Sports Company was liquidated in 1922 without ever getting to realise its great ambition of building the biggest football stadium in the country. In almost everything else, however, the Reds were at the cutting edge of history in those traumatic years immediately before and after the great divide in 1921. For many, the driving ambition in the club was to achieve in the south what Linfield had accomplished up north, and although they were eventually upstaged in that crusade by their near neighbours, Shamrock Rovers, there is no denying their immense contribution to the development of the game.

There was also the occasional aberration, or deviation from the norm, which brought them into conflict with football authorities, north and south, and of these none was more serious than the gaffes which landed them in hot water with the Free State Association early in 1934. They had already tested the patience of the Free State League on a couple of occasions before they were handed a stiff fine for allegedly poaching players from nearby clubs. This they refused to pay, and after several abortive attempts to resolve the situation, they were eventually threatened with suspension. With a little more diplomacy, the situation might have been resolved at that point; but then, out of the blue, came the bombshell which ensured that an expedient solution was no longer an option.

On 7 March 1934, a letter was received at the offices of the FAIFS from Shelbourne stating than in consequence of the unprecedented fine and subsequent suspension imposed on them by the Football League of the Irish Free State, the club had applied for membership of the Irish Football Association. At a time when north–south relations were at an all-time low in the wake of the insults traded during the failed unity Conference in Belfast, that was a cardinal offence, and within hours of penning the letter, they realised they had gone too far. The fact that Shelbourne were at the very core of the dispute which had ultimately brought the FAIFS into being, lent an added element of irony to the crisis now erupting, but that fact was almost certainly lost on Council members, as they prepared to deal with their biggest challenge so far.

On 27 June 1934, members of the Senior Council met to determine the club's fate, and having listened to a full review of the case, they ruled that Shelbourne's action was in direct contravention of the rules and objectives of the Football Association of the Irish Free State. It was therefore decided that "Shelbourne FC be suspended for a period of 12 months, starting on 27 June 1934. It was further determined that the following members of the Committee of Shelbourne FC, Messrs T. McCormick (President), P. Guileful (Chairman), J. Taylor (Hon Secretary), B. Healy (Hon Treasurer), P. Lynch, T. Cullen, J. Finnegan and T. Litton be suspended from ever taking part in the management of any club or affiliated body in football, under the jurisdiction of the Football Association of the Irish Free State."

Council members elaborated on the case in the course of the Association's annual general meeting at the Mansion House two days later, when the Hon Secretary, Jim Brennan, standing in for Jack Ryder, told delegates that the IFA had been informed that they were not empowered to accept the affiliation of the Dublin club. In the event of the IFA doing so, he assured them the issue would be pursued vigorously. Power was vested to the incoming Council to re-examine the suspension if required, but another proposal, that the action of the outgoing Council be endorsed, was carried by 25 votes to 4.

Chapter Eighteen

For the first time in almost 40 years, Shelbourne were out of senior football, with their place in the Free State League for the 1934–35 season going to Waterford. Nor was there any joy for the south Dublin club when the suspension came up for review a year later at a meeting of the FAIFS Council on 12 June 1935. A proposal that the ban on the club be lifted and that the Council appoint a commission of not less than three members, to investigate the circumstances of the dispute between the club and the Association, was declared lost. As a result of that decision, a new club, Reds United, based in the same area of Ringsend and including several former members of Shelbourne, was elected to membership of the Free State League in the 1935–36 season, eventually finishing fourth in the table behind Bohemians, Dolphin and Cork.

In October of that year, sensing that the tide of public sympathy was now beginning to run more strongly in their favour, the club made another abortive attempt for reinstatement, but it wasn't until 5 February 1936 that their efforts were finally crowned with success. It followed another intervention by their near neighbours, Shamrock Rovers, who, putting aside the great rivalry between the clubs, had been involved in each of their previously unsuccessful appeals. Now, following the proposition of Tom Scully, seconded by Matt Kenny, the long wait was finally ended when on a vote of fifteen to five, it was determined to restore Shelbourne to membership of the Free State League for the 1936–37 season. And once they had pledged loyalty to the FAIFS, the life ban on committee members was also repealed. It had been a costly error of judgement by the club, at a time when their action in seeking admission to the Irish League was interpreted as the ultimate act of betrayal. Within eight years of their return, the club had reclaimed the league championship title but, for some, the scars of that collision with authority would last a lot longer.

On other fronts, the relationship between the two Irish Associations remained as difficult as ever. On the credit side, University College, Dublin sought and were granted permission to play inter-varsity games in Northern Ireland, a notable advance in the light of some of the problems encountered the previous year. On the other hand, the FAIFS threatened to report the FA of Scotland to FIFA after they had cancelled a Junior international fixture in Dublin, allegedly at the behest of the IFA. There was now little or no interaction between Dublin and Belfast, a point that was illustrated in a curious protest by Shamrock Rovers. Following a game against Dundalk, they claimed that three members of the Dundalk side had represented Irish League clubs in games the previous day. Following an enquiry, however, it was established that Wilfred Andrews, Samuel Cairns and James Mosley were all eligible to play for the Co Louth club.

Because of their geographical location, Dundalk, who had previously depended on friendly games against the top Irish League teams to raise much-needed funds, found the ban on cross-border matches particularly expensive. In the circumstances, it was no real surprise when at the annual general meeting of the Association held at the Mansion House in Dublin, they tabled a proposal: "That the resolution passed at the 1931–32 AGM and embodied on Page 43 of the Association Rule book for season 1934–35, withholding permission for matches involving members and bodies affiliated to the IFA, be rescinded." After a long discussion, it was defeated by 40 votes to 34, but owing to the closeness of the voting, it was recommended that the incoming Council consider the possibility of reopening the debate.

It is interesting to note that John McMahon, a centre-half with Bohemians in the team which swept the board in Free State football six years earlier, was capped by Northern Ireland in their 1–0 defeat by Scotland in 1934. McMahon was never similarly honoured by the Free State selectors but figured in the southern inter-league team on three occasions. In two of those games, he actually played against the Irish League in matches at Dalymount and Windsor Park. As a former GAA player born in Derry, he was of course qualified to represent Northern Ireland, but at a time when the relationship between the two Associations was at its lowest point, his selection was still seen as contentious. Aside from football, McMahon enjoyed a long career in An Garda Siochana, but it is for the unusual nature of his brief international career that he is best remembered in Dublin. Free State officials were not amused by the IFA's decision to poach a player from their jurisdiction, but four years later they themselves were guilty of opportunism in capping the Dundalk player, Dicky Lunn, who was born in Northern Ireland, in games against Switzerland and Poland.

Chapter Eighteen

At a higher level, there was little indication of a thaw in the frosty relationship with England, a point which gave Billy Lacey, the part-time national team coach, some huge problems in the approach to the game against Hungary, at Dalymount Park, on 16 December 1934. Even then, Hungary were acknowledged as one of the best teams in the world, probably the strongest in Europe, and home advantage notwithstanding, the consensus was that it would require an immense exercise in concentration and commitment to beat them. Based on the experience of an international career which spanned three decades, Lacey worried that the absence of his English-based players would tip the scales still more heavily in the Hungarians' favour.

Irish Football Association authorities, dismayed by what they interpreted as Dublin's unwillingness to negotiate a deal at the failed Belfast Conference, had launched an intensive lobbying campaign with the other British Associations, designed to reduce the FAIFS to a position in which they would have to rely exclusively on local players for international games. By contriving a situation in which the FA of England would put pressure on clubs to refuse clearances for their Irish-born players to return home for such fixtures, they hoped to force the Association back to the negotiating table, in a much-weakened situation. That scenario was not lost on Jack Ryder, and on 7 November 1934 he sent preliminary letters to English clubs, seeking the release of players for the game against Hungary. In doing so, Ryder stressed the need to uphold the prestige of the game in Britain and Ireland with a good result against the Hungarians, but he suspected that because of the fallout from the football split in Ireland, some of the club managers would not be disposed to co-operate. Because of this, Larry Sheridan was directed to travel to England to speak with the managers involved.

In little more than a week, Ryder discovered that his worst fears were about to be realised when he received a letter from Frank Buckley, manager-secretary of Wolverhampton Wanderers, stating that because of the friction between the English FA and the FAIFS, he believed that it would not be possible to release their player, Charlie Greene, for the game. A subsequent message from Buckley confirmed that Wolves directors had sought a ruling in the matter from London, and shortly afterwards Dublin was notified officially of the player's unavailability. Greene was never invited again to play for the Free State.

Central to Lacey's match plans was the presence of Arsenal's Jimmy Dunne at the front of his attack, and to this end Ryder wrote to Sir Frederick Wall, President of the FA of England, asking him to use his good office to persuade the Highbury club to clear the Dubliner to play in the game. It was at best a forlorn hope and the response in the negative can scarcely have surprised anybody. Leeds United likewise refused permission for Charlie Turner and Harry Duggan to face the Hungarians, but perhaps the biggest disappointment of all was Everton's action in declining to make Alex Stevenson available. In time Everton would change tack so dramatically that they became the biggest provider of players for Ireland teams, but it was a vastly different story in the mid-1930s, when they were perceived in Dublin as supporting the stance of the IFA in Belfast. In the course of his travels in England, Larry Sheridan had made direct contact with Mr P. McKenna, President of the English Football League and a member of the Everton Board of Directors, who told him it was his belief that the English League would not prevent players travelling to Dublin for the game.

Alas, the reality proved otherwise and, like the others, Stevenson was refused a clearance. That struck a raw nerve with many Irish people, for the skilful inside-forward, a Dublin Protestant and later one of Glasgow Rangers' star attractions, compared favourably with Dunne when it came to measuring the Free State's assets in international football. What annoyed the supporters of the southern team was that at times when Everton were refusing to co-operate with the FAIFS, the player was invariably made available by the club for selection by Northern Ireland. This led to widespread speculation that because of his religious beliefs, Stevenson was unwilling to play on Sundays, an allegation which he subsequently repudiated. In fact, he didn't play for the south again until 1946, when he was dramatically recalled following a late reshuffle of the team which faced England at Dalymount Park, but it is a measure of his reputation that he was subsequently appointed as the FAI's national coach with responsibility for coaching the international team.

All of this left Lacey more heavily dependent on local talent than would otherwise have been the case for the match against Hungary and it showed in a sub-standard performance against accomplished opposition. Joey

Donnelly and Paddy Bermingham got the goals in a 4–2 defeat which
scarcely reflected the visitors' superiority over a home team which included
just three players based in Britain, Dick Griffiths (Walsall), Willie Fallon
(Notts Co) and Paddy Moore of Aberdeen. After a spate of goals at the start
of his international career, the sun was already beginning to set on Moore's
tragically short time at the top, a consequence of his increasingly futile
struggle with alcoholism. In a letter to the FAIFS dated 31 December, the
Aberdeen manager, Joe Travers, said that he hadn't seen Moore since the
Hungary game two weeks earlier and asked to be recouped for the money
he had loaned the player to travel home to Ireland for the match.

Moore would again be embroiled in controversy at the end of the season,
when the national team was involved in a two-match tour of Switzerland
and Germany. In his official report on the 1–0 defeat in the first game in
Basle on 5 May 1935, Larry Sheridan revealed that the Aberdeen player
had not observed the 11 p.m. curfew imposed on players on the eve of
the game, and that he surprised team officials by opting out of the match
with an injury he hadn't previously reported. "I am satisfied," wrote
Sheridan, "that if Moore had taken his place in the team, a victory would
have resulted for the Irish Free State. It is perfectly evident to me – and
my opinion may, perhaps, be shared by other officials – that the action of
Moore in this case, taken in conjunction with previous exploits on similar
occasions, makes it obvious that he is apparently incapable of appreciating
the honour bestowed on him in being called on to represent the State in
international games. It seems to me that the free holiday comes first with
this player, the prestige and honour of his country, nowhere."

Moore was recalled for the 3–1 loss to Germany three days later but,
significantly, he failed to hit the target in any of his remaining games in
the green jersey. It is a measure of the manner in which he interacted with
the public, however, that long after his untimely death in 1951, his name
continued to be associated with some of the most memorable days for the
national team.

Holland visited Dublin for the final international match of 1935 and
it occasioned the first radio broadcast of a football game by the national
station, 2RN. With no experienced commentator sufficiently qualified to
do the broadcast, 2RN asked the Association to put forward the names of

Council members who might be interested in taking on the assignment of radio commentator for a fee of four guineas. Eventually, Dr Barry Hooper, erstwhile medical officer with the team, was chosen to commentate in preference to several Council members, and the repercussions of that decision were such that permission was withheld by the Council for broadcast facilities for a number of games subsequently.

The fixture formed part of a big weekend for sport in Dublin, being preceded by the rugby union international between Ireland and New Zealand at Lansdowne Road, and by arrangement with the Irish Rugby Football Union, the Dutch football party was invited to watch the All Blacks in action. The comprehensive nature of New Zealand's win would have done nothing to improve the mindset of the Irish for the confrontation at Dalymount Park 24 hours later, but the rugby tourists were said to be delighted to receive an invitation to join the post-match football banquet in the Gresham Hotel.

Even allowing for the disappointment of a 5–2 scoreline in favour of the Dutch team, the radio coverage made this match something of a watershed in the evolution of Irish football. However, it was overshadowed by the passing of Jack Ryder who died, after a long illness, a few days before the game. Ryder is recalled as one of the founding fathers of football in Ireland after becoming involved with the Leinster Football Association in 1904, and he filled a highly influential role in promoting the game south of the border after the notorious split in 1921.

On 15 January 1936, just a fortnight after the Association's new offices were opened by the FAIFS President, Sir Oliver Grattan Esmonde, at D'Olier Chambers, D'Olier St, Dublin, a ballot was held to decide between the eight applicants for the vacant post of Secretary of the FAIFS. It resulted in victory for Joe Wickham, who defeated his nearest challenger, Larry Sheridan, by eleven votes to seven. Others who participated in the ballot were Messrs R. Balbirnie, D. Fogarty, T. Heeley, J.T. Kelly and S.R. Prole, a significant personality in League of Ireland football, first with Dundalk and later Drumcondra FC.

Chapter Nineteen

London's Stance Challenged

London's perceived indifference to Dublin's indignation in their refusal to treat the Irish Free State Association as equal partners in the administration of football in Ireland reached new heights in 1936, when Norwich City outraged many thousands of Irish people by signing two of Cork's most talented players, Owen Madden and Jackie O'Reilly, without reference to the club. Madden had just made his international debut against Hungary, and while O'Reilly was still only on the threshold of a career which would bring him two international caps, he, too, was central to the club's hopes of establishing Cork as a focal point of the game in Ireland.

Cork's immediate reaction was to suspend both players and refer the matter to the Council of the FAIFS. After unanimously agreeing that Norwich had been guilty of an illegal approach to the players at a time when they were still contracted to play for Cork, it was decided (1) that the case be referred to the English FA, pointing out that the players had incurred automatic suspension under Rule 40 by entering into negotiations with Norwich City while still under contract with Cork, and (2) that the players involved were precluded from assisting any club, until such time as those suspensions were lifted. To their thinly veiled astonishment, however, they discovered that the authorities at Lancaster Gate were not prepared to recognise the suspensions, effectively inviting other clubs in England to follow suit. That situation was intolerable and, inevitably, it ended up in a legal wrangle which would do nothing to enhance the image of the sport.

Some time earlier, Joe Wickham had written to Stanley Rous, Secretary of the FA of England, in the hope of persuading him to use his office to rationalise the anomalies existing in Irish football, and requesting that he look again at London's preferential treatment of the Irish Football

Association, which Wickham described as a "sham". In a predictable reaction to the Madden/O'Reilly controversy, Norwich hinted that, in future, they would not accommodate the Irish Association by releasing players for international games, but after the matter had been referred to Senior Counsel for legal advice, it petered out, without either party being fully satisfied. The effect of the episode, however, was to drive another wedge into the relationship between Dublin and London and, by extension, encourage Belfast in their stand-off with the FAIFS.

Within weeks of taking over Jack Ryder's old job as Secretary of the FAIFS, Joe Wickham made it clear that two of his priorities on the international front would be to prevent the IFA claiming the exclusive right of the title "Ireland" in their international fixtures and to bring pressure to bear on them to abolish the practice of selecting southern players in their team. And he promptly gave substance to those pledges by unilaterally changing the name of the southern team to "Ireland" for the meeting with Switzerland at Dalymount Park on St Patrick's Day, 1936. By doing so, he hoped to provoke a reaction from FIFA which would settle the designation of Irish teams once and for all, but in this he was proved wrong.

In August of that year, he travelled to Berlin for FIFA's Annual Congress, confident that his decision would be questioned by some delegates and determined to defend it to the hilt. In fact there was no reaction from the floor and on his return to Dublin, he was able to claim that FIFA's Executive Committee was taking no action against "our decision to play under the title of Ireland". He had to admit, however, that the Executive Committee was not in favour of the issue being debated at Congress at a time when the IFA was at pains to stress that teams representing the FAIFS should still be called the Irish Free State. From Wickham's perspective, that title was now redundant, and from then until Dublin seceded from the British Commonwealth in 1949, the Secretary was militant in his assertion that any title other than Ireland, in relation to the southern team, was incorrect. With the rival Associations now sending out teams claiming the same designation in international football, there was understandable confusion in both Britain and mainland Europe, but not enough, apparently, to force either Dublin or Belfast to retreat from core principles.

With Scotland, as anticipated, rejecting an invitation to return to

Dublin for a friendly game, for what would have been the first time since 1913, it was left to Switzerland to provide the opposition for a rebuilt Irish team at the start of a five-match programme in 1936. A year earlier, the Swiss had recorded an unexpected 1–0 win at Basle, and the prospect of revenge enticed an expectant crowd of 32,000 through the turnstiles at Dalymount Park. The occasion marked the first appearance of Bill Gorman, a fine full-back from Sligo, whose international career would eventually straddle the Second World War, one of only a handful to do so. The bigger attraction by far, however, was the return of the Arsenal player, Jimmy Dunne, whom posterity would recall as one of the most gifted of all Irish centre-forwards. Dunne's only previous appearance in the team had been in 1930, when he marked his entry to international football in the grand manner, by scoring two of the goals in a 3–1 win over Belgium in Brussels. The blond Dubliner was perhaps the most notable victim of the political war between Dublin and Belfast, with first Sheffield United and later Arsenal refusing him permission to play for the southern team for the most spurious of reasons. In the course of his six-year absence from the Free State side, he made six international appearances for the IFA, damning evidence of the manner in which English clubs discriminated against Dublin.

With Paddy Moore in the prime of his short career in the early 1930s, Dunne's absence was not as expensive as it might otherwise have been. However, there was no disguising the fact that at a time when they were desperately trying to impress Europe with the quality of their performances, the Free State team had to make do without one of the outstanding players of his generation. All of which heightened the sense of occasion now as William "Sacky" Glen led out the home team – and, in the manner of his calling, Dunne did not disappoint. Involved in almost everything that mattered in the game, he linked with Freddie Horlacher to produce the goal which would eventually decide the match and wipe the slate clean for the indignities visited on the Irish in Basle some 10 months earlier.

Next up was the end-of-season tour which took in games against Hungary and, for the first time, Luxembourg. Originally a third international fixture, against Germany, was planned, but in the end the programme was rescheduled and the German Federation sent a team to Dublin in October of that year. On an afternoon of torrential rain in Budapest, Ireland produced an outstanding performance in restricting Hungary to a 3–3 draw which, given the rating of the home team, probably eclipsed the achievement of the Irish against Spain in Barcelona five years earlier. Dunne again got on the scoresheet, hitting the target early in the game, and in Luxembourg he contributed two of the goals which launched the visitors to a 5–1 win. In every sense except finance, it had been a remarkably successful tour for the Irish party, one which was duly acknowledged across Europe as "identifying the competitive spirit of the Irish". Because of the bad weather, the attendance at the Hungarian game fell a long way below expectation, and the outcome was a loss of almost £700 on the tour, a significant setback at a difficult time for the Association.

At the annual general meeting of the FAIFS, held in the Engineers' Hall in Dawson St, Dublin on 30 June 1936, Sir Oliver Grattan Esmonde TD was re-elected as President of the Association for the sixth consecutive year. Addressing the meeting, he referred to the posture the IFA was adopting in international games and said he considered it was illegal for that organisation to misrepresent the country by their use of the name Ireland. Just four weeks later, however, the Council was passing a vote of condolence to his relatives after he had been found dead in his Dublin home by a servant. His sudden passing stunned the city, for the previous evening he was on his feet addressing Dail Eireann. The last titled member of the Oireachtas, he had served the Association well, particularly in the years immediately after the split when he used his influence at the Department for External Affairs to canvass Government support for the FAIFS. Shortly after being elected to succeed Grattan Esmonde at the annual general meeting in June 1937, Lord Holmpatrick resigned and was replaced by Dr W.F. Hooper.

Whereas his predecessor as Secretary, Jack Ryder, had interacted only infrequently with the press, Joe Wickham was quick to recognise the importance of the printed word, co-operating with the local press whenever feasible and using his office to denounce the English-based newspapers circulating in Ireland. A case in point was his fiery rubbishing in January

1936 of a report in a London newspaper suggesting that the main reason the IFA would not co-operate with the FAIFS was because the latter body insisted in staging its home international games on Sundays. Later that year, he wrote to Allied Newspapers Ltd, publishers of the *Sunday Chronicle* and *Sporting Chronicle*, complaining about their lack of coverage of the end-of-season tour of Hungary and Luxembourg. Of the 3–3 draw with Hungary, the top-rated team in Europe, he wrote: "Contrary to the English FA's experience, we didn't do badly and, after the game, the Hungarians paid us the compliment of saying that we fought harder, and with more spirit, than any of the British teams which had played in Budapest."

Within weeks, he was in contact once more with the *Sunday Chronicle*, which alone of the English Sunday papers continued to call the national team the Irish Free State instead of what he considered its proper title of Ireland. He interpreted this as "either the paper's total ignorance of Irish football or, as might be interpreted here, a definite bias against our Association". He also reprimanded the Press Association for saying that Tom Davis was playing in his first international game when he turned out for the IFA's team against England at Stoke in November 1936, ignoring the fact that he had already been capped twice by the Dublin organisation at that point. In an astonishing reply, the Press Association said that (in Britain) a distinction had always been drawn between games on mainland Europe and those in the international tournament, i.e. the British home tournament.

Ironically, Davis, who played with Oldham Athletic in England, had come to the notice of the IFA selectors by scoring twice in Ireland's summary 5–2 dismissal of Germany at Dalymount Park just weeks before his call-up by them to face England. He was among the goals again when Hungary came to Dublin in December to return Ireland's visit to Budapest in May, but on this occasion it proved something of an anticlimax for Irish supporters. In sharing the spoils with the Hungarians in the first game, the men in green had performed at a level which earned them much praise across Europe, but this occasion would prove a lot more difficult for them. Forewarned by that 3–3 draw, Hungary attacked from the start and were 3–1 in front early in the second half before Ireland really got going. From there to the end, they pinned the visitors in their own half but an injury to Paddy Moore, in his last appearance in a green shirt, deprived them of the scoring power which might at least have earned a draw after Davis converted a penalty to complement Willie Fallon's early strike.

The first major decision of the FAIFS Council in 1937 was to accept an invitation to compete in the World Cup championship in France the following year. Despite the failure to build on Paddy Moore's spectacular four-goal spree in the game against Belgium and the 5–2 defeat at the hands of Holland in Amsterdam, the initial Irish involvement in the championship in 1934 had been judged a success, and with the prospect of greater progress now, the proposal to enter for a second time was unanimously approved by the FAIFS Council.

The build-up to the competition could scarcely have been more impressive. A Jimmy Dunne goal earned a 1–0 win over Switzerland at Berne, in the first of two tour games in May, and then six days later Davy Jordan and Johnny Brown found the net for an even more impressive 2–0 victory over France in Paris. Ironically, Jordan and Brown were both born in Northern Ireland and their selection by the FAIFS provoked protests from the IFA in Belfast.

That was the form of potential giantkillers, and with goalkeeper Tommy Breen, later to emerge as a highly controversial figure, keeping a clean sheet on each occasion, the signs were encouraging. Before the draw for the preliminaries was made, the FAIFS informed the championship organisers that "having regard to the existing circumstances in Spain and the involvement of Irish factions on either side of the civil war there, it would be unwise to include them in our group". As it happened, the Irish team was drawn to meet Norway in a two-legged tie, with the winners to meet Poland for the right to play in the final.

Unfortunately for the Irish, both legs of the Norwegian tie were played on Sundays, which inevitably meant problems in securing the release of their English-based players. The advent of closed club dates to facilitate the availability of players for competitive international games was still fifty years away, and the outcome was that the selectors were forced to include no fewer than nine home-based players in their team, including newcomers Mick Hoy (Dundalk) and Tommy Donnelly (Drumcondra), who both hailed from Northern Ireland. This had the effect of further infuriating the

IFA, who insisted that the southern body was not entitled to select players from north of the border.

Norway, whose achievement in reaching the semi-finals of the Olympic football championship in Berlin the previous year had stamped them as one of Europe's better teams, dominated the game in Oslo against a weary Irish team, whose performance betrayed the physical effects of a long boat and train journey to the Norwegian capital. Thanks to some outstanding saves by George McKenzie, deputising for the injured Breen in goal, and the profligacy of the home attack, the Irish escaped with a 3–2 defeat, a scoreline which flattered them somewhat. Jimmy Dunne, by this stage back in Dublin with Shamrock Rovers, obtained one of the visitors' goals, but Norwegian Federation officials later claimed he was ineligible to play because of his earlier appearances for Northern Ireland. They didn't lodge an official protest, however, and Dunne retained his place in the Irish side which faced them in the return match at Dalymount Park four weeks later.

Also chosen in the side was Tommy Breen, by now fully recovered from injury. Breen, from Drogheda, had started his career with Newry Town before joining Manchester United. Capped for the first time by the FAIFS during the European tour the previous May, he also won caps from the IFA selectors, who saw him as the natural successor to their celebrated goalkeeper, Elisha Scott. After playing for the northern team against England three weeks earlier, he was retained for their meeting with Scotland at Aberdeen. The problem was that the Scottish game was scheduled for 10 November, just three days after the World Cup match, and IFA officials, upset by what they interpreted as southern arrogance in selecting northern players for the game in Oslo, now saw an obvious chance to turn the tables on Dublin.

They informed Breen that they were not prepared to countenance the risk of his being injured for the game in Scotland by taking part in the World Cup fixture, and if he wished to pursue what promised to be a long career with their team, he would have to withdraw from the southern side. After pondering the problem for some time, Breen contacted the FAIFS Secretary, Joe Wickham, to inform him that he was withdrawing from the World Cup match. Breen's decision to play for the IFA, because of what Wickham termed "the immediate material advantage of doing so", was seen in Dublin as a gross act of betrayal. Manchester United accepted no responsibility in the matter, lodging an official complaint with the FAIFS over a newspaper article which suggested that they had been responsible for the player's decision. It would be another eight years before a goalkeeping crisis forced Dublin to recall Breen, and then only for a brief period. Significantly, he made just two appearances for Northern Ireland after the satisfaction of the political victory occasioned by his participation in the Scottish match had begun to recede.

McKenzie, entitled to be disappointed by the selectors' decision to drop him after an outstanding performance in Oslo, was recalled to take Breen's place in an Irish line-up which featured the first international appearances of two of the enduring legends in Irish sport, Jack Carey and Kevin O'Flanagan. Alas, the victory that a nation coveted eluded them, with Reider Kvammen, a policeman in Oslo when he wasn't playing football, scoring twice to earn his team a 3–3 draw and an aggregate 6–5 victory. The World Cup campaign had been a short journey of distinction which would be replicated on several occasions in the second half of the twentieth century.

Chapter Twenty

Changing Titles

Joe Wickham's fixation about the designation of the teams sent out by the rival football associations and, in particular, Dublin's claim to have their sides entitled Ireland rather than the Irish Free State, received a significant boost with the new Constitution Bill enacted by Eamon de Valera's government in 1937. Now, for the first time, the territory within the remit of the government in Dublin was to be known as Eire or, in the English language, Ireland.

After risking the wrath of the British Football Associations for so long, he could at last advance a valid reason for his action in the spring of the previous year, in persuading the Council of the FAIFS to endorse his proposal of the Association's teams competing as Ireland in international football and, by extension, debunking the IFA's assertion that they alone were empowered to use that title. Commenting on the consequences of the Constitution Bill, the *Irish Times* noted that far from resolving the complexities of the football dispute, the reality of two international teams, each purporting to represent Ireland, would merely exacerbate the situation.

That was an opinion which resonated well with Belfast, but for the power brokers at the southern Association's new offices at D'Olier Chambers, in Dublin's D'Olier St, the new legislation provided the imprimatur of legitimacy for all that had gone before. Wasting no time, Senior Council members voted unanimously in December 1937 that the organisation should revert to its former title of the Football Association of Ireland and notify FIFA accordingly. An Irish press report quoted a message from the United Press Agency in Geneva, stating that the League of Nations had received formal notification that under Article 4 of the new Irish Constitution, which took effect on 29 December, the name of the State had been changed. The Agency report noted that under League of Nations practice, this change in name is implemented automatically "as was the case in Persia's change of title to Iran".

The reaction of the Associations affiliated to the British International Board to that change of title was predictably mixed. The English FA, anxious to be seen as a conciliatory influence, acknowledged the letter courteously; no responses were forthcoming from Scotland and Wales; and a letter from Charles Watson, Secretary of the IFA, stated that following a meeting of the Association's Emergency Committee, he had been instructed to inform Dublin "that we cannot recognise your Association using the word Ireland in your new designation and will continue to communicate with you as the Football Association of the Irish Free State". Wickham's response was equally curt, stating that as the Irish Free State no longer existed, Belfast's action was meaningless.

Later Dr Hooper, acting in his new role as President of the FAI, wrote to his English FA counterpart, William Pickford, reminding him that following the new Constitution of 1937, London now recognised the title of Ireland politically and the same status should be applied in football by the British Associations. Acknowledging the request, Pickford had high praise for the merit of Ireland's victory over Switzerland, adding, "Whatever differences there may be, we still look on all the Irish, in a sense, as one of the family." In October 1938, Pickford made his excuses for not being able to arrange a personal meeting with Hooper and informed him "that at a recent meeting of the Council of the FA [of England], it was decided to uphold the IFA's right to use the title of Ireland in international competition". For all the diplomatic niceties, it seemed that in football neither London nor Belfast had any intention of abandoning core principles.

Acting on the stance adopted by Wickham at the FIFA Congress in Berlin two years earlier, the Football Association of Ireland selectors again stretched the contentious eligibility issue by including three northern-born players, Johnny Brown, Harry Baird and Walter McMillan, in their squad for their games against Czechoslovakia at Prague on 18 May 1938 and Poland at Warsaw four days later. Brown, who made ten appearances for

Northern Ireland in spells with Wolves, Coventry and Birmingham City, had apparently crept in under the radar for the southern team the previous year, when he won his first cap against Switzerland and then scored in the 2–0 win over France in Paris. Initially, Coventry cleared him to join the Ireland party in Prague and Warsaw, but then, by order of the FA of England, both he and Baird were withdrawn. McMillan, a former team-mate of Baird's at Manchester United, was also pulled out by his club, Chesterfield, on the pretext of flu.

Asked to justify their action in barring the players, the English Association claimed that it was based on a decision taken at the 1923 Conference in Liverpool and endorsed at the most recent meeting of the British International Board at Llandudno just two months earlier. In fact, the minutes of the Llandudno meeting reveal that the IFA's letter, requesting the Board to uphold the rule preventing the southern body from selecting northern players, was received too late to be put on the agenda. Instead, delegates discussed the matter informally, but the conclusion in Dublin was that the absence of the three players was no more than the payback for happenings in 1937.

Significantly, the selectors filled the vacancies by recalling Joe O'Reilly, Kevin O'Flanagan and Jimmy Dunne. These were three patriarchal personalities in local football, and their omission from the original squad suggested to some that the selectors had summoned the northern trio purely to score political points. If they did, they were due for another shock when a passport problem forced the uncapped Barnsley full-back John Everest to withdraw just before the boat set sail. Not surprisingly, perhaps, the team fell apart on the tour when, after restricting Czechoslovakia to a commendable 2–2 draw, they were routed 6–0 by Poland, by far their heaviest defeat, in the second game in Warsaw.

Following quickly on their elimination from the World Cup at the hands of Norway, this setback did nothing to foster hope of improvement, but then, out of nothing, came a sharp revival. On 18 September 1938, just four months after the nightmare in Warsaw, the Irish team recorded a 4–0 win over Switzerland at Dalymount Park. The match was given an added sense of occasion by the presence of Dr Douglas Hyde, in one of his first major public appearances since his inauguration as the first President of Ireland some months earlier. Seated alongside Eamon de Valera and Oscar Traynor, a member of de Valera's cabinet who would later be appointed as the President of the Association, Dr Hyde was entitled to be well pleased with his first visit to an international football game. Shortly afterwards, however, he was informed that he was being removed by the Gaelic Athletic Association as one of their patrons, because of his attendance at Dalymount Park. This decision was interpreted as a gaffe of significant proportions by Croke Park and was suitably derided as such in a leader in the *Irish Times*.

If the victory over the Swiss was opportune, the one which followed two months later was even sweeter. Neither the Irish players nor the people who supported them had quite forgotten the embarrassment of Warsaw and the manner in which Poland toyed with Charlie Turner's team. Now the Poles were due at Dalymount for the return match in November 1938 and a huge crowd turned up to witness the Irish team's attempt to exact revenge. They would not be disappointed. Deriving inspiration from the noise in the stadium, Ireland took the hapless visitors off their feet by the pace and weight of their early attack, with Willie Fallon and Jack Carey scoring inside the opening 15 minutes. Jimmy Dunne added a third, and for all the technical skills of the Polish team, they were beaten 3–2. That was a performance to savour, the more so since it yielded gate receipts of £2,023-10-6. The Association's response to that windfall was to make a further investment of £500 in the purchase of 4% Land Bonds.

Unfortunately, Dicky Lunn, an amateur player with Dundalk who was winning his second cap at left-half in the Polish game, saw none of that money. Lunn's inclusion for the game with Switzerland was a source of contention, for he was born in Portadown and, as such, did not legally qualify to play for the southern team. He was found guilty of a misdemeanour some time after the Polish fixture and eventually fined £3-3-0, a sum he refused to pay. Approached on the matter, Dundalk FC officials informed the Association that the money should be deducted from Lunn's fee for playing in the game, only to be reminded that the player had been selected, and took part in the match, as an amateur. Normally, amateur players received a suitably inscribed gold medal worth three guineas. In this instance, however, Lunn received nothing because of what was termed his "general conduct".

The team's sharply improved performance could be attributed at least partly to the influence of Matt O'Mahoney of Bristol Rovers, who had taken over Charlie Turner's old role at centre-half earlier in the year. O'Mahoney, another tall man, now afforded goalkeeper George McKenzie a lot more protection and his performance in the Swiss game was such that Northern Ireland saw fit to select him for their meeting with Scotland at Windsor Park three weeks later. Imagine the FAI's surprise when they subsequently received a letter from the player, informing them that he had been selected by Northern Ireland, but if this jeopardised his chances of further international honours from Dublin, he would forgo the northern invitation. This was too good a public relations coup to ignore and, without the permission of the player, Joe Wickham gave the letter to some journalistic friends for reproduction in the Dublin newspapers. It later emerged that the letter had been a prank perpetrated by some of his Bristol Rovers team-mates, leaving O'Mahoney with embarrassing questions to answer when he eventually travelled to Belfast. Pointedly, he was never again invited to play for the northern team.

Ever since England visited Belfast in 1882, Dublin had been the only other city to stage an international match on the island. That changed, however, in March 1939 when, in deference to the wishes of the Munster Football Association, it was agreed that Ireland would meet Hungary at the all-purpose Mardyke grounds in Cork. After the extraordinary opposition of the GAA to the development of the sport in the southern province, football had developed at an impressive rate there, typified by the achievement of the Fordsons club in winning the FAI Cup in 1926. The heyday of Cork football did not arrive until the 1940s and early 1950s, when Cork United emerged as the most successful club in the country, but long before that the city had been producing some exceptionally talented players.

The biggest problem in staging an international game in Cork was the absence of a suitable ground. The Mardyke was primarily a rugby facility and it required an expansive exercise in planning to upgrade it for a major football occasion. Even then, the FAI were forced to postpone the game for 48 hours after it was revealed that it would be required for a Munster Cup rugby fixture on St Patrick's Day, 1939, the original date for the historic football fixture. It was the fourth meeting in as many years with Hungary, and this remarkable rapport with one of the great football nations derived largely from the friendly relationship which the Dublin authorities had developed with Dr Henri Fodor, a highly influential voice in Hungarian sport. Dr Fodor's interest apparently extended beyond sport and, in an interesting aside, he once communicated with the FAI, requesting the address of Hubert Briscoe, the Hungarian Consul in Ireland, and asking "if there is any connection between this man and Robert Briscoe, a member of the Irish parliament. According to newspaper reports here, this latter gentleman is expected to undertake a voyage to the USA with a view to paving the way to Jewish colonisation." In his response, Joe Wickham said of Robert Briscoe, "He is a very decent fellow and has been very helpful to our Association."

Normally, one would have expected the Irish selectors to include a couple of Cork players in their team, to boost local interest, but when Norwich City contacted the FAI to say Jackie O'Reilly was available, Wickham told them, "We have already decided to award the outside right position to Kevin O'Flanagan, a young, local amateur player whom very many English clubs are anxious to sign." Owen Madden, the other Cork player involved in the notorious action which took them to Norwich without the permission of Cork FC, was stated to be injured. That left Tim O'Keefe, who had himself been embroiled in strife with the FAI at the start of his international career, as the only obvious Cork-born player in contention for a place in the team.

The problem was that O'Keefe, by now playing with Raith Rovers in Scotland, was required to assist his club against Glasgow Rangers the day before the international match, and to get him to Cork and enable him to play for Ireland in his hometown would require a meticulous exercise in planning. It was arranged that O'Keefe would make a three-hour train journey to the port of Stranraer immediately after the club game, catch the overnight ferry to Larne, where he would be collected by Tommy Priestley, a Shelbourne player living in Belfast, and travel by road to Dublin. The last stage of the marathon journey, the three-hour rail journey to Cork, would get him there just an hour before the scheduled 3.30 kick-off. Alas, it never happened. The ferry was two hours late arriving in Larne, and the grand plan, surely one of the most difficult ever devised for a player hoping against hope to represent his country in front of family and friends, had to be abandoned.

In truth, O'Keefe wasn't the only player whose place in the team was placed in jeopardy by a crowded programme. Soon after it became clear that the rugby game would have to take precedence over the international football fixture at the Mardyke, League officials reclaimed their right to stage a representative game on the national bank holiday, and what better way to do so than with a first ever meeting with the Scottish League at Dalymount Park. The Scots, wholly dismissive of the standards of football south of the Irish border, still paid their hosts the compliment of sending a squad of mature international players to Dublin and could scarcely believe the evidence of their own eyes as they slumped to a 2–1 defeat, against a team of part-time professional players.

Five members of that triumphant Irish team, Mick Hoy (Dundalk), Kevin O'Flanagan (Bohemians), Jimmy Dunne (Shamrock Rovers) and the St James Gate pair, Joe O'Reilly and Paddy Bradshaw, promptly cleaned their boots after the match and immediately left for Cork to face the Hungarians two days later. Clearly the adrenalin was still pumping on their arrival there, as Bradshaw and Jack Carey plundered the goals which earned Ireland a highly creditable 2–2 draw with the unofficial champions of Europe.

Following the visit of an FAI delegation to Britain to lobby support there for a political solution to the football split in Ireland, Wickham wrote to J.W. Dulanty, High Commissioner for Ireland in London, stating that they had met with blunt refusals from two of the most powerful figures in the FA of England, William Pickford, the President, and Stanley Rous, the Secretary, and expressed the opinion that only diplomatic intervention at the highest level would now resolve the situation. In November 1938, Wickham again contacted Dulanty, stating that the presence of Dr Hyde and Mr de Valera at the game against Poland four days earlier testified to the importance of football in the affairs of the country. He also informed him that de Valera had become interested in the dispute between the two Irish Associations. In further correspondence, Wickham noted that

Pickford's successor as President of the FA of England was the Earl of Athlone and requested Dulanty to furnish any additional information which might become available as they prepared for the next meeting of the British International Board in May 1939.

In his response, the High Commissioner said that he had further conversations with "the gentleman I mentioned in earlier correspondence" and hoped to be able to report the outcome of his diplomatic approaches shortly. He urged that this information be treated as confidential. On 15 April 1939, Dulanty said that he had made further contact with his intermediary, later revealed as the Duke of Devonshire, who informed him that if the matter were hurried unduly, it could prejudice the outcome. A copy of a letter from Devonshire to Dulanty confirmed that there were no easy avenues at diplomatic level, to end the dispute. Devonshire referred to a story in the *Irish Independent* the previous Monday to the effect that prominent clubs affiliated to the IFA were contemplating moves to bring about a settlement. He suggested that before he made an official approach to the relevant authorities, "It may be wiser to wait and see if anything emanates from this unrest." In a covering letter Sean Nunan, Secretary at the office of the High Commissioner, asked how Dulanty should reply to Devonshire.

In his response, Wickham informed the High Commissioner that the clubs' unrest derived from a bad financial season in the north, but said that the IFA had already told these clubs that they intended to maintain their current position in the British international system. He repeated the necessity to put pressure on the FA of England, whose final meeting of the season would be held in a matter of weeks. Further correspondence from Dulanty in May 1939 held out little hope, however, of an early solution to the problem. In the event, Devonshire was unable to have a planned meeting with the Earl of Athlone before his departure to South Africa. In his absence the Dominions Office had made approaches to the FA of England and concluded that there was no prospect of official intervention producing the desired outcome. Dulanty informed Wickham that he had written to J.P. Walsh, Secretary at the Department of External Affairs, to similar effect.

Having been effectively snubbed by England at diplomatic and sporting level, the FAI was in no mood to tolerate British protests of insensitivity in pressing ahead with arrangements for their European tour in May 1939, which included a game against Germany at Bremen. Soon after the split in 1921, at a time when they were still hoping to curry favour with the FA of England in the hope of gaining admission to the British International championship, the football authorities in Dublin were guilty of distorting the truth when turning down a request for a game against Germany. Now, the situation was starkly reversed. Germany, at an advanced stage of their preparations for war, were still attempting to promulgate their political ideologies through sport, and with most of Europe, including Britain, unwilling to facilitate them, the FAI stepped into the breach.

After drawing 2–2 with Hungary, an outstanding result by any yardstick, at Budapest on 19 May 1939, they journeyed on to Bremen for a game there five days later which would prove to be the last organised by the German Football Federation before the outbreak, four months later, of the war which would engulf Europe. The Irish party cannot have been unaware of the political dimension of the occasion, but even they must have been taken aback by the climate of militancy in and around the Weser Stadium on match day. A programme of political speeches, music and more speeches lasted for almost two hours, and by the time the teams emerged from the dressing-rooms, the arena was in a state of ferment. It was, in essence, a day when the norm didn't apply, and the Irish players were accorded a huge ovation after giving the traditional Nazi salute during the playing of the German National Anthem.

This was in line with pre-match instructions, and afterwards Joe O'Reilly recalled the reaction of the player standing next in line to him, Jimmy Dunne, an avowed Republican. "As we stood there with our right arm outstretched, Jimmy kept saying to me, 'Remember Aughrim. Remember 1916.' By the time the anthem finished, I wasn't quite sure who was more agitated, the Germans or us."

In the course of his official report on the tour, Wickham noted that the tricolour flew side by side with the swastika at the match venue, adding: "We also, as a compliment to our hosts, gave the German salute to their anthem as well as standing to attention for our own. We were informed that this would be much appreciated by their public, which undoubtedly it was. At the post-match banquet, the German Minister for Sport gave us a cordial welcome and paid a special tribute to our playing the game as arranged, despite, what he termed, the untrue press reports regarding the position in Germany." Paddy Bradshaw's goal earned Ireland a creditable 1–1 draw, but this was one of those fortunately rare occasions when the extraneous events off the pitch totally eclipsed the athletic action on it.

It was a controversial ending to a traumatic period in Irish football. On his return home, Wickham set in train negotiations for games against Spain, Italy and Romania over the following two years, but having witnessed the turmoil of Bremen, he cannot have been surprised to discover that these were quickly overtaken by other, more deadly events.

Chapter Twenty-One

Peace with England

Club authorities on either side of the border were not to know it at the time, but their decision in 1938 to restart the inter-league series between the League of Ireland and the Irish League, after a break of eight years, would yield handsome dividends when the dark clouds of the Second World War were rolling around Europe in the first half of the 1940s.

After the conflict started in September 1939, international football was one of the immediate casualties. Countless thousands of people were deprived of a precious source of entertainment, while the principal source of revenue for the development and promotion of the game worldwide was also removed. And once it disappeared from the sporting calendar, even the most affluent national football federations began to struggle.

Neither the Irish Football Association nor the Football Association of Ireland could ever be classified as affluent, and when the bad days came, they were ill prepared to cope. The suspension of the British international championship meant that Belfast now had to look elsewhere for funding, and in Dublin the abrupt termination of the European link had the effect of focusing minds on the ever-present threat of bankruptcy. The irony was that out of the turmoil of the deadly conflict elsewhere came an awareness of the need to park their differences and work out a common plan of survival.

For the first time in twenty years, the two rival Associations were seen to be working in harmony – and it showed in many different ways. When Belfast suffered its darkest night of terror on the occasion of a German air blitz in 1940, not only did units of the Dublin Fire Brigade race north to help put out the fires raging across the city, but in a gesture designed to help alleviate some of the distress, St James Gate immediately agreed to play a fundraising match in the northern capital, a decision which was acclaimed by the *Belfast Telegraph* as a "splendid example of the brotherhood of sport".

Among the solutions put forward to generate revenue for football in both jurisdictions was the introduction of an inter-city club competition at the end of the local season. It proved an instant success, with the visits of teams like Linfield and Belfast Celtic attracting big crowds in Dublin and the forays of Shamrock Rovers and Bohemians for two-legged ties in Belfast likewise stimulating unusual interest north of the border. Yet the biggest attractions in those times of undisguised penury were the inter-league games, held twice yearly at Dalymount Park on St Patrick's Day and Windsor Park on Easter Monday.

The precursors of the inter-league matches were the inter-provincial meetings of Leinster and Ulster, seldom less than eventful in the pre-split era and at least partly influential in the eventual decision of the Leinster FA to go its separate way in 1921. In certain aspects, the old differences were as pronounced as ever in the inter-league fixtures, with some of the Dublin newspapers designating the Irish League team as the "North East Regional League" and those in Belfast labelling the opposition as the "Free State League". In fact, the first representative match arranged for Dalymount Park in 1940 was billed as an Ireland selection against a Scottish XI, which was hugely ironic inasmuch as the Scottish Football Association had avoided Dublin like the plague in peacetime. And a further twist was provided by the inclusion in the Scottish team of the Clyde half-back Ned Weir, who had made his international debut for Ireland against Hungary in Cork the previous year.

For all the reservations harboured in Dublin about Scottish football officials, that type of fixture could never be expected to hold the sharp competitive edge of a north–south one, and so it was that a big Bank Holiday crowd turned up for the first wartime meeting of the rival Leagues, on Monday, 18 March 1940 at Dalymount Park, a fixture which had to be postponed for 24 hours because of the Irish League's aversion to playing matches on Sundays. Chosen in the home team were local folk heroes like Jimmy Dunne, Joe O'Reilly, Paddy Bradshaw and the celebrated Bohemians goalkeeper Charlie Landers; and among the opposition were Jack Vernon, Jimmy McAlinden and Billy McMillan, all of whom would later play for the south on the resumption of international football. Now Paddy Bradshaw and John Buchanan secured the goals which gave the League of Ireland a 2–0 win, but in the ensuing years the Northern League would gain a slight advantage.

Of the Inter-City Cup tournament it can be said with some certainty that, as well as being the original one, it was the best of the north–south competitions in the post-split era. Dundalk beat Shamrock Rovers in the first final in 1942 and the winners of those that followed were Shamrock Rovers (4), Bohemians, Glentoran and Belfast Celtic. Sadly, with the total breakdown in relations between the FAI and IFA, the competition lapsed in 1949, and while attempts were made to revive cross-border tournaments in the ensuing sixty years, none quite held the appeal of those stirring games back in the 1940s.

When the curtain eventually fell on the Inter-City Cup, it was partly the product of the tension existing in the Irish League following the notorious scenes in 1948 which ended in Belfast Celtic retiring from football. Of all the passionate derby meetings with arch-rivals Linfield down through the years, none quite compared for emotion with that at Windsor Park on St Stephen's Day, 1948, when Bob Bryson, the Linfield centre-half, had to be carried off following an accidental clash with Jimmy Jones of Belfast Celtic. During the half-time break, it was announced over the public address system that Bryson's leg had been broken in the incident, and the effect was to inflame the crowd still further. Two players, Paddy Bonnar (Belfast Celtic) and Albert Currie (Linfield), were ordered off as matters gradually spiralled out of control in the second half, and when the referee whistled for full time with the scores tied at 2–2, Jones was attacked by some fifty spectators as he sought to escape to the sanctuary of the dressing-room.

Unfortunately, he was caught and thrown over the retaining wall into the terraces, where he was knocked to the ground and kicked. It required four operations to reset his broken bones, and he was to spend the next seven weeks in hospital as surgeons battled to save the shattered limb. Eventually, they succeeded, but the fallout from the incident was such that Belfast Celtic announced they were resigning from the League. The whole unsavoury episode had the effect of heightening sectarian tension in football north of the border and, among other things, it convinced legislators in the south that the Inter-City Cup competition was no longer viable. Celtic never again participated in the Irish League, but as befitted a club which was involved in so many extravagant occasions, they took their leave in the grand manner by embarking on a 10-match North American tour.

This built to a suitable climax when, with the help of three southern players, Tom "Bud" Aherne, Robin Lawlor and Michael O'Flanagan, on loan from Bohemians, they defeated the Scotland national team 2–0 in New York. Aherne had been the author of one of the more memorable quotes on the occasion of that horrific day in Windsor Park when he said, "I knew we were in trouble when, after Linfield had equalised, I saw a policeman throw his helmet in the air."

With an unprecedented number of people enlisting for military service during the Emergency in 1939–45, Ireland vs. the Army became an established wartime fixture in Dublin and it helped the FAI to remain solvent in an era of so much deprivation. In each of the six years of the conflict, they returned a small profit, no mean achievement when it is recalled that FIFA, the world governing body, almost went broke in the same period. The downside was that with so many young men joining the Army, the number of civilian clubs in Dublin dropped sharply, a point illustrated in the records for the usage of football grounds in the Fifteen Acres of the Phoenix Park during that period. The deprivations of war, and the consequent hardship imposed on people, were of course sharply felt in football, with the rationing of petrol impacting severely on motorised travel. Among the other items rationed for the duration of the war were clothing and footwear, and it led to a remarkable decision taken by the FAI's Junior Emergency Committee in January 1943. On a unanimous vote, members of the FAI's Junior Council agreed to provide family clothing coupons to enable the Association to purchase from the sports outfitters J.W. Elvery a set of jerseys and shorts for the first ever Junior international game against Northern Ireland at Dalymount Park.

If for no other reason than the necessity of leaning on each other for survival, the levels of antagonism between Dublin and Belfast were markedly lower during the Emergency, and it showed when the resumption of international football heralded a new start for sport in 1946. Seven southern players, Tommy Breen, Jack Carey, Sean McCarthy, Kevin O'Flanagan, Alex Stevenson, Davy Walsh and Paddy Waters, were selected by Northern Ireland for the "victory international" series that year. More significant by far, however, was the inclusion of four northern players, Billy McMillan, Jack Vernon, Walter Sloan and Jimmy McAlinden, in the squad for the FAI's Iberian tour in June. A fifth, Davy Cochrane, withdrew because of his aversion to travelling by air. It was not, of course, the first time that Dublin had poached players from the north, but it was the first occasion that the IFA, in formal session, had agreed to facilitate this.

What brought about this U-turn in policy was not immediately clear, but it was probably down to the influence of the Belfast Celtic legislator, Austin Donnelly, who was now at the helm of affairs in the IFA after being elected President of the Association the previous year. Given the heritage of Belfast Celtic and their predominantly Catholic and nationalist following, it made sense for Donnelly to endear himself to Dublin and, more importantly, those closer to home at Celtic Park by striking up a better relationship with the southern body. Jack Carey would later recall the Iberian tour as one of the happiest he had made with Ireland, one in which the contribution of the northern contingent was significant.

Carey was the only survivor from the Irish teams of pre-war years, but thanks to the input of Captain Tom Scully, Shamrock Rovers' representative on the selection committee, Peter Farrell was, against all expectations, chosen to lead out the team for the opening tour game against Portugal at Lisbon on 16 June 1946. That was all the more illogical by virtue of the fact that Carey was responsible for coaching the starting eleven as well as the three players who sat on the bench, Con Martin (Glentoran), Eddie Gannon (Shelbourne) and Michael O'Flanagan (Bohemians). Thanks to an inspired performance by left-winger Rogerio de Carvalho, who scored one goal and then set up two more for his front-line colleagues, Portugal were three up before goalkeeper Ned Courtney was injured and forced to hand over the goalkeeper's sweater to Con Martin after 30 minutes.

Courtney, an amateur player with Cork United who combined football with his career as a soldier, suffered more than most on his international debut, and while Martin didn't come under anything like the same pressure when the visitors were playing with the wind in the second half, he did sufficiently well to warrant retention for the second game against Spain in Madrid a week later. In between stints as an emergency goalkeeper, Martin was a full-back or centre-half at the start of his career with Drumcondra, but thanks to his height and an earlier involvement in Gaelic football, he proved a first-class goalkeeping replacement for the hapless Courtney.

Against Spain, Jackie O'Reilly, who hit a late consolation goal for the Irish in Lisbon, kept his place at outside-right in an unchanged team from that which finished the Portuguese game, and with Martin pulling off some superb saves, including one from his Real Madrid namesake, Ireland emerged as improbable 1–0 winners, thanks to a finely taken goal from Walter Sloan eight minutes before half-time. Con Martin's performance was such that he was approached after the game by a representative of Real Madrid, enquiring if he would be interested in signing for the club, but as he later recalled, "I didn't give it a second thought because I couldn't speak Spanish."

Apart from sustaining a minimal loss of £55 on the tour, the FAI could scarcely have wished for a more exciting return to international football, and just eight weeks after their return home it got even better. In a move born of hope rather than confidence, Joe Wickham contacted Stanley Rous, Secretary of the Football Association of England, enquiring if England would agree to play in Dublin for the first time since 1912. He based the request on the fact that, if ratified, it would form the perfect centrepiece for the FAI's Silver Jubilee celebrations, and suggested that it could be staged on Monday, 30 September, just two days after England played Northern Ireland in Belfast. He assured Rous that in the event of a favourable response, they would receive a big welcome from Irish people in what would be the first international game at Dalymount Park since the suspension of international football in 1939.

Given the difficult nature of Anglo-Irish negotiations, there was no reason to anticipate a favourable reply, but a week later came the cable which changed the face of that relationship. Rous confirmed they were prepared to accept the invitation, "providing we have first-class hotel accommodation and the financial details of the fixture are right", but urged that the information be treated as confidential for the moment. Days later, Wickham responded that he had made a provisional booking for the England party at the Gresham Hotel, "one of the best in Dublin", and offered them half the gate receipts with a match guarantee of £1,000. By return of post, the fixture was confirmed and the capital braced itself for its biggest sporting attraction in almost half a century.

Was this a belated return for all the diplomatic posturing which appeared to have gone unrewarded in the years leading up to the interruption of international football, or did the positive answer have more to do with basic issues – like the enjoyment of good food and the comfortable quarters which Dublin was ready to provide? In September 1946, England was still enchained by wartime rationing, and the prospect of escaping the dreary routine, if only for a couple of days, clearly appealed to many. In his autobiography, published shortly before his tragic death in the Manchester United air disaster in 1958, Frank Swift, the England goalkeeper, wrote of "the joy in being served a five-course meal, the best any of us had eaten in years".

A major policy shift of these dimensions had to be more deeply rooted, however, and in this context the political pressures exerted in 1938–39 were almost certainly influential. Eamon de Valera obviously thought so, for in a break with tradition he agreed to host a formal reception for the England party at Government buildings on the eve of the game. So too did Radio Eireann, who promised to broadcast as much of the game as the 5.30 kick-off would permit. They stressed, however, that it would be necessary to interrupt the live commentary to facilitate a schools programme at 6 p.m. and the evening news half an hour later, but the commentator, Mr (Eamonn) Andrews, would summarise the missing part of the coverage when the transmission resumed at 6.50 p.m.

A letter from FIFA welcomed the news that England were travelling to Dublin after such a long absence and expressed the hope that the fixture would mark the start of a better relationship between the FAI and the FA of England.

With at least some members of the Ireland squad which had played in Portugal and Spain likely to be named in the northern team for the Windsor Park fixture against England, it was arranged that these players would travel to Dublin with the England party by train on the morning after the game. They would then be transported by a fleet of taxis from Amiens St (Connolly) railway station to the Gresham Hotel because, as Wickham put it, "private motor coaches are not yet on the road". At that point, the pre-match arrangements could scarcely have been more encouraging; but then, perhaps inevitably, things began to go wrong. Mindful of the IFA's decision to make their players available for the Iberian tour, Wickham, without reference to Belfast, wrote directly to English clubs seeking the release of their players.

One of them was Peter Doherty, the Derry-born inside-forward who was regarded by many of the older generation of football supporters as the finest Irish player of them all. Doherty, a player with the skill of a George Best and the strength and courage of Nat Lofthouse, bore favourable comparison with the celebrated England inside-forwards of the time, Raich Carter and Wilf Mannion, and was the jewel in the crown as far as the FAI was concerned in their ambition to select fully representative teams. He had not been available to join the Iberian tour, but now, with the permission of his club, Derby County, he clearly prized the opportunity of playing in a green shirt in Dublin.

Within three weeks of Derby County confirming that clearance, however, Wickham received a letter from his IFA counterpart, J.N. Small, in which he wrote: "With reference to our private conversation on the telephone, I discussed this matter with my chairman, Mr Donnelly, and he thinks that in view of your previous application being for matches in Portugal and Iberia [only], it would be judicious to make a further application to keep the matter strictly in order." Wickham's handwritten note at the end of Small's letter stated that he had phoned Small merely to acquaint him of the FAI Committee's earlier decision on the subject. "They [the Committee] considered that they should be free to select any Irishman in their team and would not be dictated to by England, in the matter." Then, in quick succession came letters from Portsmouth, Arsenal and Belfast Celtic stating that McAlinden, Sloan and Jack Vernon would not now be available to play at Dalymount Park.

Chapter Twenty-One

The reasons for that volte-face have been a subject of vexed debate ever since. There is no evidence to suggest that the FA of England intervened directly in the matter. Neither can it be assumed that Donnelly, who within another two years would be replaced as IFA President, was personally responsible for the decision after his enthusiastic support just months earlier. More likely by far is that England's acceptance of the invitation to come to Dublin had seriously weakened the wall of resistance with which Northern Ireland, Scotland and Wales were able to persuade the British International Board to confront the FAI over its demands for change in the past. Now the strongest and most influential member of the Board was extending the hand of friendship to an organisation they had formerly perceived as hostile. The fact that Peter Doherty, Northern Ireland's most high-profile player, was being sought to showcase the validity of FAI's claim to select northern players, merely aggravated the climate of unease in Belfast, and they acted accordingly in blocking Doherty's clearance in an incident which went unreported in the build-up to the game.

In one instance, at least, the IFA was prepared to accommodate Dublin. Responding to a request from Wickham, in the matter of the fees to be paid to match officials on the resumption of international football, they said they were paying the referee £20 and the two linesmen £3 for their meeting with England.

In the aftermath of Belfast's action, the FAI was forced to revise their team as a matter of urgency, and in addition to Peter Farrell and Tommy Eglington, they now sought the release of a third Everton player, Alex Stevenson, to fill the inside-left position originally reserved for Doherty. Stevenson's last appearance for the southern team was in the 2–0 defeat by Holland in Amsterdam 14 years earlier, a protracted absence which, apart from club prejudices, was interpreted by some, incorrectly, as an indication of a lack of commitment. Now, with no attractive options available to the selectors, he found himself back in favour in his native city.

Also recalled from the wilderness was Tommy Breen, who had incurred the wrath of the great majority of the football public by opting out of the World Cup game against Norway in 1937 in order to play

Above: A moment of undying fascination for Northern Ireland fans as England goalkeeper Gordon Banks, preparing to clear, is outwitted by the skill and athleticism of George Best at Windsor Park in May 1971.

Above: Liam Brady prepares to deliver another accurate cross at the summit of his career with the Republic of Ireland. Despite making 72 international appearances, Brady never played in the finals of a major championship.

Left: Norman Whiteside, at 17, was the youngest player to appear in the 1982 World Cup finals in Spain. He had developed into a key member of the team by the time they again qualified for the finals in Mexico four years later but recurring injuries forced him into premature retirement.

Above: Gerry Armstrong puts his name on one of Northern Ireland's most important goals, capitalising on a defensive error to hit the winner in their World Cup meeting with Spain at Valencia in 1982.

Above: Billy Bingham, seen here celebrating another big Northern Ireland performance, was a valuable member of the team which reached the World Cup finals in 1958 and later, as manager, he led the team to two more finals in 1982 and 1986.

Above: Pat Jennings, an inspirational goalkeeper for Tottenham and Arsenal, won the first of his 119 Northern Ireland caps against Wales in 1964 and took his leave of the big stage after the World Cup meeting with Brazil in Mexico in 1986.

Above: Ray Houghton, one of Jack Charlton's first acquisitions on becoming manager of the Republic of Ireland team in 1986, set the scene for days of high revelry in West Germany with an unlikely winner against England, in the 1988 European championship finals at Stuttgart.

Right: A fine illustration of Paul McGrath's power in the air. Like Andy Townsend, McGrath was viewed as a pivotal personality in the squad put together by Jack Charlton.

Above: Jack Charlton, flanked by his assistant, Maurice Setters, salutes the travelling Irish supporters, as he leaves the pitch at the end of the World Cup quarter-final tie against Italy in 1990, in Rome's Olympic Stadium.

Above: Packie Bonner guesses right to stop a penalty from Romania's Daniel Timofte, a save which, coupled with David O'Leary's successful spot kick minutes later, earned the Republic of Ireland a place in the last eight in Italy in 1990.

Above: Ray Houghton again in the spotlight, this time with the goal which surprised Italy and gave the Republic of Ireland the perfect start to their 1994 World Cup finals programme, in the Giants Stadium in New Jersey.

Above: Roy Keane, an inspirational team captain for Manchester United and seldom less than controversial in the closing phase of his Republic of Ireland career, culminating in his decision to return home just days before the start of the 2002 World Cup finals.

Above: David Healy emerged as the most lethal striker in the 2008 European championship qualifiers with 13 goals to his credit. Healy's remarkable achievement was to take Colin Clarke's record of 13 goals for Northern Ireland, to 35 by the end of 2011.

Above: Howls of protest from Shay Given, Keith Andrews, Kevin Kilbane and Paul McShane, as Thierry Henry's infamous handball goes unnoticed by the match officials and France eliminate the Republic of Ireland in a play off in Paris, for the finals of the 2010 World Cup.

Left: Shay Given, the Republic of Ireland goalkeeper, who became the most capped Irish player of all time, by winning his 120th cap in the return game with Estonia in November 2011.

Above: Green For Go as Damien Duff, Robbie Keane and John O'Shea celebrate the Republic of Ireland's qualification for the finals of the 2012 European championship and the promise of another colourful summer for the team's supporters.

with Northern Ireland in the British championship. Breen was by now attached to Shamrock Rovers in the League of Ireland, but he owed his controversial recall to the fact that Con Martin, never more than a reluctant goalkeeper, was required to deputise for Jack Vernon of Belfast Celtic at centre-half.

Chosen at right-half was a newcomer, Willie Walsh of Manchester City, who had played for England at schools level. Asked to check out Walsh's Irish qualifications, Jack Carey reported initially in the negative, only to discover subsequently that he was in fact born in Dublin. Walsh would go on to be capped by Northern Ireland, and when he moved to New Zealand towards the end of his career, he also played for that country, giving him a unique record of representing four different jurisdictions. The most remarkable feature of the team, however, was the inclusion of the O'Flanagan brothers, Kevin and Michael, in the front line, the first time since Dublin attained its football independence that siblings had appeared in the same Ireland team. Kevin, a doctor in London when he wasn't playing for Arsenal, arrived in Dublin only hours before the kick-off to discover that his brother had been summoned from his place of work as a late replacement for the injured Davy Walsh. The following year, the brothers were chosen in Ireland's rugby union team, a truly astounding record which has never been matched in any country.

After the policy of neutrality pursued by the de Valera Government during the war, the fixture was also seen as a bridge-building exercise politically, a point emphasised not merely in the pre-match reception hosted by the Taoiseach but also by the presence of the President, Sean T. O'Kelly, for the pre-match introductions and the rare spectacle of the Tanaiste, Sean Lemass, seated in the stand.

England had emerged as runaway 7–2 winners in Belfast, but now, playing their second game in 48 hours, they found the going a lot more difficult. The overflow crowd provided a carnival atmosphere for the return of big-time international sport in the capital, and with the game still goalless at a late stage of the second half, they groaned collectively when Stevenson's shot struck the crossbar. And the full cost of that near miss would come sharply into focus just seven minutes before the end of the game when Tom Finney, making his international debut on the right wing in the absence of the legendary Stanley Matthews, scored the winner for a relieved England team.

England's share of the £3,557 gate receipts amounted to £1,761, and the visitors were said to be so impressed by the Irish team's performance and the hospitality accorded them, including the presentation of a replica of the Ardagh Chalice, that follow-up stories in the press suggested the fixture could well become an annual one.

Chapter Twenty-Two

Joy in Liverpool

One of the by-products of England's first game in Dublin in 34 years was that they experienced at first hand the anomalies of a system which, thanks to the IFA's insistence in selecting players born in the south for their international teams, meant that players could with apparent impunity represent two countries at the same time. That flew in the face of sporting convention, but it wasn't until confronted by the practicalities of Dublin's long-felt grievance that the FA of England deemed the actions of the Belfast Association to be impractical.

At Dalymount Park, Jack Carey and Bill Gorman lined up for the second time in 48 hours against the English, on this occasion for a different jurisdiction, while Tom "Bud" Aherne, who wore the No. 3 shirt for the Irish team in Belfast, was one of the nominated reserves for the match in Dublin. And that, for the first time, prompted stories in newspapers circulating in Britain that the IFA was in breach of FIFA regulations in their choice of such players for games in the British championship.

Joe Wickham, as ever, was anxious to seize every opportunity to have the problem discussed at the highest level, and his big opportunity came in July 1948 when, following the decision of England, Scotland, Wales and Northern Ireland, to rejoin FIFA after a break of twenty years, the Annual Congress of the world governing body was held in London. Some three weeks earlier, the FA of England had discussed the Irish issue and the minutes of their Council meeting on 3 July 1948 stated: "It was reported that the IFA had not accepted the FA's offer to discuss the matter in Conference with the other Associations to try and reach an agreement and, if necessary, frame a new one, in substitution of a purported agreement made in 1935, of which there is no tangible evidence. It was agreed that the secretary should write to the Irish FA and the FA of Ireland saying that having regard to the proposal of the FA of Ireland to be made at the upcoming FIFA Congress and the Football Association's wish to play matches against the two Irish Associations, the Committee would welcome an assurance that the Associations concerned, would in future, restrict the selection of their players to that area over which they have jurisdiction. If that assurance was not forthcoming, the Committee would be compelled to recommend to Council a course of action to be adopted."

That appeared to mark a significant change in London's perspective of the Irish problem and its historical support for Belfast, and it encouraged the FAI in its belief that they would get a sympathetic hearing at the FIFA Congress to be held on 27–28 July. Addressing delegates at the Congress, Mr John McBride of the Irish Football Association said that since the IFA, in common with the other British Associations, had withdrawn from membership of FIFA, the name of their jurisdiction had been changed from Ireland to Northern Ireland and asked by whose authority this action had been taken. Dr I. Schricker, FIFA's General Secretary, explained to the international delegates that there were two Irish associations affiliated to FIFA and stressed that in changing the name of the IFA's jurisdiction, they had no intention of depreciating the Association.

Speaking on behalf of the FAI, Mr Jim Brennan stated that the 1927 FIFA Congress in Helsinki, at a time when the four British Associations were still in membership of the world governing body, had adopted the proposal submitted by his Association to change their rule book by inserting after the words Irish Football Association, and before the word Ireland, the word Northern. He added that there was nothing irregular on the part of either the Secretary or Executive Committee of FIFA in doing this and, on behalf of the FA of Ireland, he protested against any alteration of the statute of 1927. Mr Brook Hirst, of the English FA, submitted that the paragraph as drafted by the Secretary was perfectly in order and did not represent an insult to the IFA. Congress agreed with this view.

A subsequent proposal by the FAI that the IFA be restricted to selecting players from their own jurisdiction for all future games, including those in the British championship, was defeated. In games other than those in the British championship, FIFA's eligibility rules would, however, strictly apply.

Mr Brennan asserted that his Association controlled 26 of the 32 counties on the island of Ireland and said that the only means of resolving the issue was to bring it to arbitration. Mr Seeldrayers of FIFA's Executive Committee responded that if FIFA were asked by both parties to arbitrate in the matter, they would of course do so. Otherwise they could not interfere.

At a subsequent meeting of the Council of the FA of England it was determined that (1) they were prepared to play matches against the FA of Ireland; (2) in the interests of players born in Ireland and playing with English clubs, it was essential that agreement be reached regarding the country for which they played; and (3) English clubs were concerned about the dual demands being made on such players. A lengthy discussion took place during which it was pointed out that under the terms of a previous agreement, "Eire" was given dominion status and that the Irish FA therefore considered itself free to select players born in a dominion as, indeed, other British Associations had done. It was decided, therefore, to defer the whole matter pending a statement with regard to the "political constitution of Ireland". Joe Wickham resented that reference to dominion status, but he returned from the Congress reassured in the belief that the world of international football had now a better appreciation of the Irish problem and that redress could soon be on the way.

After the high excitement of the game against England, there was an added spring in the step of the average Irish football supporter at the dawn of the New Year in 1947 – and it helped minimise the effects of one of the harshest winters on record. For months, snow and ice played havoc with the best-laid plans of the various sporting organisations, and when Spain arrived in Dublin in the first week in March, the playing surface at Dalymount Park was still littered with the remnants of the straw which had been brought in to protect it against long nights of biting frost. For all the preventative measures, however, the pitch was scarcely playable on match day, and with the capacity crowd spilling on to the touchlines, it was only after much cajoling that the English referee, Jack Barrick, permitted the game to go ahead. It was a setting designed to unnerve even the most intrepid travellers and, for the second time in nine months, Spain succumbed. On this occasion, Davy Walsh inflicted most of the damage by scoring twice and with Paddy Coad adding another goal, the home team was fully deserving of a 3–2 win.

Out of that game came a greater awareness of the security problems inherent in any big sporting occasion. Privately, FAI officials confided they were fortunate that no serious accidents had occurred, and when Portugal arrived in the first week in May 1947, to return the visit of the Irish team to Lisbon the previous year, a more efficient set of arrangements was in place. On the pitch, however, nothing had changed, with Correia and Araujo hitting the goals which gave the Portuguese another clear-cut win. And when, in Lisbon just over two weeks later, Portugal replicated that 2–0 victory over an Irish team which included Drumcondra team-mates Kevin Clarke and Benny Henderson on their international debuts, the Irishmen may have sensed that they had indeed stumbled on a bogey team. To compound a disappointing Iberian tour, Spain came from behind to win 2–1 at Barcelona on 30 May 1947, defeating Ireland for the first time in five meetings, and Jack Carey, by now in charge on and off the pitch, knew for certain that the road to international fulfilment had many twists.

The suspension of international football for seven years ate into the careers of many talented players who, cut off in their prime, never quite fulfilled their potential. A handful of truly great performers made the transition, however, and one of them was the modest, gently spoken Carey. Long before the arrival of total football, the Dubliner was the epitome of versatility at club and international level. In a marathon 16-year career with Manchester United, he played in 10 different positions and, 60 years on, he is still regarded as one of the founding fathers of the club's worldwide empire. When he lifted the English FA Cup following their 4–2 win over Blackpool in the 1948 final, it was their first success in the competition since 1909, and five years later he led the club to the First Division championship title, thus ending a wait of 42 years. The morning after that achievement, the *Manchester Guardian* hailed it as one of the city's finest hours and eulogised the parts played by Carey and the team's venerable manager, Matt Busby.

Playing in the green of Ireland, north and south, Carey was the pride of the race, a consummate professional in the heat of the most torrid battles and a splendid ambassador for the game when he wasn't directing operations on the pitch. Those qualities were recognised in the grand

manner when, in May 1947, he was chosen to captain the Europe team
which played Great Britain in a fundraising game for FIFA at Hampden
Park. It was the biggest manifestation to that point of the growing respect
commanded by the teams sent out from Ireland. Ironically, his Ireland
team-mate Jack Vernon was chosen in the British team and it was Vernon
who had the last laugh when they beat the European selection 4–1.
In extenuation of his team's poor showing Carey, who had travelled to
Amsterdam the week before the game to meet some of his players, said
that because of the diversity of the team members, they were unable to
communicate properly, either before or during the game.

In another significant development in May 1947, the first schoolboy
international game was staged in Dublin. Although the Minor grade had
been in existence long before the Second World War, the administration
of competitions for schoolboys was haphazard. In August 1947, however,
Paddy Reilly, a tireless worker in the management of Junior and under-age
football, moved that the Association appoint a special committee to control
this category of football. It was a predictable reaction to a remarkable
game at Dalymount Park where, inspired by superb performances from
Billy Duffy and Billy Quinn, who both signed for Arsenal after the game,
and fellow Dubliner George Cummins who scored four times, Ireland
trounced England 8–3 in the fixture marking the arrival of international
schoolboy football in the capital. The English got their revenge with a
7–0 win in London two years later, but in 1951 Ireland were back with a
bang, beating the host country 8–4 in Liverpool. On this solid base was
built the structure which, many years hence, would produce European
championship wins for Ireland at Under 16 and Under 18 level.

Another important decision taken in 1947 saw Ireland re-enter the
Olympic football championship in London the following year. It was
in this competition, in Paris in 1924, that the infant Free State had
tested the water in international football; and now, 24 years later, it
was again Bohemians who would provide the bulk of the team. In all,
they contributed five players to the squad managed by Jack Carey, but
significantly Michael O'Flanagan was not among them. At that stage
of his eventful career, the younger of the famous O'Flanagan brothers
was concentrating on rugby, having shared in Ireland's historic Grand

Slam success just months earlier, and his absence showed as Ireland were eliminated in the preliminary stages of the Olympic competition.

Even as the English influence in Irish football began to diminish, the political landscape shifted. In 1937, the Constitution of the Irish Free State was replaced by the Constitution of Ireland, written under the supervision of Eamon de Valera and adopted by referendum on 1 July 1937. Under its terms, Ireland was declared to be a "sovereign, independent, democratic state", while curiously retaining its membership of the British Commonwealth. Contemporary political analysts interpreted this as a mere sop to the Westminster Parliament, but if that was regarded as something of an irrelevance in the world of conventional politics, it continued to militate against Dublin's efforts to be treated as a wholly independent body by the British football authorities. The dominion status clause introduced at the Liverpool Conference in 1923 as a means of allowing the British International Board to end their suspension of the Football Association of Ireland, may have seemed a convenient way of expediting that solution, but for the next 25 years it would continue to hamper the aspirations of those who resented London's preferential treatment of Belfast.

Then, within a year of the overthrow of de Valera's Government, a new Coalition Administration led by John A. Costello introduced the Republic of Ireland (1948) Act which took Ireland out of the Commonwealth, to be followed soon afterwards by the British Government's Ireland Act (1949), guaranteeing the status of Northern Ireland. Now, with the political demarcations defined more precisely, FIFA moved with greater conviction to remove the anomalies which had infuriated Jack Ryder and his successor Joe Wickham for so long, and the practice of the IFA selecting southern players in their teams would end in a matter of months. A recurring source of grief was being closed off, and one can only guess at Wickham's inner thoughts when, in July 1948, he responded to an invitation from the FA of England to attend a Conference of Dominion States in London, with a curt rejection.

Despite the differences which existed between the FAI and the other British football bodies, there was, one sensed, an undercurrent of mutual respect between London and Dublin; and some eight months after rejecting that invitation, Wickham was pleasantly surprised to receive

a letter from Stanley Rous, Secretary of the FA of England, conveying
the news that at a recent meeting of their International Committee, it
was agreed to invite the FAI to send their international team to play in
Liverpool later in the year. Rous proposed two dates, Monday,
19 September, or Wednesday, 21 September, with an evening kick-off.

It was an invitation which the FAI could never have anticipated, and it
was of course accepted with alacrity. Belfast, Glasgow and Cardiff might
still be out of bounds for an international team from Dublin, but here was
the most powerful of the home Associations rolling out the red carpet,
and Wickham fairly revelled in the unexpected seal of approval. After the
match had been confirmed for Goodison Park, on the latter of the two
suggested dates, FAI officials were in contact with British Railways and the
B & I Steampacket Company, in anticipation of the biggest exodus of Irish
football fans to that point and confirming that the official party of 40, led
by the President, Oscar Traynor, formerly a member of de Valera's cabinet,
would travel by boat to Liverpool.

The match was already being hyped by the press as the most important
ever undertaken by the FAI. England, conscious of their narrow margin of
victory in the last meeting of the countries at Dalymount Park three years
earlier, resolved to put their strongest team on the pitch at the start of the
build-up to their first appearance in the World Cup finals in Montevideo
the following summer. The Irishmen, for their part, were hoping to use the
game to build some momentum for the closing phase of their qualifying
programme for the same competition.

For all the promise of a new, more friendly relationship between the
Associations, Joe Wickham still found cause to write to Stanley Rous two
months before the fixture, complaining about the hosts' designation of
the match as one between England and Eire. Wickham claimed that in
previous international games, they had played under the title of Ireland.
At no time was it correct to call the team Eire, as this was the Gaelic name
for Ireland. He requested that they not now be designated as Eire, as
there would be objections to it in Ireland. In a courteous response, Rous
apologised for any offence caused but said the FAI should realise that
the English FA had to differentiate between this match and their annual
fixture with Northern Ireland which, for many years, had been billed as

one against Ireland. Recognising Dublin's difficulties in the matter, he now proposed to advertise the game as one between England and the FA of Ireland and expressed the hope that the matter would be clarified in future years.

In releasing Peter Desmond to join the Irish team, David Jack, the Middlesbrough manager, attached a rider that, like his club-mate Arthur Fitzsimons, Desmond didn't do himself justice on his return to the club after the recent game against Finland. He stated that both players looked jaded and he attributed this to their travels with the Ireland team. Fitzsimons was not included in the team to play England because, as Wickham explained, "The Selection Committee think he is a bit young for this class of football." In confirming an arrangement for the Irish players to work out at Everton's training ground on the day before the fixture, Wickham made a semi-apology to the club secretary, Theo Kelly, for the selectors' decision to play Peter Farrell out of position at inside-right. He said the reason for this was that Farrell would literally add weight to the front line as well as profiting from playing alongside his Everton colleague Peter Corr on the right wing.

In the event, the training arrangements didn't quite go to plan. Newspapers reported that only seven Irish players turned up for a session at Southport on the eve of the match. Farrell and Corr had trained with their Everton colleagues at the same venue earlier in the day, while neither Con Martin (Aston Villa) nor Davy Walsh (West Bromwich Albion) had reported to the team hotel by the time the depleted squad set off for Southport. It wasn't the type of scenario to foster hope for a good result the following day, but out of this shambles Ireland fashioned a victory which would reverberate around the world of sport.

Watched by a capacity crowd, they won the admiration of friend and foe alike with a blend of skill and courage that shocked the home team. They took the lead in the 33rd minute, when Bert Mozley brought down Peter Desmond as he raced into the 18-yard area to make contact with Tommy O'Connor's pass and Con Martin's powerfully struck penalty kick spun out of the grip of goalkeeper Bert Williams to cross the line. That was the signal for an all-out English attack in the second half, but with Carey marshalling his fellow defenders well and Tommy Godwin pulling off a string of fine saves the Irish held out. Then, with the clock running down, they polished their victory with a second goal, Peter Farrell linking with O'Connor to chip the ball over the advancing England goalkeeper.

It was the first occasion that England had been beaten at home by a "foreign" team, and football connoisseurs everywhere rubbed their eyes in disbelief. A couple of hours later, the Irish players went their separate ways, Martin returning to Birmingham with a coachload of English supporters, stopping for fish and chips on the way, while the two League of Ireland players in the party, Godwin and O'Connor, caught the late night boat from Liverpool to Dublin. It had been a day without precedent in Irish football and was enriched by a cheque for £3,169-8-11, representing the FAI's share of the gate receipts.

In the context of their World Cup preparations, the result was something of a disaster for England, but for Ireland it held out the hope that after a faltering start to their qualifying programme they might yet escape the consequences and make it into the finals of the first post-war competition. Drawn in the same group as Sweden, the Olympic champions from the London Games the previous year, they sensed that they needed to take at least a point from their opening game in Stockholm to keep alive their hopes of making the cut. Davy Walsh's goal, after just nine minutes, hinted at heroics in the making on a wet, windy afternoon in the Swedish capital, but before they could consolidate that advantage they were rocked back on their heels. Sune Andersson equalised from a penalty, awarded for a handball by Con Martin, Jeppson added a second before half-time, and when Liedholm scored again midway through the second half, there was simply no way back for the visitors. To compound a bad day at the office, a set of tracksuits which the FAI had purchased in Stockholm was impounded by customs on their return to Dublin, but in this instance there was a happy ending when the garments were released without charge two days later.

Their second World Cup qualifier, just a fortnight before they embarked on that remarkable escapade in Liverpool, brought them into opposition with Finland at Dalymount Park. On this occasion, thankfully, there were no rude awakenings after Johnny Gavin had put them ahead, and with Con Martin adding two more, they were good value for their 3–0 victory.

At that point everything hinged on their ability to finish their programme with two wins, and with reports of their win over England preceding them to Helsinki for the return meeting with Finland on 9 October 1949, hopes were high that they could achieve their target.

Tim Coffey of Drumcondra replaced the injured Willie Walsh in one of two changes from the team which had brought England to heel, and together with Johnny Gavin, in for Peter Corr on the right wing, he made a solid contribution in a goalless first half. Davy Walsh thought he had broken the deadlock with a goal, only for the referee to disallow it because of a foul on the goalkeeper, but with just 25 minutes remaining, Ireland eventually took the lead with Coffey setting up Peter Farrell for a fine goal. That lead was protected with relative ease until the last minute, when a mêlée in the Irish goalmouth ended with the ball in the net and the visiting players, to a man, with their hands in the air, protesting that a foul had been committed. Unmoved, the Dutch referee, Jan Bronkhorst, allowed the goal to stand, which meant that Ireland now needed to beat Sweden at home to force a third meeting with the Swedes for a place in the finals.

The pre-match signs were scarcely encouraging, with some English clubs insisting on their Ireland players staying at their clubs until after they had played for them on the eve of the World Cup game. Despite the importance of the match, the FAI had no option but to go with a ruling which would not have been accepted by any of the British Associations, but deep down they may have sensed that theirs was now a lost cause. Unable to reproduce the verve they had shown in Liverpool, the home team was a goal down after just four minutes and the scorer, 19-year-old Kalle Palmer, went on to complete the hat-trick which doomed them to a 3–1 defeat. A year which had encompassed so much history was going out with a whimper, but while they didn't know it at the time, the story of the 1950 World Cup would hold a few more strange twists for the Irish.

Chapter Twenty-Three

World Cup Refusal

The problem of players representing two different jurisdictions at one and the same time was compounded for the authorities by the fact that those fortunate enough to be selected saw no ethical difficulties in doing so. One of the exceptions, of course, was Tom Farquharson, the distinguished Cardiff City goalkeeper, who stood on his principles after making his seventh appearance for Northern Ireland in the defeat by Scotland at Windsor Park in 1925 and declared that he would never again make himself available for selection by the Belfast Association.

For a while, the Northern Ireland winger Davy Cochrane was perceived in the south as having an equally firm conviction after withdrawing from the FAI's Iberian tour in 1946. The action of the Portadown man was all the more surprising in view of the fact that in a brief spell with Shamrock Rovers during the 1945–46 season he twice played for the League of Ireland against the Irish League. His decision to skip the Iberian tour was mystifying to many, until it emerged that he'd had to withdraw from the Spanish and Portuguese games simply because he was averse to air travel. As a breed, however, Irish players prized both the chance to test their ability in international football and, just as importantly, the inflated match fee which went with the honour. For them, the politics of the game were a side issue, and the protests of English clubs in having to provide players for two distinct Ireland teams were likewise a matter of indifference in dressing-rooms around Britain.

Jack Carey, the best-known Irish player of his generation, had as many admirers north of the border as south of it. When asked on one occasion why he insisted on turning out for Northern Ireland, he replied simply that football was his trade and he would pursue that trade at every opportunity.

Challenged on another occasion about his decision to enlist in the British Army on the outbreak of the Second World War, he said, "Any country which gives me a living is worth fighting for." Carey served for a time in North Africa and Italy where, removed from military duties, he played football under the name Cario.

Con Martin, another player in demand by both sets of selectors after taking up residence in Belfast during his sojourn there with Glentoran, was also frank in his explanation for maintaining the northern link. "With a fixed wage ceiling in operation," he recalled, "there wasn't huge money to be made in football, so when the chance came to play for Northern Ireland, I didn't need a second invitation to accept." And yet, when the crunch arrived early in 1950, he was the first to nail his colours to the mast in the south and, effectively, declare that the era of dual representation was over.

The reality was that in the wake of the Northern Ireland Act being passed into law by the British Government in 1949, and FIFA, with the support of the FA of England, announcing its intention of regularising the Ireland situation, the landscape had changed so dramatically that the implementation of the new order came into effect almost immediately in the autumn of 1949. With the four British Associations by now back in the fold and ready to compete in the World Cup for the first time, FIFA announced that the British championship for the 1949–50 season would serve as a qualifying process for the World Cup. And conscious of that, the Northern Ireland selectors decided to rely exclusively on their own resources in the opening two games against Scotland and England. In each instance they suffered a heavy reverse, losing 8–2 to Scotland in Belfast and 9–2 to England at Maine Road, Manchester, five weeks later.

At that point, their hopes of going to the World Cup were effectively over, and this may have been the rationale for their amazing decision to turn the clock back and name four southern players, Tom "Bud" Aherne, Con Martin, Reg Ryan and Davy Walsh, in their team for their final game in the championship, against Wales at Wrexham on 8 March 1950. All four players had previously assisted the Republic of Ireland in qualifying games in the same competition, and the IFA now risked suspension, both for themselves and the quartet in question, by effectively requesting them to play at Wrexham.

A series of unofficial phone calls was made from Dublin on the morning of the game, reminding the players of the predicament they were in and urging them to withdraw from the Northern Ireland side. "I got a call from Dublin spelling out the consequences if I went ahead and played in the match," remembered Martin. "I listened to what the man said, but at that stage it was far too late. I couldn't let my team-mates down and leave them stranded. So I played. But by the time I returned to my club, I had made up my mind that I wouldn't play again for Northern Ireland. I enjoyed my time with them and had some good friends there. Aston Villa's chairman at the time, Fred Normansell, had friends in Dublin who didn't want me to play up there, and he effectively made the decision for me and said he would make up any money I lost by declining to play for the North. What upset him was that we had an important club game against Manchester United the same day. Apart from letting me join the Northern Ireland team, Villa released Trevor Ford, a big player for us at the time, to assist Wales. Manchester United, on the other hand, refused to clear Jack Carey for the match in Wrexham and ended up hammering Villa 7–0."

In a letter to the FAI, Con Martin confirmed his intention of severing his connections with the IFA and was promptly congratulated for doing so by Joe Wickham. Reg Ryan met with a different reaction when he returned to his club, West Bromwich Albion. Ryan told club officials of the phone call he had received in addition to a letter sent to him before he travelled to Wrexham, and this drew a sharp retort from the chairman of West Bromwich Albion, Major Keyes. In a communication addressed to the FAI, Keyes said the player had received a letter from Joe Cunningham, chairman of Shamrock Rovers, in relation to his selection by Northern Ireland and he now considered it appropriate to ask what action the Association proposed to take in the matter. Following a brief discussion at a meeting of the International Affairs Committee, it was decided that no response be made to Keyes.

Shamrock Rovers were largely responsible for orchestrating the final break with the IFA. Two weeks later, their delegate to the FAI's International Affairs Committee, Captain Tom Scully, tabled the following motions: "(1) That as and from May 1, 1950, a clearance shall not be granted to any player unless the said player signs an undertaking not to play in any international or representative game, unless it is under the jurisdiction of the FAI, and (2) That as and from May 1, 1950, any player who takes part in an international game in which the title 'Ireland' is used, unless said international game is under the auspices of the FAI, such player shall not be eligible for selection in the FAI's future international games."

That sounded the death knell for the practice of dual representation in international football in Ireland, and the end of the anomalies which had brought the game there into disrepute internationally. The irony was that when a shortage of funds forced the FAI to abandon plans to send Joe Wickham to Rio de Janeiro in June 1950 to inform FIFA's Annual Congress of their decision, the FA of England volunteered to do it for them. Yet, in a letter dated 15 March 1950, the English authorities regretted that they were not in a position to take immediate action against the IFA for fielding illegal players in the Wrexham game. Instead, they recommended that the matter be reported to the British International Board, at which they would support the FAI's protest.

A postscript to the Wrexham saga, and the FAI's decision to alter their rule book to take account of Scully's proposals, was written when Joe Wickham received notification from FIFA's Executive Committee that they had upheld a protest from the IFA that the proposed alterations were unconstitutional. Following a protracted debate, the FAI agreed to conform with the ruling from the world governing body, on the basis that a recent letter from FIFA to the Association made it clear that "the Irish Football Association is not entitled to select players born within the FAI's jurisdiction without consent". They assumed that any breach of this ruling would lead to appropriate action by FIFA.

Sweden's emphatic win at Dalymount Park seemed to have ended the Republic of Ireland's last lingering hope of playing in the 1950 World Cup finals in Brazil, but then, out of nowhere, came a faint indication that they might still play on the biggest stage of all. Following an agreement between FIFA and the British International Board, it had been determined that the two leading teams in the British championship would qualify for the finals, and even before they met to decide the winners of the title at Hampden Park in Glasgow in April 1950, England and Scotland were already assured of finishing in the top two. The problem was that before the championship started, the Scottish FA had let it be known that they would only travel to the finals if they went as British champions. At it happened, Roy Bentley's goal decided the game in England's favour and the Scots, true to their pledge, declined the invitation to take part in the Brazilian showpiece.

At first, FIFA sought to fill the vacancy for the last of the 16 places in the finals by offering it to Portugal. When they declined, other national associations, among them the FAI, were canvassed about their willingness to step into the breach, just seven weeks before the opening match in the giant Maracana Stadium in Rio de Janeiro on 24 June 1950. Thirty-two days before the big kick-off, Joe Wickham said that he had just received a telegram from "Lotsy, FIFA", asking if the Association would be prepared to compete in the World Cup finals in the event of a vacancy arising. Following a discussion, it was proposed by Myles Murphy, seconded by Tom Scully, that "we accept – providing we get a definite invitation". Mr J.J. Kane, the FAI Chairman, stated that he considered the matter "too important" for a decision to be taken at a meeting of the International Affairs Committee. However, Mr Murphy insisted on a vote being taken there and then, and it was duly carried by three votes to two. At that point, the Chairman intervened to say that before a final decision on whether to send a team to the finals was taken, the Committee would have to meet again in two days' time.

So it was that, on 25 May 1950, the Committee was back in session and Captain Scully demanded to know what instructions the Secretary had received at the previous meeting to discuss the World Cup offer; and after the Chairman had stated his views on the matter, Joe Wickham read his rough draft of the decisions taken at the meeting. The Chairman agreed with these, but Murphy disagreed with both, holding that a definite decision had been made and any attempt to alter this would be irregular and totally undemocratic. Scully supported Murphy's stance and challenged the accuracy of the Secretary's records. The Chairman held that this was a matter of great importance to the Association and, as such, it would have to be considered carefully and by the right body, which was not the International Affairs Committee. Tom Giffney furnished an account of the projected costs involved, stating that they would amount to £2,700 and "put us into bankruptcy". Murphy said he wished to register a protest against the procedure being adopted and the action of the Secretary. Jack Traynor said he was against accepting the last-minute invitation, on the basis that they would be "merely picking up the crumbs". The Chairman said that that the invitation would be placed on the agenda for the next meeting of the Association's Senior Council, but Murphy again disagreed, emphasising that a decision on the invitation had been taken at the last meeting. Eventually, on the recommendation of the International Affairs Committee, the Senior Council decided not to pursue the matter.

Throughout the history of the FAI's stormy relationship with the IFA, the League of Ireland and Irish League authorities managed to retain a relatively good relationship. There were exceptions, of course, notably in the period between 1930 and 1938, in the immediate aftermath of the failed Conferences in Dublin and Belfast, when the graph of those relations dropped sharply. And there was another rocky spell in the early 1950s, when the English Football League and Scottish Leagues were finding it increasingly difficult to maintain the tradition of annual fixtures against both the League of Ireland and the Irish League. On many occasions, these deteriorated into embarrassing mis-matches, particularly when the Irish teams were required to travel to England and Scotland. And with the League authorities experiencing growing pressure from clubs to justify the release of players for such fixtures, the long-term future of the series came under serious threat.

Eventually, it reached a point where it was suggested by the English and Scottish Leagues that the two Irish bodies should pool their playing resources, an arrangement which, in addition to providing better competition, would have the effect of placating clubs regarding the increasing demands being made on their players. Not surprisingly, perhaps, this suggestion did not sit comfortably with the authorities in Belfast. At a meeting of the International Football League Board, held in Dublin in May 1951, the Irish League was rebuked for its refusal to enter into talks with their counterparts in Dublin, for the purpose of joining forces to offer more meaningful opposition to the English and Scottish teams. Among other things, it was stressed that their continued reluctance to do so could undermine the long-term viability of the games. That warning fell on deaf ears, however, and the inter-league fixtures which, for many years, generated valuable income for both Belfast and Dublin, fell into increasing disrepute and were eventually abandoned in the 1970s.

At international level, the search for new and more attractive opposition continued apace, and early in 1951 it was announced that arrangements had been completed for a game against Argentina at Dalymount Park in May, the first time a team from South America had visited the country. The public response to that announcement was favourable, and the initial print order for 39,000 match tickets had to be increased after it was decided to erect a temporary stand to accommodate the crowd for this, Dublin's first all-ticket match. It marked the first appearance in the team of Alf Ringstead, who would go on to serve Ireland well, but a solitary goal from Labruna sufficed to win it for the South Americans.

Only marginally less attractive was the meeting with West Germany in October 1951, the first time a German national team had played in Ireland since the end of the Second World War, more than six years earlier. The last time Ireland encountered German opposition was in Bremen in May 1939, just months before the outbreak of war, and they can only have been surprised to discover that Jakob Streitle, who was in the home team on that occasion, was still holding his place in their defence at full-back. The Irish side included two new caps, Florrie Burke, the Cork Athletic centre-half, and Dessie Glynn of Drumcondra. And Glynn, who emigrated to Canada at the end of his career, found himself centre stage as an exciting game built to a suitable climax.

The Irish team appeared to have the game under control when, following an own goal by Posipal, Arthur Fitzsimons established them in a 2–0 lead before half-time. Those who thought so, however, reckoned without the battling spirit of a German team determined to re-establish themselves, and in quick succession Max Morlock and Fritz Walter, another pre-war veteran, fired home the goals which brought them level. Then, with just five minutes left, the Everton club-mates Peter Farrell and Tommy Eglington combined to send Glynn racing through for the winning goal. Even at that late stage, however, an eventful game held one more twist.

In the light of the terrible conflict which concluded only in 1945, the appointment of an Englishman, Fred Ling, to referee the match had raised a few eyebrows. And with the game in its dying moments Ling succeeded in raising the anger of the entire West German entourage after Streitle had climbed above the Irish defence to head home Gerritzen's corner kick for what appeared to be a spectacular equaliser. Instead of pointing to the centre spot to confirm the goal, however, the referee spread his arms wide to indicate that the game was over – and was immediately surrounded by the West German players. Nobody, not least the 30,000 spectators, knew what was happening out on the pitch, and journalists had to seek out the referee after the game to clarify the situation. He explained, somewhat unconvincingly, that he had blown the full-time whistle while the ball was in flight from the corner kick, and that Ireland had won the match 3–2.

The explanation didn't sit well with officials from the German Federation, but if they thought they had seen the last of Mr Ling, they were mistaken. After being overpowered 8–2 by Hungary in the pool stages of the World Cup finals in Switzerland in 1954, West Germany defied all expectations and got their act together so well that they qualified for a second tilt at the Hungarians, this time in the final. Then, to their consternation, they discovered that the most important game in the history of German football was to be refereed by none other than the aforementioned Fred Ling.

Hungary, unbeaten in international football for four years, were the warmest of favourites to lift the trophy for the first time, the more so after opening up a 2–0 lead early in the game. Remarkably, West Germany still found the reserves of character to fashion a breathtaking recovery, and with the English referee in kinder mood on this occasion, Helmuth Rahn grabbed the second of his two goals to secure a 3–2 win for Josef Herberger's German team. Three years on from the indignities of Dalymount Park, the wheel had come full circle for the men in white shirts.

Dublin's venerable stadium would be the scene of another eventful game in November 1952, when the first visit of France to Dublin for a friendly fixture evoked even greater interest than the West German match. Among other things, the occasion would be remembered long afterwards for the overspill of spectators on to the pitch and the sight of the great French player Raymond Kopa dodging between spectators as he was chased by "Bud" Aherne down the touchline before "escaping" through the tunnel to the dressing-rooms. A final scoreline of 1–1 was a source of some comfort to Irish supporters when it later emerged that the Republic had been drawn in the same group as France and Luxembourg in the preliminaries for the 1954 World Cup finals in Berne.

Unfortunately, Jack Carey had left the scene by then after announcing his retirement. His had been a career without parallel to that point, and his achievement in winning 29 caps, a huge total at a time when international fixtures were relatively sparse, epitomised his contribution to the evolution of the team. Carey was offered the job of managing/coaching the national team, but turned it down on the basis that he would need three or four days with the players before big games and his new post as manager of Blackburn Rovers would not permit him that luxury. He was the first player to win the FAI statuette for 25 international appearances and, confirming his retirement as an international player, he wrote: "No player was ever treated better by the Association than I. The statuette I got for 25 international appearances will have a special place in my home. It is better than all the illuminated addresses, gold watches, clocks and the like, because it is symbolic of Ireland and a credit to her crafts people."

Carey's influence on Ireland teams was all-pervading, and the sense of loss was accentuated when a crowd of 45,000, a stadium record, watched France run all over the home side in the first leg of the World Cup tie at Dalymount Park on 4 October 1953, a game which left few in any doubt about the eventual group winners. France were three up before Reg Ryan got the home team's first goal in the 58th minute, and the 5–3 scoreline in the visitors' favour was distorted by the fact that the remaining two Irish scores did not materialise until the last seven minutes, at a stage when the competitive element had been drained from the game.

Ireland won both home and away against Luxembourg, as expected, but their hopes of qualification were effectively shattered in that first meeting with a classy French team. To their credit, Ireland did better in the return game at Paris, holding out on this occasion for 73 minutes before Piantoni got in for the decisive goal for France.

Chapter Twenty-Four

Two Irelands

If the eligibility rules governing the selection of the two rival international teams on the island of Ireland had been clarified beyond misinterpretation by the early 1950s, the issue of the correct identification of the sides sent out by the football authorities in Dublin and Belfast continued to be as contentious as ever.

With the exception of the two meetings with England, at Dalymount Park in 1946 and at Goodison Park three years later, the FAI had been fielding teams under the title of Ireland since 1936. And as the English authorities were quick to emphasise, the reason for the exceptions was that, logically, they could not be seen to play teams from different jurisdictions in the same season, each claiming to be called Ireland.

The FAI thought they had won their case beyond further debate when, after a FIFA meeting in Paris, a spokesman for the world governing body addressed the Irish press contingent gathered in the French capital for the return World Cup meeting of the countries in the Parc des Princes on 25 November 1953. He announced that the Dublin-based organisation had been acknowledged as the one with the better credentials to the title of Ireland, and that northern teams should play as Northern Ireland. Nothing in Irish football could ever be as definitive as that, however, and no sooner had the statement been circulated in the international media, than Belfast mounted a counter-campaign.

It led inevitably to the IFA tabling a motion at FIFA's annual Congress at Lisbon in 1954, calling on the authorities to instruct the FAI to refrain from misrepresenting themselves as Ireland in international competition. In an accompanying submission, the Belfast organisation claimed that history and tradition established them as the only organisation fitted to claim the title of Ireland, and after outlining the reasons for the split and the various attempts made to arrive at a settlement, the document read: "From time to time, various suggestions were made and conferences held to formulate a working arrangement between the two Associations. These meetings proved abortive as they were bound to do, with political influences as they existed in the Irish Free State. But the position altered with the action of the Irish Free State leaving the British Commonwealth. In consequence of this, the FA of the Irish Free State forfeited all claim to any connection with the Irish Football Association and the other British Associations.

"The title taken by the once Football Association of the Irish Free State should be altered to the real name of the country over which they claim jurisdiction – that is Eire. It is important at this stage to point out that association football is not recognised as their national game which is called 'Gaelic' and is an amalgamation of association and rugby football. Although their territory may be greater in extent than that of the Irish Football Association, there are vast tracts of that territory in which no association football is played at all.

"The position today is that the Irish Football Association remains the national association and, indeed, the only association entitled to use the title 'Ireland'. Its territory may be reduced in size but in every other respect it remains unaltered. It carries the confidence of the other British associations and takes its place in the British international championship as 'Ireland' and is the only body competent to do so. The Irish Football Association has suffered many attempts at interference with great tolerance, but in every instance, they have acted within the laws and within their rights with due regard for the rights of others.

"The Irish Football Association has been accepted and recognised as one of the four British Associations since its formation seventy-four years ago and is, in fact, the fourth oldest association in the world. All it asks is to be left alone to conduct its own business in its own country as the national association recognised by the other British Associations and FIFA."

Joe Wickham, armed with a bundle of miniature maps of Ireland to enable delegates to appreciate the anomaly of the IFA governing just a sixth of the territory on the island of Ireland, and yet purporting to appropriate the title of "Ireland", said that in terms of membership the FAI was quite the bigger of the two organisations and, since the split, had expanded at a far greater rate than the body north of the border. Further, he argued that his organisation was recognised throughout the world of football as representing Ireland, with the exception of the four British countries. And he raised the ire of Belfast delegates by stating that the FA of England, by far the biggest and most powerful of these organisations, now acknowledged the validity of their claim to send out teams, representing itself as Ireland.

Notwithstanding the decision arrived at in Paris the previous year, Congress decreed that, in future, the FAI's teams be designated as the Republic of Ireland, with those selected by the IFA to be known as Northern Ireland. Although initially disappointed by the ruling, Dublin gave immediate effect to it by playing under their new title for the first time, in the friendly game against Norway at Dalymount Park, on 7 November 1954. The IFA, by now reinstated as a member of FIFA, continued to play as Ireland in the British championship and Northern Ireland in the remainder of their international fixtures. This led to protests from Dublin that FIFA was not policing its own rules effectively and that because of the continued refusal of the IFA to adhere to its new title, it should be suspended. However, with the wisdom born of their recurring failure to reconcile the warring Irish factions in the past, the governing body shrank from precipitate action, and eventually the problem was sorted by default when the British championship lapsed in the early 1980s.

The record books show that the Republic of Ireland team launched the new era with a win, Con Martin and Reg Ryan securing the goals which enabled them to overcome Norway 2–1. What they do not disclose is that the game landed the FAI in hot water with the English Football League authorities after Alex Stevenson, now in charge of the national team, had availed himself of old contacts at his former club, Everton, to persuade them to release four players, Jimmy O'Neill, Don Donovan, Peter Farrell and Tommy Eglington, for the non-competitive fixture. This led to them being withdrawn from Everton's game the previous day and, ultimately, to charges from the Football League authorities that Everton's side had been weakened unnecessarily to facilitate the match in Dublin. The episode put a heavy strain on the rapport which Dublin had developed with the Merseyside club, and it gradually became more difficult to obtain the release of English-based players for friendly fixtures.

The Irish Football Association celebrated its 75th anniversary with a gala football occasion at Windsor Park on 13 August 1955, the centrepiece of which was a game between Europe and a Great Britain selection which included three home players, Danny Blanchflower, Bertie Peacock and Jimmy McIlroy. Jack Carey had captained Europe in a similar fixture at Glasgow eight years earlier and, in line with established practice, the European Federation invited the FAI to submit the names of three players, in order of preference, as possible candidates for the team. Peter Farrell, Arthur Fitzsimons and Tommy Eglington were duly nominated by Dublin, but when the team was announced, none of the trio was included. Dublin suspected that Belfast was involved in that decision, and those misgivings hardened when the FAI was not invited to participate in the celebrations. On a point of principle, however, they decided to make a suitable presentation to the northern authorities, with Joe Wickham and Oscar Traynor, the President, attending the game in a private capacity.

Problems of a different variety surfaced later in 1955 when the FAI, not unaccustomed to adversarial situations, found themselves embroiled in controversy once more, this time involving the Catholic Archdiocese of Dublin. The first ever meeting with Yugoslavia had been confirmed two months earlier at a time when President Tito's repressive policies on religious freedom were already beginning to incur the wrath of the western world. That resentment built to a climax when some of the country's leading Catholic prelates were placed under house arrest, and after Dr John Charles McQuaid voiced reservations about the visit of the Yugoslav football team, the alarm bells began to ring for the FAI hierarchy on Merrion Square. Dr McQuaid, a powerful influence on Irish society in the 1950s, had previously intruded into sport with disconcerting effect, when actively discouraging moves to promote women's athletics in Ireland.

Now, as a close associate of the Taoiseach Eamon de Valera from their student days at Blackrock College, he sought to mobilise public opinion against the Yugoslav match going ahead. He found a strong ally in Philip Greene, the highly respected football commentator for Radio Eireann, who announced that on conscientious grounds he would not work at the game, even though the national broadcaster was apparently willing to provide coverage. Various religious groupings also made it known that they were opposed to the match going ahead, but this merely had the effect of hardening attitudes on Merrion Square. Determined not to be seen to be coerced by the religious authorities, they announced that in spite of all the obstacles being placed in their way, the fixture would go ahead at the appointed time and venue, on 19 September 1955 at Dalymount Park. There were many occasions in the course of an embarrassingly one-sided game, however, when they may have regretted that cussedness. Clearly moved by the Church's stance on the issue, thousands of football fans stayed away and the attendance was officially recorded at just over 22,000. Those who did brave the wrath of the protest groups saw the Yugoslavs win as they liked on a 4–1 scoreline.

Having turned down the position at the end of his playing career two years earlier, Jack Carey now felt sufficiently settled at Blackburn Rovers to undertake the part-time post of coaching/managing the national team. It would be difficult to overstate the esteem in which Carey was held in the game in Britain and Ireland, and his return to the Irish dressing-room was seen as a huge boost for players striving to attain greater consistency at the highest level. Victories over Holland and Norway in May 1955 were followed by a defeat at the hands of West Germany in Hamburg – results which reflected accurately the graph of the team's fortunes.

In an age when telephonic contact was accessible only to the few, the manager felt it necessary to communicate with his players by letter post in the approach to his first game in charge, a friendly against Spain at Dalymount Park on 27 November 1955. Placing the emphasis on the collective effort rather than individual skill, Carey told them that careless loss of possession was the product of self-doubt and preached the need for greater vigilance in times of stress. The message appeared to resonate with the players, and the consensus was that Spain were fortunate to escape with a 2–2 draw. Initially, Carey was paid a paltry match fee of £20, but on being informed that his Northern Ireland counterpart, Peter Doherty, was receiving more than double that amount, it was subsequently increased to £50.

The proximity of the qualifying process for the finals of the 1958 World Cup invested the start of 1956 with an added degree of urgency, and the opening warm-up match, against Holland in Rotterdam, could scarcely have gone better for the new manager. As yet, the Dutch team was not rated among the best in the world, but a 4–1 victory still represented a substantial achievement for the men in green. It marked the first appearance in the Irish team of Liam Whelan, a player of languid skills to transform any game, and Carey liked what he saw at the start of what turned out to be a tragically short international career. "He is a great prospect who will be even better when he gets faster," he wrote. "With so many alternatives available to Manchester United, Matt Busby would not have left him in his team for so long, if he wasn't good."

Competitive international football would demand a different set of priorities, however, and the Irish manager was acutely aware of the need to focus minds even more sharply for the opening World Cup qualifier, at home to Denmark on 3 October 1956. Con Martin, an iconic personality in the story of Irish football, had come to the end of a marvellous playing career and was replaced at centre-half by Gerry Mackey, a member of the talented Shamrock Rovers team which, under the direction of Paddy Coad, dominated League of Ireland competitions in the 1950s. Changes in the front line saw the inclusion of Johnny Gavin (Norwich) and Dermot Curtis (Shelbourne), and fittingly it was they who secured the goals which enabled the home team to win 2–1.

The following month, Dalymount Park staged another attractive friendly game, against West Germany, who had won the World Cup in Switzerland two years earlier. With many English clubs railing against the imposition of having to release players for non-competitive fixtures, the Irish selectors found themselves embarked on a substantial exercise in improvisation, with no fewer than seven locally based players pressed into service against the champions. Even making allowances for the experimental nature of the German team, the Irish looked to be merely making up the numbers, but to the delight of the crowd, they emerged with a 3–0 victory. Jimmy "Maxie" McCann scored the last of the goals on his international debut, but in line with the curious decision making of the era, Shamrock Rovers' artful winger was never selected again.

Taken in conjunction with the wins over Holland and Denmark, the result confirmed that the Irish team was making steady progress under Carey, but the biggest challenges had yet to be faced. The third country included in Ireland's World Cup grouping was England, and the prospect of home and away games against these time-honoured rivals created a climate of expectancy which exceeded anything that had gone before. Memories of Goodison Park and that historic success in 1949 were still fresh, and with a place in the World Cup finals at stake, it was unquestionably the biggest football occasion in Dublin in many years.

Officials at Shelbourne FC obviously thought so too, for without reference to the FAI, they made an approach to the Irish Rugby Football Union, enquiring about the availability of Lansdowne Road for the second leg of the tie in Dublin. It was the first occasion since the fixture against Italy in 1927 that the rugby stadium had been mooted as the venue for a football match, and the move quickly gathered support. The Munster FA backed the suggestion on the basis that Dalymount Park would not be big enough to cater for all the fans wishing to see the game, and added, oddly, that the switch would also encourage rugby enthusiasts to support the match. The Dublin Tostal Festival committee also made representations to the FAI on the matter, and a letter from Tim O'Driscoll, Director General of Bord Failte, stated that the fixture would attract more tourists if staged at Lansdowne Road. Inevitably, perhaps, in the light of the IRFU's policy of not playing on the Sabbath, the response to Shelbourne's initiative was negative. Dismissing the suggestion out of hand, Bill Jeffares, the IRFU secretary, said that the stadium would not be available for any game on the scheduled date, Sunday, 19 May 1957.

The first-leg match was arranged for London's Wembley Stadium on 8 May, and in anticipation of an exodus of supporters accompanying the team, the FAI was allocated 3,500 match tickets. Gate receipts in both games were to be split on a fifty-fifty basis after the deduction of expenses, and with the most expensive stand tickets at Wembley priced at two pounds ten shillings, the Irish Association was entitled to anticipate a financial windfall. To ensure an equitable return for the English FA from the Dalymount game, it was agreed to raise the charges for stand tickets to one pound five shillings, with admission to the reserved terrace and popular enclosure priced at seven and four shillings respectively.

Pointedly, Jack Carey reminded the FAI that players should be equipped with official tracksuits for the pre-match ceremony at Wembley, and to promote a better sense of team spirit, he pledged to dissuade the press from distinguishing between cross-channel and home-based players in the squad. To give weight to this point, he included seven League of Ireland players in his preliminary squad, including Tommy Dunne (St Patrick's Athletic), a son of the legendary Jimmy Dunne, who had played in the games against Denmark and West Germany, Tommy Rowe (Drumcondra) and Donal Leahy (Cork Athletic).

As it happened, the FA Cup final between Manchester United and Aston Villa was due to be played at Wembley shortly before the international. If that match were to be drawn, the replay would take place on the same day as the World Cup match and in that event it was arranged that the English authorities would have permission for the four Manchester United players named in their squad of 22, Roger Byrne, Duncan Edwards, Tommy Taylor and David Pegg, to be replaced with Maurice Norman, Dennis Wilshaw, Brian Clough and Brian Pilkington. The FAI had no contingency plans at that point for the possible loss of Liam Whelan (Manchester United) and Pat Saward (Aston Villa). As it turned out, Aston Villa defeated their rivals 2–1 at the first time of asking and the national teams were able to take the field at full strength.

A crowd of 51,000, including a big contingent of Irish supporters, turned up for the first World Cup match to be played at Wembley, and they can only have been impressed by the quality of England's first-half performance. Frequently moving at a different pace from the opposition, they were four goals in front at the interval, thanks to a hat-trick from a rampant Tommy Taylor and a goal from John Atyeo. Yet, the game was not entirely one-sided, the visitors enjoying some good spells without ever really threatening Alan Hodgkinson in England's goal. Most of Ireland's limited inspiration flowed from Joe Haverty on the left wing and, appropriately, it was the Arsenal player who set up Dermot Curtis for Ireland's only goal early in the second half. Further opportunities were spurned, however, before Atyeo completed England's 5–1 win a minute from the end. The only consolation for the FAI was that their share of the gate receipts amounted to almost £19,000.

It had been a salutary lesson in finishing by the home attack, accentuated by some inept defending by the Irish, and Carey acknowledged that to have any chance of turning the tables in the return game 11 days later, he would have to address the weaknesses exposed so painfully in London. Peter Farrell, who had skippered the team on his 28th international appearance, was replaced at right-half by Ronnie Nolan; Tommy Godwin returned to goal in place of Alan Kelly; and, most significant of all, Charlie Hurley was introduced for his first cap at centre-half to deal with the aerial threat presented by Tommy Taylor.

Hurley, born in Cork but taken to London by his family as an infant, had been due to make his debut against Spain the previous year, only to be forced out because of an injury. In the intervening period he had twice represented London in the old inter-city games, and while his club base at Millwall wasn't overly ambitious, the superbly built youngster was seen as a golden talent in the raw. And those exalted evaluations were shown to be correct when, on a warm, unforgettable afternoon in May, he walked into Dalymount Park as an unknown and left as the new Colossus of Irish football.

After Alf Ringstead had earned the adulation of the crowd by converting a cross from Arthur Fitzsimons into a precious goal within three minutes of the kick-off, the Irish team protected their advantage zealously, and with Hurley and goalkeeper Godwin rolling back wave after wave of attacks, they were still in the lead as the game entered its final minute. Then, in moments etched into the memory of all who witnessed it, Tom Finney crossed from the right and, just as he had done at Wembley, John Atyeo manufactured the space which enabled him to direct a precise header into the net for the equaliser. For all their travail in a noisy, vibrating stadium, England had snatched a draw against the odds, and it was the end of the World Cup trail for a brave Irish team which deserved better.

Two Irelands

In his post-match analysis, Carey lauded Ronnie Nolan's performance, in shutting out the threat posed by Johnny Haynes, just as he had lavished praise on Joe Haverty for his mesmeric skills on the ball in the first game. Deep down, however, his pragmatism told him that this gifted team had just squandered a rare chance of crashing the big time and making it into the finals of the World Cup in Sweden the following summer.

Chapter Twenty-Five

Belfast Upstages Dublin

Northern Ireland were among the least fancied teams when the draw for the preliminaries of the 1958 World Cup lumped the mighty and the meek together, in their pursuit of a place in the finals in Sweden in the summer of 1958. Like England, Scotland and Wales, they had renewed their membership of FIFA only 10 years earlier and, in terms of international experience, rated among the lightweights of European football at that point.

Unlike the Republic of Ireland who, in various guises, had been involved in the mainstream of European competition since 1926, the IFA participated in no more than three international games, two in Paris, and the other in Bergen, between the two World Wars. And having rejoined FIFA, they played just one mainland European country, France, before announcing their intention of throwing their hat into the ring for the biggest prize of all. Even the most optimistic of their number must have feared for their chances of survival; and yet, from this unlikely background, they succeeded where the FAI had failed and, against all sporting logic, claimed a place in the quarter-finals of the World Cup. The Wee North had arrived on the world stage years ahead of schedule, and with this achievement came an even greater reward – local bragging rights in the ongoing propaganda war between Dublin and Belfast.

Among the prime influences in their captivating adventure in Scandinavia, the contributions of Peter Doherty, the manager/coach, and his team captain, Danny Blanchflower, were the most remarkable. As a player, Doherty ranked high on the list of the all-time greats, a splendid competitor who had brought the skills of inside-forward play to a point close to perfection. Unlike other distinguished players who had gone into management, however, he was also capable of working with less gifted individuals, and it showed in his time in charge of Northern Ireland.

Blanchflower arrived at Tottenham after a varied apprenticeship with Glentoran, Barnsley and Aston Villa, but once established in London he quickly emerged as one of the most accomplished players in Britain, an inspiring team captain who would go on to lead his club to the coveted FA Cup and League Championship "double" in the 1960–61 season. Twice voted Footballer of the Year, his was a name which commanded respect throughout Europe.

In terms of club profile, Burnley's Jimmy McIlroy was another highly regarded member of the Northern Ireland team in Sweden. In the mood, McIlroy was acknowledged as a master of his craft and while it didn't always show in his 55 international appearances, his presence applied an added gloss to his celebrated partnership with Peter McParland on the left wing. By contrast, McParland was a man for all seasons, and his achievement in scoring five times in the finals marked him out as one of the most lethal finishers in the championship.

Nobody could accuse Doherty's players of enjoying an armchair ride to the finals. Drawn in the same preliminary group as Italy and Portugal, they were everybody's choice to finish at the foot of the table in this, their first venture into the big time. Portugal would go on to become one of the best teams in Europe in the 1960s, but you would never have guessed it after Billy Bingham's goal had earned the Irish a creditable 1–1 draw in the first leg of their tie in Lisbon. Weeks later, Northern Ireland confirmed that it was no flash in the pan with a rare 3–2 win over England in a British championship game at Wembley. The effect of that game was to whet the appetite for their trip to Rome to play Italy on Thursday, 25 April 1957, just days before the FA Cup final meeting of Manchester United and Aston Villa at Wembley. This meant that Doherty was forced to replace Jackie Blanchflower and Peter McParland, and it showed as Sergio Cervato's precisely struck free-kick won the game for the Italians. A week later, however, Portugal were met and mastered in a 3–0 win in the return game at Windsor Park, and when the Portuguese subsequently defeated Italy, the Irish challenge was firmly back on track.

Italy were due in Belfast on 4 December for the tie which would make or break Doherty's hopes of history, but nobody could have anticipated the drama that followed. The Italians arrived on schedule two days before the game, but fog at London airport prevented the appointed referee, Istvan Bolt of Hungary, making it to Belfast on time. Unfortunately, that news arrived too late to permit the stand-by referee, Arthur Ellis, to travel by ferry to Larne, and when the Italians refused, not unexpectedly, to allow a local referee to take charge of a World Cup match, IFA officials were left in a quandary. Eventually, it was agreed that the game should go ahead as a friendly, with the Italians returning for the competitive fixture in January. All this happened less than 90 minutes before the scheduled kick-off, and with thousands of fans already assembled in Windsor Park or en route to the ground, a mini riot broke out when it was announced that the match about to start was a mere friendly. It set the scene for an ugly, vicious afternoon in which the tackling bordered on the reckless, and after it ended in an unsatisfactory 2–2 draw, police were forced to draw their batons to restore order.

That was an ominous sign for the rearranged World Cup date of 15 January 1958, but as it turned out the elaborate security arrangements put in place for the match were unnecessary. Although an Italian player, Ghiggia, was sent off in the second half, the occasion held little of the nastiness of the match the previous month as goals from McIlroy and Wilbur Cush gave the home team a thrilling 2–1 win and the opportunity to take on the best in the business some six months later.

Even as the IFA contemplated that joyous prospect, however, another problem arose. Before confirming their entry for the championship, officials in Belfast were made aware that teams qualifying for the finals would be required to play on Sundays. And since the IFA's Articles of Association, drafted some seventy years earlier, expressly banned this practice, a major controversy now erupted, with the conservative element in the organisation questioning why Northern Ireland had entered the competition in the first place. Eventually a compromise was reached enabling Doherty's men to fulfil their destiny and the relevant rule to stay in place. Years later, however, the rule was changed and the national team is now permitted to play Sunday matches outside Northern Ireland.

When the squad eventually set off for Sweden on 2 June 1958, one of their 18 registered players, Jackie Blanchflower, was missing. The Manchester United all-rounder, who had sustained multiple injuries in the Munich air disaster four months earlier, would never play again and his loss proved doubly expensive, as injuries and the physical demands of playing five games in the space of 11 days took a heavy toll on the depleted squad.

At the finals in Sweden, Northern Ireland found themselves in a group with Czechoslovakia, Argentina and West Germany, and enjoyed the perfect start when Wilbur Cush's goal gave them a 1–0 win over the Czechs at Halmstad. Three days later they faced Argentina at the same venue, and on this occasion they found themselves on the wrong end of a 3–1 scoreline. That was a shock to the system, but a possible escape route was opened up when Peter McParland scored twice against West Germany in Malmo to earn a 2–2 draw, which meant that they would have to meet Czechoslovakia a second time for the right to go through to the quarter-finals. Harry Gregg, a heroic figure amid the carnage of the Munich disaster, had travelled to Sweden as one of the key members of Doherty's team, but an ankle injury sustained against West Germany meant that he had to be replaced by Norman Uprichard for the play-off.

Not the least of Doherty's problems was that centre-forward Billy Simpson of Glasgow Rangers pulled a muscle shortly after his arrival in Sweden and took no part in the competition. In turn, the manager awarded the No. 9 shirt to Derek Dougan, Roy Coyle and Tommy Casey without any real success; and, remarkably, Jackie Scott of Grimsby Town became the fourth player in as many games to lead the attack for the second meeting with Czechoslovakia. Scott soon swapped places with McParland, however, and the move paid off when the ebullient Aston Villa man again scored twice, the second in extra time, to secure a 2–1 win over a Czech side which had earlier trounced Argentina 6–1.

At this stage of the championship, Northern Ireland were making world headlines, the more so after it was disclosed that Uprichard had played through the pain barrier after breaking a bone in his hand, early in the play-off. Now only France, a team which scarcely compared to either Czechoslovakia or West Germany, stood between the Irish and a place in the semi-finals, but a combination of injuries and weariness would prove to be their undoing. Playing their second game in three days, they were no match for the French in Norrkoping and eventually sank to a 4–0 defeat. It had, however, been a brave foray into the unknown, and the effect was to establish Northern Ireland as a formidable football force, worthy of the respect of even the biggest nations.

An interesting postscript was provided by Harry Gregg, whose athleticism and courage in the West German game established him as the best goalkeeper in the championship. When he flew out from London to Copenhagen on the first leg of the safari, it was the first occasion he had sat in a plane since the horrors of Munich. When the World Cup eventually ended for Northern Ireland, he travelled home by air with Sammy Walker, one of the team selectors, a day before the main party left Stockholm – and it proved to be a fortunate decision. The aircraft carrying the official party developed problems, the undercarriage failing to retract after take-off, and ashen-faced passengers had to endure a lot of tension when, with all the emergency services on alert, the pilot was forced to circle the airport, jettisoning fuel for almost an hour before making a safe landing.

While Northern Ireland was making ready for heroics on the world stage, their counterparts in the south were busying themselves with preparations for a friendly game in Poland. It was no ordinary friendly match, however, as it marked the occasion of the Poles' return to international football against a western European team after all the tribulations visited on that country during and after the Second World War. Poland was by now, of course, a member of the Soviet bloc, but unlike the match against Yugoslavia three years earlier, this fixture had the approval of everybody.

Poland had played in Dublin in 1938 in a game attended by the President, Douglas Hyde, but after the trauma of the intervening twenty years, for the Poles those memories were at best blurred. In a letter to the FAI enquiring about the colours of the national flag, Roman Gielda, Secretary of the Polish Football Federation, wrote: "You'll kindly excuse me this question but the flag and all the gifts from you in 1938 have been lost in the unexpected destruction of our town [Warsaw] in 1939. If possible, send us a little paper flag to enable us to make a flag in the right proportions." Complying with this request, Joe Wickham wrote: "We have not yet decided how we will travel. The tragic Manchester United air disaster at Munich [25 days earlier] has made travel more awkward, so we're uncertain if we'll go by air or by boat and train. Any suggestions?"

A crowd of more than 100,000 turned up in the Slaski Stadium in Katowice on 11 May 1958 to celebrate a historic occasion, and they saw Ireland twice take the lead before being caught out by a late equaliser. By all accounts, the visitors had the better of the exchanges and as Bill Murphy reported in the *Irish Independent* the following morning, "The Irish players left the pitch at the end of the game with the chants of Bravo, Bravo, ringing in their ears." Jack Carey was clearly moved by the occasion too, stating in his official report: "It was fitting that our Association should be the first to resume international games with this predominantly Catholic country."

The Irish suffered a 3–1 loss in their second tour game against Austria in Vienna three days later and in his player assessments, Carey remarked that of the three goals scored on tour, Dermot Curtis secured two of them as well as creating the opening for the third obtained by George Cummins. Of Curtis, he wrote: "His main asset is his nuisance value, but he's not fit enough to sustain his efforts. I think he smokes too much."

In 1959 the inaugural European Nations Cup competition, later rebranded as the European championship, attracted only a limited entry and was run on a straight knockout basis. It was the Republic of Ireland's lot to be drawn with Czechoslovakia in the only preliminary two-leg tie, and mindful of the fact that Northern Ireland had twice beaten the Czechs in the course of the World Cup finals the previous year, Carey was hopeful of progressing. A 2–0 win in the first leg at Dalymount Park substantiated those hopes, but in the second, alas, old failings came back to haunt them and three second-half goals, following a successful fourth-minute penalty taken by goalkeeper Stacho, gave the home team a 4–2 win on aggregate.

The introduction of John Giles to the team against Sweden at Dalymount Park in November 1959 was reassuring proof that the youth policies put in place by the FAI were producing results. Giles, a member of a family with a proud record in football, had long been hailed as an outstanding talent who, with average luck, would mature into a valuable member of the national senior squad. In the past such predictions had often proved misleading, with young players, set down in unfamiliar settings at English clubs, failing to make the transition from under-age competition. That fate was never likely to befall the youth from Dublin's north inner city, however, and even before breaking into Manchester United's first team, he was promoted by Carey for the Swedish match.

Sweden, beaten on home territory by Brazil in the World Cup final the previous year, fitted comfortably into any list of Europe's better teams at the time, and just four days before the Dublin assignment they proved it by beating England 3–2 at Wembley. That presaged a difficult afternoon for the home team, but inspired by an impressive long-range strike by Giles which cut into an early two-goal lead for the Swedes, the Irish team went on to win 3–2 with two further goals from Dermot Curtis.

Disturbingly, however, the ensuing years saw the supply of young players with the requisite attributes to reach the top beginning to dry up, and in those circumstances the FAI delegates were enthusiastic in their support for the proposal at FIFA's annual congress in Tokyo in 1964, to change the eligibility rules governing selections for international football. As a consequence of the changes approved in Tokyo, players born elsewhere were qualified to represent the country of their ancestors. In time, the FAI made astute use of what came to be known as the "granny rule", but they were certainly not alone in exploiting the additional opportunities provided by the new legislation. Initially, the IFA appeared to resist those benefits, but gradually they too began to trawl through the credentials of those British players who, unable to win a place in their national team, sought other outlets to progress to international football.

Critics argued, with some validity, that the revised eligibility rules militated against those locally born players harbouring hope of representing the country of their birth. In October 1963, a League of Ireland selection had humbled what was, in effect, a full England team at Dalymount Park, reinforcing claims that local players were not being treated fairly by the international selectors. In the end, however, expediency won out and, almost by definition, full-time professionals were rated by the decision makers as superior to part-time rivals.

Shay Brennan, a name forever identified with Manchester United's brave efforts to regroup after the horrors of the Munich air crash, was the first Irish player to benefit from the new rule. Born in Manchester of parents from Carlow, he was included in England's preliminary squad of 40 for the 1962 World Cup finals in Chile and would later go on to partner Tony Dunne at full-back in the Old Trafford team which won the European Cup for the first time in 1968. Carey had identified him as a player who could have an important contribution to make to the Irish defence, and at his request Joe Wickham wrote to Denis Follows, Secretary of the English FA, on 12 April 1965, asking if his Association had any objection to Brennan playing for Ireland. The response, three days later, was positive. Follows said he had discussed the matter with the England manager, Alf Ramsey, who informed him that the player was unlikely to be called up by England, and there was therefore no objection to the FAI utilising his services under the new FIFA regulations.

The qualifying process for the 1966 World Cup finals in England afforded Brennan an early opportunity to justify Carey's confidence in him. The Republic was drawn in a group with Spain and Syria, but with the latter country heavily militarised at the time, it was always questionable if they would be in a position to stage a World Cup match. After much procrastination, they eventually withdrew, reducing the group to a straight contest which was, effectively, a rerun of the European championship meetings of Ireland and Spain the previous year.

The first leg of the tie brought out a crowd of 42,000 for the evening kick-off at Dalymount Park on Wednesday, 5 May 1965. That was a measure of the interest created by the inclusion of four Manchester United players in the team, with full-backs Brennan and Dunne fronting club-mate Pat Dunne in goal and Noel Cantwell deployed at centre-forward. Cantwell's inclusion at the front of the attack was designed to ruffle the refined defence of the Spaniards, and just after the hour the tactic paid off. Iribar, an experienced international goalkeeper, took his eye off the ball as the big Cork man charged at him and could only help Frank O'Neill's free-kick into the net for the goal which separated the teams at the finish.

It meant that, even if they lost the return game in Seville in October, the Irish team was guaranteed a third chance to top the group. That possibility was not lost on Joe Wickham, and long before the second match, he had opened negotiations with his opposite number in the Spanish Federation, Antonio Ramirez, about a likely venue for a play-off. Ramirez suggested, somewhat naively, that in the event of Ireland losing in Seville, they should stay on in Spain to save travel costs and play the match 48 hours later. After dismissing this out of hand, Wickham suggested London as a neutral venue, with the Spanish Federation nominating Lisbon. Further suggestions by the Spaniards that a play-off be staged in Paris were countered by an Irish preference for Amsterdam, but with time of the essence and FIFA becoming increasingly irritated by the delay in reaching a settlement, word filtered back to Dublin that in the event of no agreement within another 48 hours, the parent body was ready to impose an order on the teams to play in Paris. Determined to make the best of a bad situation, Wickham contacted Madrid again, ahead of the FIFA deadline, and indicated they would be prepared to play in the Parc des Princes in the French capital, if allowed to retain the entire gate receipts.

This offer was accepted, and immediately the FAI were exposed to charges that they had squandered the opportunity of qualifying for the World Cup finals for a small bundle of silver. Critics claimed that in accepting Paris as the venue, the Association had consciously turned the play-off into a home game for Spain because of the relatively easy access to Paris for their supporters. The authorities in Dublin responded that in settling for the French capital they were, at worst, assuring themselves of a big pay night, but the controversy would endure long after the 1966 World Cup championship had run its course.

Irish hopes of digging out a decent result in Seville were dealt a huge blow when an injury forced Charlie Hurley out of the game. Hurley was central to their hopes of survival in a siege situation, and in his absence the selectors were forced to recall Cantwell from his front-line role to play at centre-half, with the uncapped Shelbourne player Eric Barber chosen in attack. Surprisingly, in the circumstances, it was the Irishmen who made the early running, and after having an early "goal" disallowed, Andy McEvoy, one of the most accomplished finishers in British club football in his time, opened the scoring midway through the first half and then had a legitimate penalty claim rejected. However, two goals from Pereda approaching half-time changed everything, and when he completed his hat-trick early in the second half, Spain were out of sight and on their way to a 4–1 win.

The doomsday scenario of a play-off in Paris had now materialised, and Hurley's ongoing absence did nothing to help the Irish cause. With at least 30,000 Spanish supporters in a crowd of 35,731, it had, indeed, all the trappings of a home match for Spain, and spurred by tidal waves of noise, they dominated for most of the game. It is testimony to the resilience of the Irish defence on the night that the scoreline was still blank going into the final 10 minutes, with the tie apparently headed for extra time. Then the ubiquitous Pereda popped up once more and when Cantwell and Mick Meagan failed to deal with his cross, Ufarte seized the chance to send the Spanish fans into ecstasy. The Republic of Ireland had again come up short in a major competition, but the compensation was that the FAI retained the entire net gate receipts of £7,448, a significant boost at a time of economic stress for the Association.

Chapter Twenty-Six

Changing of the Guard

Apart from some traumatic events on the field of play, the 1960s were notable for the developments which saw significant changes in personnel in the administrative structures of the two Irish organisations. Harold Hartrick Cavan OBE had been appointed President of the IFA in 1958, but it wasn't until the following decade that he began to mature into the senior statesman who would, in time, rise to the second highest post in the hierarchy of international football as senior vice-president of FIFA.

In tandem with Billy Drennan, Secretary of the Association, Cavan would influence the policies of the IFA for much of the next fifty years. He was an astute legislator who, with Victor Ferris at his side, was also for many years the selector in charge of the international team. Yet, when the winds of change began to blow, Cavan was directly responsible for the introduction of a team manager, an appointment which would soon make his selection duties redundant. Although it was his club Ards, through the sponsorship of Harold Black, which was responsible for the introduction in 1968 of the Blaxnit Cup tournament, the first cross-border competition since the Inter-City Cup twenty years earlier, he was perceived in the south as an old-fashioned conservative who, above all else, prized the link with London and the security afforded by membership of the British Board.

In Dublin, the unexpected death in 1966 of Oscar Traynor, a Belfast Republican who served in several of Eamon de Valera's governments, deprived the FAI of a respected President who, away from politics, loved football with a passion which would serve the game well. He was replaced by Donagh O'Malley, one of the most popular of all Irish politicians, and if his term of office did not last nearly as long as that of his predecessor, O'Malley's influence on the Association was considerable. History recalls

him as the most reforming of all Ministers for Education in the Republic of
Ireland for his introduction of free second-level education and later free bus
transport for students living in rural areas.

A rugby player of some substance in his native Limerick, O'Malley
was also deeply interested in football, and at a time when the educational
authorities in Ireland were guilty of turning a blind eye to the action of
Christian Brothers and others involved in education, in promoting Gaelic
Games to the exclusion of other sports in the more densely populated
areas, he was an admirable leader in the campaign to shame those schools
involved. This blatantly prejudicial policy was illustrated most powerfully
when Liam Brady, later to develop into one of Europe's best players, was
expelled from St Aidan's Christian Brothers school in the Dublin north
side suburb of Whitehall, after choosing to captain the national schoolboys
football team in Wales in preference to playing in a Gaelic football match
for the school.

That outrageous ruling, later reversed, highlighted the injustice of the
educational system as it applied to sport, but it was Donagh O'Malley's
appointment as Minister for Education in 1966, which marked the start
of an orchestrated campaign to break the stranglehold which the GAA had
carefully contrived in first- and second-level educational institutions. At the
time Seamus O Riain, a schoolteacher by profession, was President of the
GAA, and Jim Barry, a prominent member of the Cork GAA Board, was
one of the more vociferous defenders of the control the Association exerted
in the choice of school sports. That struck a raw nerve with many, and
ultimately it was O'Malley's public rebuke of Barry, in a policy-defining
statement on education and sport in January 1967, which empowered
other organisations to adopt a more militant stance in the manner in which
they interacted with schools in protecting the interests of all sports.

"Equal opportunity of education for all our children should also give
them an opportunity of playing games of their choice," O'Malley told
Barry. "I want to emphasise that there are people playing games besides
those you support, who are quite entitled to call themselves just as good
Irishmen. Or do you suggest that we should not cherish all our children
equally but continue to create a feeling among our children that they are
'Shoneens' because they play certain games?"

On O'Malley's untimely passing in 1968 at the age of 47, Neil Blaney became the third Fianna Fail minister to be appointed to the highest office in the Association and for those who would dare question the Association's nationalist ethos and conveniently seek to dismiss it as a monument to the partition of the country, the choice of three heavyweight personalities in the main Republican political party was significant. In their different ways, all three would leave their imprint on the organisation. However, the biggest loss of all to the FAI was unquestionably the death of the General Secretary, Joe Wickham. As befitted a man who gave a lifetime of service to football, he died on active service after collapsing during the half-time break in the friendly international against Poland at Katowice on 30 October 1968.

After succeeding Jack Ryder in 1936, Wickham went on to become the longest-serving administrator in Europe, a person of great presence, who was instantly recognisable in every corner of Europe. Like Harry Cavan, he was a coachbuilder by trade, and while still a young man he became active in the trade union movement. As a player, he assisted Midland Athletic and, for a short time, Bohemians, but it was as an administrator, first with the Football Association of the Irish Free State and then the FAI, that he earned his reputation as an iconic figure in the Irish game. On his death, Eamon de Valera would describe him as one of the country's finest ambassadors, "a man who never lost an opportunity to promote the image of Ireland abroad".

For close on twenty years Wickham fought, at times it seemed single-handed, for the right to use the word Ireland in the designation of his Association. It looked a readily attainable aspiration but, no less than the right to acquire equality in the eligibility rules obtaining in the selection of the national teams sent out by the two Irish Associations, it would prove a long, unrewarding mission until the relevant legislation was amended in 1954. His abiding passion, however, was to establish the rightful place of the FAIFS and, later, the FAI in the history of the country, and to debunk the propaganda of those who took unto themselves the title of custodians of Irish culture. For him, the gibe of garrison sport was a cheap, despicable attempt to dismiss the contribution of football and its followers in the making of the new Ireland. De Valera, as we have seen, would acknowledge

that contribution in full in 1968, speaking of the General Secretary as
"a pivotal influence in an organisation which has played its part in the
history of our country"; and two years earlier, the President had expressed
his personal endorsement of the plans the FAI was putting in place for the
50th anniversary of the 1916 Rebellion. Wickham was seen by some of his
adversaries in Belfast as a stubborn, uncompromising figure who shifted
only grudgingly from entrenched positions, but no less than Harry Cavan
on the other side of the border, his record of service will stand the test of
time.

Belfast wasn't the only place where Joe Wickham was viewed as an
abrasive adversary. There was, for example, the ongoing dispute with RTE,
in which he and his committee members never relented in their efforts to
get what they regarded as their rightful share of air time from the national
broadcaster. Going back to the pre-war era of 2RN, the relationship
between the FAI and the broadcasting authorities had always been a tetchy
one, with permission for radio coverage of international games occasionally
being withheld. The football organisation was not alone in this, for even
then the suspicion was that the decision makers in 2RN were biased in the
manner in which they promoted the interests of the GAA.

That perception persisted long after the deprivations of war had eased,
but it flared again in 1962 after Michael O'Hehir, RTE's Gaelic Games
and racing commentator, had been appointed Head of Sport at the
station. It was the FAI's case that the combination of O'Hehir's dual roles
made it difficult to secure an equitable share of air time, a charge which
was emphatically rejected by Montrose. At the heart of the dispute was
radio coverage of sporting events at weekends and the manner in which
the Athlone wavelength was allocated. In particular, the FAI was enraged
by decisions in the early 1960s to restrict radio coverage of the FAI Cup
finals to the Dublin and Cork wavelengths while broadcasting that day's
GAA games on the more powerful Athlone band. Eventually, with the
increasing emphasis on television coverage of sport and the requirement
to work harder to cultivate the goodwill of all organisations, the problem
evaporated.

On domestic issues, Wickham was fair but unflinching, and it may
be significant that within 12 months of his passing, the method of

selecting the national squad had changed dramatically. For at least two years previously, established members of the national team had been campaigning to bring the FAI into line with other national Federations and appoint a full-time manager of the team who would be solely responsible for selections. It was an argument which did not overly impress Council members, who saw in it an abrogation of the rights which had been vested in them.

Noel Cantwell and John Giles were among those who believed that the old system had outlived its usefulness, and Cantwell, in fact, was being touted as the man best suited for the proposed new post following the resignation of Jack Carey as manager/coach in 1967. A charismatic personality, first at West Ham and later Manchester United, the big Cork man was acknowledged throughout Britain and Ireland as the acceptable face of football. Allied to his considerable skills and knowledge of the game, it made him a standout candidate for the task of building on Carey's legacy.

After an involvement of almost thirty years with the national team, Carey had relinquished the part-time position because of an increasing workload with his club, Nottingham Forest. "It is with considerable regret that I request my name should not be put forward for re-election for the 1967–68 season," he wrote. "It is a very sad moment for me to have to break a direct connection with the FAI since I was honoured with my first international cap in 1937." In his reply, some 18 months before his death, Joe Wickham wrote: "To you, I am to extend the grateful thanks of the Association for your splendid service over so many years, first as a player and then as manager. You have always maintained your prestige as a sportsman and we have always been proud of you."

Cantwell, who was in the process of ending his playing career with Manchester United, applied for the vacancy created by Carey's departure, with the blessing of his manager, Matt Busby. In his formal letter of application he wrote: "To be manager of our international team would be my greatest honour, and if appointed, I would strive to make our country a world class force." He was not to know it then, but just a couple of months later Jimmy Hill would resign abruptly as manager of Coventry City, and Cantwell, then chairman of the Professional Footballers Association in

England, pipped his old West Ham team-mate Malcolm Allison for the coveted £7,000-a-year post. That appointment changed everything and within a year of being chosen to replace Carey, he resigned, citing the pressures of life as the manager of a First Division club as the reason.

Among other things, it convinced the FAI of the impracticality of appointing an English club manager to undertake the job on a part-time basis, and at the Executive Committee meeting which followed Cantwell's departure, Charlie Walsh proposed and Frank Davis seconded a motion that in future any such appointment should be home-based. He then moved that Mick Meagan, who happened to be in charge of his own club, Drogheda, at the time, be named as the new manager/coach, the first to have an input into team selections, and it was endorsed unanimously. Initially, Meagan, a player of impressive ability who was widely respected across the spectrum of football, merely sat in at meetings of the selectors, but eventually he assumed full responsibility for this function. It is interesting to note that two years earlier, two of the national team selectors, Captain Tom Scully and Jim Younger, were moved to deny a press report that when they went to watch a training session at Milltown, on the eve of a game against Czechoslovakia on 21 May 1967, they failed to recognise two of the players they had chosen.

How Joe Wickham, had he survived, would have viewed the developments which led to Meagan's appointment, is questionable. Nor would he have been hugely impressed when Pat O'Brien's proposal at a meeting of the Senior Council on 14 November 1969 – "That this Council intimates to the Irish Football Association that it considers the time opportune for a meeting between representatives of both Associations, with a view to discussing the possibility of fielding one all-Ireland team in future European and World Cup competitions" – was defeated on a 14–12 vote. It was the first time in the history of the Association that a proposal on these lines had been rejected, and it represented a significant shift to a policy of amicable co-existence.

In the event, Meagan met with only limited reward in his new role, but in extenuation of his record he could point to the fact that he inherited probably the least effective group of players since the early years of the Association. He was replaced two years later by Liam Tuohy, who would claim a big World Cup win over France in 1972, and a 1–1 draw in the return game in Paris, as irrefutable proof that he was building a competitive squad before handing over the reins to John Giles in 1973.

The other big event of 1971 was not of the FAI's making but rather a convincing testament of the new rationale informing GAA opinion. At the end of a long, often lonely battle to highlight the inequity of Rule 42 of the Association's official rule book, Tom Woulfe's persistence was finally rewarded with the amendment of the legislation governing the playing or watching of "foreign" sports. Woulfe, a Kerryman who emerged as one of the more influential personalities in Gaelic Games affairs in the capital, had long endured the ire of some of his peers in raising the question of the Ban, as it came to be known, on an annual basis before it became fashionable to espouse the cause. And the fact that the seal of approval was applied during the presidency of Pat Fanning, one of the more strident supporters of the divisive rule, at the annual Congress of the Association in Belfast, merely heightened the significance of the occasion.

In time, it would lead to the GAA's historic decision to hire out Croke Park for the staging of big football and rugby fixtures, but the most important benefit of all was to allow the interaction which enabled young people to alternate their sporting interests, a right which had been denied their predecessors for close on eighty years. The decision was warmly welcomed by those they had perceived as a threat to their sports for so long, and it would play a huge part in producing the climate of ecumenism which enriched Irish sport in the early years of the twenty-first century.

The early years of Giles's reign were punctuated with some good performances. The South American tour in 1974 was notable for the fact that they were highly competitive in a 2–1 defeat by Brazil in Rio de Janeiro and again in going down 2–0 to Uruguay in Montevideo. The tour ended with a 2–1 success over Chile in Santiago, raising hope that after the deep trough of the late 1960s, the graph of the national team's results was on the climb again. And that feel-good factor duly hardened into conviction when Don Givens completed a hat-trick to give the home team a 3–0 victory over the Soviet Union in a memorable European championship game at Dalymount Park on 30 October 1974. Unfortunately, a 2–1 defeat by 11 Dinamo Kiev players representing the

Soviet Union in the return game in Kiev, followed three days later by a shock 1–0 reversal at the hands of Switzerland in Berne, doomed Irish hopes of qualifying for the European finals, but the consensus was that Giles and his players were on the right road.

Dublin's frustration over their failure to make the cut for the finals of any of the major championships throughout the 1970s was matched by a similar sense of disillusionment north of the border. After the high hopes fostered by their remarkable Scandinavian odyssey in 1958, Northern Ireland would struggle for the next twenty years, a decline all the more remarkable in so far as it coincided with the arrival on the international stage of George Best.

In the red shirt of Manchester United, Best was frequently acclaimed as one of the most exciting players in the world, whose skills on the ball were matched only by his immense courage. With the notable exception of the game against Scotland at Windsor Park in 1967, however, he never quite made the same impact in his 37 appearances for Northern Ireland, at a time when they could call on other talented players of the quality of Johnny Crossan and Terry Neill.

For the Republic of Ireland, a World Cup grouping with France and Bulgaria fired renewed ambition of making the cut for the finals in Argentina in 1978, and the opening assignment, away to France in Paris on 17 November 1976, was at once inviting and intimidating. With the young Arsenal trio of Liam Brady, Frank Stapleton and David O'Leary bringing an added element of class to the team, expectations were high entering the Parc des Princes, but once again the hopes of a nation were not to be realised. In a game in which inspiration was often a distant second to perspiration, the Irish were undone when a mistake by Giles ended with Michel Platini firing the French into the lead early in the second half. A debatable offside decision erased what looked to be a legitimate goal from Stapleton soon afterwards, and in their increasingly urgent pursuit of an equaliser, the visitors fell prey to a breakaway goal from Bathenay two minutes from the end, to allow the French to put a deceptive gloss on the margin of their victory.

That defeat would be avenged, in part, by Liam Brady's winning goal in the return game at Lansdowne Road five months later, but when Bulgaria, assisted by some benign refereeing decisions, triumphed 2–1 in an ill-tempered match in Sofia and then heaped further misery on Giles by salvaging a goalless draw in the second-leg game in Dublin, the Irish were again cast in the role of onlookers for the showpiece finals, won by the host country in Buenos Aires the following summer.

Giles, by now back in Dublin to head a resurgence by Shamrock Rovers, didn't have much trouble in motivating his players following the draw for the preliminaries of the 1980 European championship. For the first time since the "split", the two Ireland teams were headed for confrontation in a group which also included England. Set down in this situation, the other two countries involved, Bulgaria and Denmark, may have felt like intruders.

The Northern Ireland troubles were still raging in 1979, and when the European championship pairings were announced, there were many who accused UEFA of insensitivity for refusing to keep the two Irelands apart. The special security measures in operation on match day in Dublin included a strict limit on the number of visiting fans from the north, and those who did make it into Lansdowne Road for the afternoon kick-off found themselves segregated and heavily policed throughout, in a restricted crowd of 46,000. The occasion attracted as much interest from news journalists as their sporting counterparts, with many noting the decision of the Taoiseach, Jack Lynch, to absent himself from the attendance for both the Northern Ireland and England games. At a time of attempted political bridge-building, this was interpreted as curious, but members of the FAI Council were quick to make the point that Lynch, in fact, had never attended any international football match.

Fortunately, Dublin was spared the excesses of violence which marred the European Cup meeting of Dundalk and Linfield at Oriel Park just weeks later, a sequel to the Mountbatten murders in Co Leitrim, and an uneventful goalless draw left Danny Blanchflower, the Northern Ireland manager, feeling a lot more satisfied than John Giles. Some 4,000 additional spectators were admitted to Lansdowne Road for the next European game against England on 26 October 1978, when Gerry Daly's goal enabled the Irish team to escape the consequences of Bob Latchford's early score for England. All the same, two home draws were undeniably

damaging to their hopes of going through to the finals. England duly
won the return game with two goals from Kevin Keegan, and Giles knew
for certain that all the escape routes had been closed off when Gerry
Armstrong's winner was celebrated in raucous fashion by Northern Ireland
supporters at Windsor Park.

After almost seven years in charge, Giles had not succeeded in effecting
the big breakthrough in championship competition, and in April 1980
he resigned, to be replaced in the short term by Alan Kelly and then, on
a more permanent basis, by Eoin Hand. Giles's achievement was to bring
Ireland into line with comparable countries in streamlining the structures
for international football, but he still departed in some disillusionment.
Before taking his leave, Giles had supervised an unconvincing 3–2 win
over Cyprus in Nicosia at the start of the qualifying process for the finals of
the 1982 World Cup in Spain. At the time, the Cypriots were numbered
among the least accomplished of all European teams, and fears expressed
after the match that Ireland's failure to win more decisively could come
back to haunt them proved, unhappily, to be well founded.

After a 1–0 defeat by Argentina in May 1980, a game which marked
the first appearance of Diego Maradona in the South American team,
Eoin Hand's term in charge of the Republic's team started promisingly,
with a 2–1 win over Holland at Lansdowne Road. The Dutch, beaten
finalists in each of the two preceding World Cups, were at that point in the
process of rebuilding their squad, but it did not disguise the dimensions
of the task confronting the home team after Tahamata had left goalkeeper
Gerry Peyton stranded for the opening goal early in the second half. It
wasn't until 11 minutes from the end that Gerry Daly levelled the scores,
and then, just five minutes later, Mark Lawrenson swooped to head
the winner from Liam Brady's free-kick. The Irishmen would go on to
complement that performance by salvaging a 2–2 draw in the return game
in Rotterdam, but vital lapses of concentration and a couple of highly
controversial refereeing decisions in the games in between proved ruinous.

Michael Robinson, on his international debut, had what seemed a
legitimate goal disallowed before Zimako scored late in the game to give
France a 2–0 success in Paris; and referee Nazare of Portugal was accused of
being hoodwinked by Belgium's veteran Eric Gerets in the incident which

led to Jan Ceulemans poaching the only goal, three minutes from time, in a crucial game in Brussels. In the end, competition for the two qualifying places on offer in the group condensed into a three-cornered struggle involving France, Belgium and Ireland – and, cruelly, it was Hand's squad which lost out on goal difference.

That tantalising failure would endure as evidence of the FAI's misfortune in missing out on the big time, the more so since it removed the unique opportunity for the two Irish Associations to be represented in the finals of the World Cup. Just as they did in Sweden in 1958, Northern Ireland, who had won the British championship for only the second time in 1981, confounded their critics with some big performances in a qualifying group which included Portugal, Sweden, Scotland and Israel. A goalless draw in Tel Aviv represented a less than inspiring start for the team, now under the management of Billy Bingham, but from there on it was full steam ahead, with home wins over Portugal and Sweden, draws, home and away, with Scotland, aided by Israel's shock 4–1 win over the Portuguese, unlocking the gate to the promised land.

Set down in the heat of a scorching summer in Valencia, Bingham's team, built on the cornerstones of the diverse skills of Martin O'Neill and Sammy McIlroy in midfield, the forthright threat of Gerry Armstrong up front and, not least, the wholly reassuring athleticism of Pat Jennings in goal, grew from the status of no-hopers to produce one of the major upsets of the 1982 World Cup championship. As a consequence of draws against Yugoslavia and Honduras, they had to surprise the host country Spain to be certain of progressing in the competition. After many frustrating failures to match pedigree with performance, this was the tournament in which the Spaniards sought to fulfil their destiny in football, but if the growing optimism in the home camp was designed to unnerve Bingham, it certainly didn't show.

With the pragmatism which had ever been at the heart of his philosophy, the manager based his strategy on frustrating the temperamental Spanish players with cool, disciplined defence. With Chris Nicholl and John McClelland dominating their penalty area, Jimmy Nicholl and Mal Donaghy holding the flanks and Jennings growing in confidence with each passing minute, they discharged the first part of their brief to the letter. The second, more difficult exercise was to catch the home team on the break, but two minutes into the second half the home supporters in Valencia's Luis Calderon stadium were reduced to stunned silence when Gerry Armstrong pounced on a goalkeeping mistake to produce one of the most celebrated goals in the history of Irish football.

After protecting that lead in varying degrees of skill and good fortune for the remainder of the game, Northern Ireland were through to the next round of the competition, but having drawn 2–2 with Austria, their fairytale ended in a 4–1 defeat by France. For the officials accompanying the Irish team, it had been an assignment which surpassed all expectations. Proof of that was provided by the fact that when they embarked on the journey to Spain, they took just three sets of shirts with them, for the exchange between players at the end of each match. Thus, when they qualified for the second series of games in the competition, they were forced to make urgent calls to Belfast, asking for additional playing gear to be dispatched to Spain without delay. Given the lowly position from which they started, it had been an adventure which caught the imagination of people everywhere and, for the first time since 1958, Northern Ireland were back among the elite of the sport.

Notwithstanding the element of frustration in the Republic's elimination, the IFA was now seen to be back in the ascendancy, and the plot of the World Cup competition which followed did nothing to alter that perception. After the high promise of the 1982 campaign, the southern team struggled to rediscover the verve which had brought them so close to qualifying for the finals in Spain. On this occasion they flattered to deceive after Mickey Walsh's goal had given them a 1–0 home victory over the Soviet Union in the opening qualifier. Away defeats at the hands of Norway, Denmark and the Soviet Union, followed by a goalless draw at home to Norway, cost them their chance of playing in the finals in Mexico, however, a failure which would also cost Eoin Hand his job.

Northern Ireland, by contrast, made a poor start to their qualifying campaign, losing 1–0, in the tiny town of Pori, to a Finnish team that had not won any of their previous 22 games. That appeared to presage difficult times ahead for Bingham's team, but in spite of going down to Mark Hateley's goal in their Windsor Park meeting with England, they performed sufficiently well in their games against Romania and Turkey to put themselves in a position where they went to Wembley for the last match, needing only a point to make the cut for the finals in Mexico. England were the dominant team on the night, but thanks to another imperious performance by Pat Jennings, the Irish team got the result they wanted and, after a tense goalless draw, they were on their way to central America.

Mexico in the summer was always going to be difficult, and ominously for Northern Ireland, they found themselves once more in the same group as Spain. Brazil were the automatic favourites to top the table and when the men in green could only draw 1–1 against rank outsiders Algeria in their opening match, they were living on borrowed time. Spain duly took their revenge with a 2–1 success in Guadalajara, which meant that Northern Ireland would have to salvage at least a point from Brazil at the same venue to have any chance of qualifying. That was a tall order for any opposition, doubly so for a side beginning to run on empty, and when the South Americans emerged with a 3–0 victory, it was all over for Bingham and his players. To make the occasion still more poignant, Pat Jennings announced his retirement after the match, not the kind of departure the great man deserved. In 119 international performances, he had proved himself to be probably the most effective Northern Ireland player of all time.

Chapter Twenty-Seven

The Charlton Years

With Eoin Hand's contract completed and an obvious desire for change among the more influential decision makers, the FAI's Executive Committee had much to ponder as they contemplated the challenge of reviving the fortunes of the Republic of Ireland in international football at the start of 1986.

Compared to their courageous battle against the odds in Spain four years earlier, Northern Ireland had not done particularly well in the most recent World Cup championship in Mexico. Yet, compared to their southern counterparts, they were in a different league at that point after qualifying for the finals for the third time in less than thirty years. The Republic, on the other hand, had never made it on to the big stage, and that statistic rankled with people who contended, with some logic, that with a much bigger player base than the Association north of the border, they ought to be doing better.

Two developments in quick succession would change all that. First, the FAI negotiated a major corporate sponsorship deal with Opel (Ireland), the first in the Association's history; and then, soon afterwards, they let it be known that if necessary, they were prepared to look at the candidatures of non-nationals in their search for a successor to Hand as national team manager. Even for an organisation accustomed to running a tight ship in terms of expenditure, the Association had been experiencing severe cash flow problems by the mid-1970s, and in 1977 Dick Doran, the Honorary Treasurer, reported that the finances of the organisation were a cause of serious concern with expenditure outstripping income by £14,262 for the preceding eight months. At that stage, the full-time staff at their Merrion Square headquarters numbered no more than three persons and yet, at the nadir of their financial difficulties, they were forced to seek a loan from one of their affiliate bodies to pay the wages at the end of the month. Further, the terms of John Giles's reappointment as national team manager stipulated that he was not permitted to name a squad of more than 16 players, a telling commentary on the monetary troubles besetting Joe Wickham's replacement as General Secretary, Peadar O'Driscoll.

It was against that background that the Opel deal materialised in 1986 as a result, it has to be said, of a grandiose investment plan which went seriously wrong. The plan was centred on a nationwide lottery, offering the prize of a luxury car every month for a defined period. As it turned out, this did not attract sufficient subscribers to make it feasible, and Opel (Ireland), who were to have provided the vehicles at a discounted rate, offered instead a straightforward sponsorship deal. That was the brainchild of the managing director of Opel (Ireland), Arnold O'Byrne, a man from the football heartland of Sandymount/Ringsend who would go on to broker probably the most successful sponsorship deal in Irish sporting history.

Fortified by that development, the Association moved quickly to appoint a manager. Among the non-nationals interviewed by Des Casey, the FAI President, and Dr Tony O'Neill in the preliminary process were Bob Paisley, Jack Charlton, Pat Crerand, Billy McNeill and Graham Lee. Two former holders of the post, Liam Tuohy and John Giles, headed the list of Irish applicants, which also included Noel Cantwell, Theo Foley, Jim McLoughlin, Mark Lawrenson and Paddy Mulligan. After a convoluted selection process the list was reduced to four, Paisley, Charlton, Giles and Tuohy; and after Paisley, a former manager of Liverpool, had topped the first ballot, Charlton eventually emerged as the man charged with the responsibility of delivering on the hopes of a nation in international football.

Soon afterwards, the permanent staff was augmented by the arrival of Dr Tony O'Neill, who would replace Peadar O'Driscoll within the year, and Donie Butler, who in the newly created post of Commercial Manager would shortly announce an enhanced sponsorship deal with Opel, worth £500,000 over a period of four years. The key personnel were now in place to drive the organisation forward, on and off the pitch, and from this encouraging base the Association headed for the Promised Land. Jack Charlton's forthright style of management was not always appreciated in the first year of his stewardship, but all that would change on a dreary afternoon in Sofia in November 1987.

In spite of their failure to beat either of the two top-seeded countries in the group, Belgium and Scotland, on home terrain, the new manager devised a match plan sufficiently clever to earn a historic 1–0 victory over the Scots at Hampden Park in February 1987; and when they defeated Bulgaria with goals from Paul McGrath and Kevin Moran in their final qualifying game at Lansdowne Road on 14 October, they still held a slim mathematical chance of going through to the finals. That depended on Scotland, by now out of contention, surprising Bulgaria in hostile territory four weeks later, a prospect so tenuous that Charlton chose to go fishing on the day of the game, rather than stay home to monitor news of events in far-off Sofia. Imagine his surprise, then, to be told on his return that Hearts part-timer Gary Mackay had scored in the dying minutes to give the Scots a 1–0 win which would reverberate around Europe. The Republic, unfancied even by their most fervent supporters, had arrived at the top of the group table by the most devious of routes, and within days the country had begun to ready itself for the jamboree which would be the European championship finals in West Germany the following summer.

For an organisation accustomed to low-budget operations, the logistical challenges flowing from European qualification, not least the matter of the bonuses to be paid to the players and technical staff, were considerable. And it is a measure of the improving nature of the relationship with the IFA that Northern Ireland officials offered to pass on the benefit of their experiences in the 1982 and 1986 World Cup finals to assist their Dublin colleagues. Back in 1981, the last in the series of meetings to explore the possibility of fielding an all-Ireland team had broken up in frustration, with the FAI pointing the finger at Harry Cavan as the main obstacle to progress. By 1985, however, the relationship had improved sufficiently for the Irish League to approve the bold decision to admit Derry City to membership of the League of Ireland. The club had withdrawn from the Irish League following a game against Ballymena United at the height of the civil and political unrest in Northern Ireland in the early 1970s, and the decision, approved by UEFA, to allow them to play south of the border, was now interpreted as a major advance.

Jack Charlton also had problems, albeit of a different nature, as he anticipated the biggest challenge of his managerial career to that point. Mark Lawrenson, arguably the best player, pound for pound, in British club football at the summit of his career, learned early in 1988 that he would never play again because of an Achilles tendon problem, dating back to Liverpool's game against Wimbledon in March of the previous year. Add to that the loss of Liam Brady, a name respected across Europe at the height of his club career in Italy but now back in English football with West Ham, as well as the premature retirement of Lawrenson's Liverpool club-mate Jim Beglin, and the cumulative impact on a relatively small squad was severe.

Even so, nothing could diminish the enthusiasm sweeping the country after the draw for the first series of games in West Germany had lumped Ireland with England, the Soviet Union and Holland. With the top two teams in each of the two groupings to progress to the semi-finals, a winning start was essential to have a realistic chance of making the cut, and that lent an added element of urgency to the opening game against England at Stuttgart on 12 June 1988, a date destined to be written into the folklore of Irish football. A vast army of travelling supporters ensured that there were at least 15,000 Irish fans in the Neckarstadion when Frank Stapleton led out the team, and they could scarcely have dreamed of a better start, with Ray Houghton's looping header putting the Irish ahead within five minutes of the kick-off.

With players of the quality of Tony Adams, Bryan Robson and Gary Lineker deployed down the spine of the team, it was inevitable that England would come back strongly, and so it proved as wave after wave of attacks broke on the solid defence of Mick McCarthy, Kevin Moran, Paul McGrath and, not least, Packie Bonner in goal. The countdown to the finish may well have been the longest ever for an Irish game but, in the end, frayed nerves held and the green hordes were able to celebrate a historic win.

A minimum of two points were now required from the remaining two games, and the first of them came in an exciting 1–1 draw with the Soviet Union at Hanover, a performance which was rightly identified as one of their best away from home. Even without the injured McGrath, the Irish team played with sufficient composure to lead at half-time through a goal from Ronnie Whelan. With better luck, the lead could have been more substantial, and spurned chances for Tony Galvin and John Aldridge proved expensive when Oleg Protasov equalised to give the Soviets a point they didn't deserve. Effectively, it meant that Ireland now had to win their remaining game, for in the event of a draw with Holland at Gelsenkirchen, the Dutch would progress on a marginally better scoring differential. With the match venue located relatively close to the Dutch border, it was something of a home fixture for the men in the orange shirts, and it showed with 40,000 of their supporters easily outnumbering the Irish fans. For all that, however, Jack Charlton's team was still in with a chance until a mishit shot from Ronald Koeman was deflected by Wim Kieft past a stranded Packie Bonner for the only goal.

By any measure, it was a fortuitous goal for Holland and cruel in the extreme for an Irish team who had fought like Spartans to prolong their interest in the championship. With just seven minutes left in the game, it was never likely that Ireland would score twice, and the sense of grievance deepened when the two qualifiers from the group progressed to the final, in which Holland defeated the Soviet Union 2–0 to claim their first major title. The consolation for the FAI was a cheque from UEFA for £637,261.45 – huge money for an organisation which had teetered on the brink of insolvency just 10 years earlier.

With their place in the top echelon of European football at last firmly established, Charlton now viewed qualification for the finals of the 1990 World Cup, in Italy, as an attainable target. To get there, they would have to validate that new status in a group which, in addition to Spain, Hungary and Malta, included Northern Ireland. Ten years earlier, the northern team had emerged on the high ground after their two European championship games, restricting the home team to a goalless draw at Lansdowne Road before Gerry Armstrong delivered his much-acclaimed winner in the return game at Windsor Park.

Jack Charlton's arrival, and the heroics which ensued in West Germany, had not wholly removed the scars left by Armstrong's goal, and it lent an added element of significance to the meeting of the teams in the first leg of the World Cup qualifier at Windsor Park on 14 September 1988. It was the Republic's first game since the European championship defeat by Holland, and the mood of the fans could not have been more different from the high revelry of the crowd in Gelsenkirchen. With a massive security presence in the Belfast stadium there was little light relief, and in those circumstances, a dull, goalless draw somehow seemed fitting.

For followers of the southern team, the return game at Lansdowne Road 11 months later brought a lot more joy. Needing a win to stay on course for a place in the finals, the home team started nervously before Ronnie Whelan's goal, approaching the half-time break, settled his team-mates. Two more followed from Tony Cascarino and Ray Houghton in the second half, and in the end the Republic's win was comprehensive enough to preclude any excuses by the visitors. Victory over Malta in Valetta in their last game confirmed their second placing in the group table behind Spain; and so, for the first time, the Republic were on their way to the World Cup finals.

By a curious coincidence, Charlton would find his team confronted once more by two of the three countries they had faced in the European championship finals, England and Holland. And, just as in West Germany, they would open their programme against England, this time in Sardinia, and after a novel fixture against Egypt, their final group match would be against the Dutch. After the heroics of Stuttgart, Big Jack was acutely aware of the threat posed by Bobby Robson's English team. Robson could claim with some justification that they had been caught on the hop by a fired-up Irish side in Germany: now they were ready and fully committed to deal with anything the opposition might throw at them in the Sant'Elia Stadium in Cagliari.

In Stuttgart, Robson's game plan had been undone by Houghton's goal after only five minutes. Now the boot was firmly on the other foot, with Packie Bonner having to bend his back and retrieve the ball from his net inside eight minutes. A mistake by Steve Staunton was compounded when Chris Waddle's cross floated over two defenders to enable Gary Lineker to score. The badge of Charlton's teams was their capacity to look challenges in the eye and ask why not, and they recovered their poise sufficiently quickly to be full value for Kevin Sheedy's second-half equaliser.

The Irish fans packed into the stadium were entitled to be satisfied with what they had seen, and following a boring, goalless draw with Egypt, the smile was back on their faces after Niall Quinn's late strike for a 1–1 draw with Holland sufficed to earn the Irish a place in the knockout stages of the championship. The bonus of that golden goal was that it would open the way to one of the undying days of grandeur in Irish football, when Packie Bonner's save, followed by David O'Leary's firmly struck penalty, gave Ireland victory over Romania in Genoa in the first ever shootout in the World Cup.

By now, the Ireland manager held a nation in the palm of his hands. Even people with only a peripheral interest in sport enlisted in the small army of supporters accompanying the squad on its travels, and conspicuous among them were a large number from north of the border. This was markedly different from Northern Ireland's experience in their 1982 and 1986 World Cup adventures in Spain and Mexico respectively, when the number of southern people travelling with them probably didn't exceed more than a couple of dozen. Now, with the IFA's teams embroiled in all kinds of difficulties in their efforts to rediscover old glories, northern people made up possibly as much as 5 per cent of the fans converging on Rome for the quarter-final tie with Italy in the city's Olympic Stadium.

Alas, for all the goodwill pouring down from the stands, the Irishmen's sack of dreams was now almost empty, and while their character and commitment remained constant, they were never able to summon the skills needed to impose themselves on the critical struggle for midfield control. The Italians, for their part, were less than brilliant in winning by a solitary goal from Toto Schillaci, but few could advance claims of a miscarriage of justice as Ireland exited the championship. In spite of that disappointment, the players were greeted by a crowd thought to be in excess of 250,000 on their return to Dublin.

Jack Charlton later admitted to being mildly embarrassed by the numbers who turned out, but the effect was to convince him that Irish people, north or south of the border, are passionate about their sport. And the manner in which Big Jack and his players had captured the imagination of young people would be reflected in the statistics provided at the annual general meeting of the Association in July 1991, when Sean Connolly, the

General Secretary, remarked on the explosion in the numbers now playing football. He confirmed that there had been an increase of more than 40 per cent in recent years, with current figures of 125,000 registered players and 3,200 clubs in every corner of the country.

Much of the charisma of Charlton and his squad derived from the manner in which they had competed against England in both the European and World Cup championships. Apart from swelling the coffers of the FAI, the England games served to boost the self-belief of players who, in another era, perhaps might have been intimidated by the lessons of history. Now, incredibly, the Republic and England were drawn together for a third consecutive occasion when they found themselves in the same grouping for the preliminaries of the 1992 European championship. Poland and Turkey were the other teams in the group, but inevitably it was the fixtures with England which grabbed the public's attention.

After a 5–0 trouncing of Turkey at the start of their programme, Charlton summoned all his big-name players for the meeting with England, in front of another sell-out crowd at Lansdowne Road on 14 November 1990. Tony Cascarino's goal 11 minutes from the end earned the home team a 1–1 draw, which reflected accurately the pattern of a disappointing game, and the scoreline was to be replicated in the return match which attracted a crowd of 83,000, paying a record £1.25m, at Wembley Stadium four months later. This time it was Niall Quinn, getting on the end of Paul McGrath's cross, who rescued the Irish, but on the count of scoring chances created, they were aggrieved not to have won. It meant that both teams went into the final series of games on 13 November with realistic chances of qualifying, only for the Irishmen, 3–1 winners over Turkey at Istanbul, to be left crestfallen by Gary Lineker's late winner for England in Poland.

The mood of the players on the return journey to Dublin was one of deep depression. For the first time in three competitions, they had failed to qualify for the finals, and the manner of England's late reprieve, when all seemed lost for them, merely heightened the sense of frustration. All that would change, however, when the draw for the preliminaries of the 1994 World Cup put them on course for two more meetings with Northern Ireland in a group completed by Spain, Denmark, Albania,

Lithuania and Latvia. The away legs of the ties with Denmark and Spain were soon identified as the most difficult in Charlton's programme, and having scored four times in their opening assignment, at home to Latvia, the players fulfilled their defensive brief to the letter with goalless draws in Copenhagen and Seville. The home match against Northern Ireland was next up on 31 March 1993, and the Republic duly replicated a 3–0 win, four years earlier, with goals from Andy Townsend, Niall Quinn and Steve Staunton.

Failure to improve on a 1–1 scoreline in the return game with Denmark hinted at trouble in the making, however, and when they sank to a 3–1 defeat against Spain, their first home loss in a competitive game since the 4–1 thrashing by Denmark almost eight years earlier, fears were being openly expressed about their ability to make the cut for the finals in the United States in the summer of 1994. In the end, it all came down to the last series of games to decide which of the top three teams in the table, Spain, Ireland and Denmark, would miss out. Summarised, it meant that the Republic had to take at least a point from their meeting with Northern Ireland at Windsor Park, and also hope for favourable results elsewhere, before confirming their trans-Atlantic travel plans.

The security situation in Northern Ireland had worsened appreciably in the months and weeks before the game on 17 November 1993, increasing speculation that it might have to be taken out of Belfast and staged at a venue in mainland Britain. Eventually, the IFA, acting on the advice of security authorities in the city, decided they should retain their home advantage, setting in train a massive security operation which meant that a ring of steel protected the players and officials on match night. The FAI purchased 400 match tickets but decided against selling them to team supporters, who were urged by police authorities on both sides of the border to stay away from the match. It all made for an unreal setting, heightened by a verbal spat between the two team managers, and when Jimmy Quinn put the home team in front with a spectacular strike just 16 minutes from the end, it looked as if the Republic had come to the end of the road.

The crowd of 11,000 was ecstatic, but in a last throw of the dice Charlton withdrew Ray Houghton and sent on Alan McLoughlin for his first competitive international appearance in two years. Joyously, for the hundreds of thousands watching the match on television south of the border, the gamble paid off when the Portsmouth player got on the end of a misdirected clearance to fire a thrilling equaliser into the back of Tommy Wright's net. Taken in conjunction with Spain's 1–0 win over Denmark in Seville, it meant that the Republic edged past the Danes on goal difference for the second qualifying place in the table, and another summer of high drama was in the offing. As they locked the gates of Windsor Park that night, Jack Charlton braced himself for more heroics, while Billy Bingham headed for well-earned retirement after rendering Northern Ireland yeoman service as player and manager.

Six years earlier, the Republic of Ireland had derived huge inspiration from the achievement of beating England in their first game in the European championship finals in Stuttgart. Now, in New York's Giants Stadium, they would be offered a similar opportunity to make an immediate impression after the draw for the finals paired them with Italy first up, followed by games against Mexico and Norway. The team's performances in the concluding stages of their qualifying programme had been worrying, however, and on the short coach journey from the Forte Crest Hotel at Dublin airport to the main terminal building, I recall a conversation in which Charlton, uncharacteristically, expressed apprehension about the task awaiting them. "I think we'll do well to qualify from the group," he said, "but if we can pull one big performance out of the bag, it will go some way towards tempering the disappointment of our supporters back home." In the event, those words would prove prophetic.

In seven previous meetings with Italy, Ireland had come up short every time, and supporters didn't need reminding that it was the Italians who ended Irish dreams of World Cup glory in 1990. In the only meeting of the countries in the intervening period, Italy won 2–0 in a US Cup tie in Boston, and now nobody doubted either their ability or their commitment to heap more misery on Charlton's team. Established patrons of the Giants Stadium merely added to the sense of impending disappointment by reminding anybody who cared to listen that New York, with its big Italian population, represented something of a home venue for the team in blue.

Whatever the eventual outcome, it soon emerged that the last assumption would be proved wrong on this occasion. From early morning, Irish fans were making their way towards New Jersey, and by kick-off time there could be little doubt that green was the predominant colour in the stadium. It was a setting fertile for the spectacular, and just as he had done in Stuttgart, Ray Houghton thrilled the crowd with the early goal which would find its way into folklore. In attempting to clear a long delivery from Denis Irwin, Franco Baresi, the veteran AC Milan defender, only succeeded in heading the ball back into danger and, from the edge of the penalty area, Houghton executed the chip shot over stranded goalkeeper Gianluca Pagliuca with such precision that a commentator later likened it to one of golfer Jack Nicklaus's famed wedge shots.

From that base, Ireland might have been expected to rediscover their form of Italia '90 but, alas, the Italian result was as good as it got for Charlton and his players. Forced to report for a noon kick-off in the torrid heat of Orlando, they were defeated 2–1 by Mexico in their next game six days later, and while a goalless draw with Norway was good enough to qualify them for the round of 16 in the championship, it was felt by many that they were living on borrowed time. Sadly, the pessimists were proved right, for ordered back to the infamous Citrus Bowl in Orlando, the Irishmen never got their game together against Holland and were eliminated by goals from Dennis Bergkamp and Wim Jonk. It had been a brave journey against the odds but, deep down, the manager sensed that the glory days were fast running out.

Some twenty months later, the ghosts of US '94 would return to rock the foundations of the FAI, but in the meantime there was the challenge of upholding Ireland's hard-won prestige in the qualifying process for the 1996 European championship. A 4–0 win at home to Liechtenstein in the opening match was no more than anybody expected. Less predictable by far was that they would duplicate that scoreline in their second match against Northern Ireland at Windsor Park some six weeks later. It was the most emphatic victory by either side in the series of games between the two Irish Associations and flowed from goals by John Aldridge, Roy Keane, John Sheridan and Andy Townsend. To their credit, Northern Ireland, now under the management of Bryan Hamilton, recovered sufficiently to draw 1–1 in the return game in Dublin on 29 March 1995, a match overshadowed by the traumatic events at Lansdowne Road six weeks earlier.

Normally the visit of England, for what was grandiosely billed as a friendly fixture with a difference, should have been a celebration of Ireland's outstanding progress as a footballing nation. Instead, it descended into one of the darkest days in Irish sport after a section of the England supporters rioted, causing the Dutch referee to abandon the game after just 27 minutes, at a stage when the home team was leading with a goal from David Kelly. Louis Kilcoyne, the FAI President, would later describe it as one of the saddest occasions in the long history of the game in Ireland, and among the immediate consequences was a review of the security arrangements in place for all international games.

A 1–0 home win over Portugal, courtesy of a goal from Steve Staunton, meant that qualification for the European finals in England was still a realistic prospect, but that all changed in the space of eight bleak days in June 1995. A goalless draw against the part-time professionals of Liechtenstein in Eschen was among the most disappointing results of the Charlton era and when it was followed by a wretchedly tired performance against Austria at Lansdowne Road, resulting in a 3–1 defeat, even those close to the team were admitting to worry. Their apprehension was justified, for Peter Stoger put his name on a brilliant hat-trick, to replicate the Dublin result in the return game in Vienna, and then Portugal swamped the Irish 3–0 on an evening of torrential rain in Lisbon, which left Charlton depending on Northern Ireland defeating Austria on the same evening in Belfast, for the Republic to have a chance of snatching the second of the qualifying places on offer in the group.

Northern Ireland, 4–1 ahead at one stage of the game, duly held on to dismiss the Austrians 5–3, and the Republic were through to a play-off with Holland at the "neutral" venue of Anfield for the prize of a place in the European finals in England the following summer. Given the startling nature of the collapse in the second half of their qualifying programme, it was a bonus they didn't deserve, and Big Jack, ever the pragmatist, sensed the worst as he packed his bags and headed for Liverpool. No less than other members of his technical team, he was astounded at the erosion of the self-belief which had once been the main characteristic of the teams he sent out, and even before the kick-off in Liverpool, he had already resolved that, in the event of losing the game, he would quit.

Forced to go without the injured duo of Roy Keane and Niall Quinn, he looked on in anguish as Holland, built on the axis of the Ajax team which earlier in the year had won the European Champions League and then the World Club Championship, took an early grip on the game, strong enough to squeeze the heart out of the Irish side. Two goals from a youthful Patrick Kluivert gave the Dutch a deceptively easy 2–0 win, and with Irish fans refusing to disperse at the end of the match, Jack Charlton, accompanied by his assistant, Maurice Setters, re-emerged from the dressing-room to wave an emotional farewell to the supporters he had grown to love.

At that point his intention was to resign in the first week of February, when he would have been 10 full years in the job. At a time when managers, club and national, were regarded as highly expendable, that would have been regarded as the ultimate seal of approval on an appointment which represented one of the shrewdest ever negotiated by the FAI. That was the perception of the vast majority of the public whom the England World Cup winner had attracted to his cause, and the man himself, by now approaching his 61st birthday, considered that his record of achievement gave him the right to name the date and place of his departure. The fact that there was no international fixture scheduled until the last week of March 1996 appeared to strengthen the case for a delayed announcement.

Unfortunately, some in the FAI hierarchy thought otherwise. They reckoned, not without some logic, that the sooner his replacement was nominated, the better the preparations would be for their next big competitive assignment, the 1998 World Cup. So it was that, on 21 December 1995, they summoned him to a meeting in Dublin at which the atmosphere was said to be tense. Eventually, however, Charlton put his name to a formal statement confirming his resignation, and the most successful era in Irish football was over. The fallout from that announcement was considerable. The perception that Charlton had been pushed not only outraged a large chunk of the public but appeared to cause a rift within the organisation itself.

Starting with the resignation of the General Secretary, Sean Connolly, who had not been directly involved in the Charlton fiasco, it erupted into a full-blown public debate when Louis Kilcoyne, the President, and Joe Delaney, Honorary Treasurer, two of the central personalities in the controversy, resigned after a nine-hour meeting in the Westbury Hotel on 8 March 1996 following allegations of irregularities in the marketing of match tickets during US '94. At the core of the controversy was the action of a foreign agent who absconded with money handed over in the bartering of match tickets. It emerged that Joe Delaney, who claimed that he was acting with the approval of the executive officers of the Association, had personally met a shortfall of £210,000 in this matter, and his success in securing match tickets for Irish fans in the exchange was publicly acknowledged by Charlton. In spite of this, however, his resignation and that of Kilcoyne were accepted, whereas the meeting refused to accept those of Pat Quigley, Senior Vice-President, Michael Hyland, Vice-President, and Des Casey, Honorary Secretary, all of whom stated that they were unaware of any illegal payments being made.

Chapter Twenty-Eight

Saipan Calling

Following the installation of Mick McCarthy as the new national team manager and the appointment of Pat Quigley to succeed Louis Kilcoyne as President of the Association, the FAI was given a timely opportunity to distance itself from the peripheral damage sustained during the night of the long knives in the Westbury Hotel. A census revealed that the total of registered players had increased to more than 175,000 in 1996, and that team numbers had grown to over 10,000, all of which reflected the remarkable expansion of the game at schoolboy and junior level. Donie Butler, the FAI's Commercial Manager, who had been involved in organising the census, offered the view that football was now the leading participant sport in the country.

Ironically, Butler would himself part company with the Association before the end of the year, and an even bigger development saw Bernard O'Byrne appointed to fill Sean Connolly's old post as General Secretary. Brendan Menton jnr. became the Honorary Treasurer and, thus renewed, the organisation embarked on a programme designed to polish its slightly tarnished image. The new regime lost no time in beginning to implement the findings of the Ray Cass Consultancy report, which recommended the fundamental restructuring of the decision-making process within the Association. One of the key issues addressed was the advisability of dismantling the old Executive Committee and replacing it with a Board of Management. This was interpreted as an important step in professionalising the running of the organisation.

Another significant decision taken by the new regime was to pour cold water on the recurring suggestion that the troubled Wimbledon FC might relocate to Dublin. Sam Hammam, Wimbledon's colourful chairman, had indicated that in the event of the FAI granting the requisite permission, the club might be prepared to build a new stadium in Dublin. That would be the pitching point of their application, but League of Ireland clubs were quick to object on the basis that it would impact adversely on local football. An earlier generation of football legislators had railed against the idea of televised football games in Britain being transmitted south of the Irish border, and their successors were not about to countenance the even bigger threat of Premiership games being staged in Dublin. Teams like Manchester United, Liverpool and Arsenal with their strong Irish connections might be popular attractions in pre-season fixtures, but the notion of their playing competitive games there, was anathema to those involved in domestic football. In this instance, the Irish protestors found a willing ally in the Football Association of England in their campaign against the audacious Wimbledon move, and eventually the idea was dropped.

An even bigger issue at FAI headquarters in the 1990s was that of finding a suitable home for international football in Dublin. Starting in the modern era with the game against Italy in 1971, the Association had used Lansdowne Road for its bigger fixtures, finally closing the gates on Dalymount Park for senior international matches after the meeting with Morocco in 1990. While the refurbished stadium in Phibsboro was ideal for the requirements of Bohemians' club games, it did not meet the security standards laid down by FIFA for bigger occasions. The same problem existed in Belfast, where Windsor Park, a stadium which in its prime in the 1950s housed huge crowds for games in the British championship, was beginning to fall into disrepair. There, however, the need was not so urgent, for unlike the situation in the south, the twin effects of the Northern Ireland troubles and a steep slide from the standards set by Billy Bingham's teams meant that international attendances could now frequently be measured in four figures.

On irregular occasions in the previous 15 years, the possibility of building a specialist football stadium had been raised by some of the more progressive elements in the FAI, only to founder, inevitably, because of a lack of funding. The higher profile of the game during the Charlton years, however, and a corresponding increase in the State funding available following the introduction of a National Sports Council and the subsequent provision of a seat at the Cabinet table for sport, meant that by 1998 the long-held aspiration was now becoming a distinct possibility. Much of the initial speculation was that it would be located in the Phoenix Park, if the Government proceeded with plans to build a National Conference Centre there, but it soon emerged that the latter building was being planned for Dublin's Docklands.

On 20 January 1999, Bernard O'Byrne, venturing where others had baulked in the past, announced that the FAI proposed to go ahead with plans for a purpose-built stadium for football at City West on the outskirts of Dublin. He said that an agreement had been reached to proceed with the project with five partners: the Mark McCormack Event Management Agency, Deutsche Bank, HBG, a construction company with a proven track record in this area, Deloitte and Touche, the accountancy firm, and RHWL, the architects. He said that the all-seater, 45,000-capacity stadium, with a number of ancillary facilities, would have a removable pitch and a retractable roof, enabling it to be used on a round-the-year basis.

In a separate development, Bertie Ahern, the Taoiseach of the day and an ardent supporter of sport in general, announced plans for an 80,000-capacity National Stadium to be sited at Abbotstown in Dublin 15. Ahern expressed the hope that the FAI would become one of the anchor tenants of the project, but it soon became clear that the football organisation was committed to its ambitious plans for the City West project, by now being branded as Eircom Park, thereby establishing a sharp division of interests. Eventually, after a long series of planning objections, not least those relating to the proximity of the stadium to Baldonnel airport and the effects the height of the stadium complex could have on operations there, the Eircom Park project was abandoned at considerable cost to the Association. In time, the National Stadium project at Abbotstown also fell by the wayside because of objections by the Progressive Democrats party, junior partners in a coalition government with Fianna Fail, and all this led, some years later, to the construction of the new National Stadium on the existing site at Lansdowne Road.

Removed from the complexities of football politics, Mick McCarthy was quickly recognised as a success in the difficult role of filling Jack Charlton's boots. Football, and the increasing profile of the national team worldwide, was seen by many as an important component of the Celtic Tiger era; and, as such, it was crucial that McCarthy, an inspirational team captain in his playing days, should go on delivering the results to keep pace with the image of a nation on the move. After the trauma of defeat in the play-off with Holland for a place in the finals of the 1996 European championship, the immediate priority was to regroup in time for the preliminaries of the 1998 World Cup, and among the young players introduced by the new manager were Kenny Cunningham, Gary Breen, Ian Harte and Jason McAteer, all of whom would figure prominently for the greater part of the next 10 years.

The evidence of the first two World Cup qualifiers, away to Macedonia and Romania, was scarcely reassuring. After opening the scoring through Alan McLoughlin after only eight minutes, they succumbed to a 3–2 defeat in Skopje, and a 1–0 defeat by Romania in Bucharest was marked by a penalty miss by Roy Keane. In the end, Keane's error would prove expensive for taken in conjunction with the failure to improve on a goalless draw at home to Iceland and a similar result with lowly Lithuania at Lansdowne Road, it meant that they had to settle for second place and a difficult play-off against Belgium. That would prove a fruitless mission, with Belgium's Luc Nilis emerging as the star of the two-legged tie after he had neutralised Denis Irwin's finely executed free-kick for a 1–1 draw at Lansdowne Road and then delivered the winner in a 2–1 victory for the Belgians in Brussels.

That was a bitter pill to swallow, the more so since it marked the retirement of the team captain, Andy Townsend, from international football and, equally significant, the swansong of Ray Houghton, whose goals against England and Italy would be recalled long after he ceased to be active. Ironically, he had combined with Townsend to score the last of his six Ireland goals in the game at Brussels but, alas, it counted for nothing after Nilis had hit the target 16 minutes from the end. Even as one generation of heroes departed into the shadows, however, another crop of gifted players emerged when McCarthy accentuated his rebuilding programme in a friendly game against the Czech Republic at Olomouc on 25 March 1998. Among the newcomers that evening were Robbie Keane and Damien Duff, two of the better-known names to graduate from the Brian Kerr football academy, who would emerge as international celebrities in their own right in the years which followed.

Kerr, who had learned his coaching skills at the foot of Liam Tuohy, was a gifted manager in the renaissance of St Patrick's Athletic in League of Ireland football in the 1990s, but it was his achievement in leading the country to victory in the European Under 16 and Under 18 titles, the first to achieve the double in the same season, which secured his place in history. Playing in only his second competitive game, Robbie Keane scored twice in the 5–0 rout of Malta in a European championship qualifier and over the next 13 years would more than double Niall Quinn's record of 21 goals for the Republic.

Jack Charlton had enjoyed his share of luck en route to becoming the Republic's most successful manager, but there were times, during the qualifying process for the European championship finals in Holland and Belgium at the start of the new millennium, when McCarthy could have felt that he was being made to pick up the bill for the good fortune of his predecessor. Davor Suker derailed the Irish challenge to top their group in one of the more critical qualifying matches by scoring a dramatic winner for Croatia, three minutes into injury time in Zagreb's Maksimir Stadium; and then, even more cruel, Macedonian defender Goran Stavrevski headed a spectacular goal to deny McCarthy a win at precisely the same stage of the game at Skopje. The price the Irish manager had to pay was a play-off with Turkey, then beginning to develop as a formidable force in football, and ultimately it proved too much. Lee Carsley's handball enabled Tayfur Havutcu to convert the late penalty which cancelled Robbie Keane's strike just minutes earlier in the first meeting with the Turks at Lansdowne Road, and that precious away goal would ultimately suffice to put the Turks through after a goalless draw in the return match, on a nasty, intimidating evening in Bursa's Ataturk Stadium.

Two play-off defeats were enough to tax the patience of even the most forbearing of managers, but McCarthy, unbroken, drove on and had his persistent endeavours rewarded in the qualifiers for the 2002 World Cup. Taking a leaf from Charlton's manual for survival in playing the most difficult games at the start of a qualifying programme, the Irish manager chose to open with a visit to Amsterdam to play Holland before taking on Portugal in Lisbon. A 2–2 draw against the Dutch was generally interpreted as a good result, but Roy Keane later emerged from the dressing-room to castigate his team-mates for surrendering the two-goal lead which Robbie Keane and Jason McAteer had given them. It was a different story in Lisbon, with Ireland rallying well in the last quarter and Matt Holland scoring 17 minutes from the end to earn a 1–1 draw and a valuable point against Portugal. That scoreline was replicated in the return match with the Portuguese, but the home crowd knew for certain that the Irish were on their way to another play-off, this time against Iran, when McAteer's goal sufficed to beat the Dutch in Dublin, and send them to the top of the group table in the process.

Iran, whom Ireland had defeated 2–1 at Recife in the course of their South American tour in 1972,were largely an unknown quantity for McCarthy, but in spite of winning the first leg of the tie at Lansdowne Road with goals from Ian Harte and Robbie Keane, the manager sensed that the return fixture at Tehran could be difficult. For one thing the team captain, Roy Keane, was out injured and, even more ominously, Iranian crowds had a reputation of being hostile to visiting teams. As it happened, the Irish defence survived comfortably and while Yahya Golmohammadi scored an injury-time winner for the home team, Ireland qualified on a 2–1 aggregate. McCarthy and his senior players had come good at the third time of asking, and now all eyes were focused on the World Cup finals in the Far East in the summer of 2002.

For the third occasion in four World Cup championships, the Republic were qualified to play on the biggest stage of all, and given that in the 1998 competition they were eliminated only after that agonising play-off with Belgium, it confirmed their place among the top European nations. And in a curious fashion, the deep disappointment of losing out in Brussels and the tears which were shed in the dressing-room in the wake of that 2–1 defeat, merely served to heighten the sense of fulfilment as the official party returned to Dublin from Tehran. For the first time in World Cup history, the finals were being staged in the Far East, with the final scheduled for the International Stadium in Yokohama, Japan.

Different countries will have different reasons to recall FIFA's decision to decide the winners of football's most coveted accolade on unfamiliar terrain, some eight years before they pushed out the boundaries yet again by taking the Jules Rimet trophy for presentation in South Africa. For Irish people, it will be forever remembered for the notorious Saipan incident and the chain of events which led to the team captain, Roy Keane, upping and leaving the training camp at the start of the final phase of their build-up to the finals. For McCarthy and his advisers, everything had gone to plan, with three warm-up games against Russia, Denmark and the United States all ending in victories. The last part of the preparations would see the Irish team take part in Niall Quinn's testimonial game at Sunderland, followed by a match against Nigeria at Lansdowne Road three days later, before their departure to the island of Saipan the following morning.

Roy Keane sought and was given permission to miss the Sunderland fixture, was replaced in the second half of the Nigerian match and scarcely looked like a man fired by the excitement of leading out his country in the World Cup finals, as the group assembled at their Dublin airport base and made ready for the first leg of a long journey to Saipan, 12 hours later. Saipan, a holiday island some three hours by air from Tokyo, appeared to be the ideal base to acclimatise before moving on to Izumo a week later. It was chosen by McCarthy and the Irish management team largely on account of its relative isolation, and as much to protect Roy Keane from the prying eyes of the media as anything else. There were, indeed, no unwelcome intrusions by the press on the squad's arrival there, but it quickly emerged that this was the least of the player's worries. From the late arrival of the squad's playing gear in Saipan, to the unacceptable state of the training ground, to management's decision to exempt the two goalkeepers, Shay Given and Alan Kelly, from taking part in an eight-a-side game, the team captain let it be known that he was dissatisfied with what he considered to be the slipshod nature of the preparations.

Eventually, he indicated that he wished to return home for personal reasons, changed his mind a short time later, and then repeated his initial request at a stormy meeting of players and management. McCarthy finally grew tired of attempting to placate his team captain and made arrangements for him to return to Manchester the following day – setting in train one of the biggest controversies in the history of Irish football.

For some, the combative Manchester United skipper embodied all the qualities of successful team captaincy, a natural leader who set the standards for the national side, on and off the pitch. For others, he was a divisive influence, a player who only rarely reproduced his imperious performances for Manchester United when clad in a green shirt. For them, his action in walking away from the honour of leading his country into the finals of the World Cup championship would, in the context of sport, come close to the ultimate act of disloyalty.

The issue would split public opinion at home as never before, but the consensus was that the manager had acted correctly, erring only in his decision to revisit the subject on several occasions subsequently when he might have been better advised to keep his counsel. The crisis left behind a distinctly unhappy atmosphere in the media's relationship with management, but it could scarcely be construed as weakening Ireland's level of performance on the pitch.

In terms of experience, the replacement midfielder, Mark Kinsella, didn't even begin to compare with Keane, and yet his partnership with Matt Holland evolved to the point where the absence of the Manchester United player made no adverse difference. It could even be argued that it improved the Irish build-up, in the sense that it made for less predictability in the team's strategies, which too often dictated that everything be routed through Keane. It was Holland who came up with the goal which gave the Irish back their self-belief in the opening game against Cameroon in Niigata, angling his shot beyond the reach of goalkeeper Boukar Alioum after Patrick Mboma's goal had given Cameroon an interval lead.

The 1–1 draw, against a team which epitomised the upsurge in the skills of African teams, was reasonably well received, but it meant that a defeat in the next game against Germany in the Kashimas Stadium at Ibaraki would leave McCarthy with a huge challenge if he was to emulate Jack Charlton's achievement in qualifying for the knockout stages of the competition. Germany had beaten England in a group game at Wembley on their way to the finals, and while the team did not perhaps compare with the side which recorded the last of their three World Cup triumphs in 1990, it was still regarded as one which could have a major influence in determining the new champions.

Players of the quality of Oliver Kahn, their veteran goalkeeper, Dietmar Hamann and the emerging duo of Michael Ballack and Miroslav Klose gave them an undisputed element of class, and it was the Polish-born Klose who put the Irish in trouble in the first instance, swooping in characteristic fashion on Ballack's pass to beat Shay Given after just 19 minutes. That was ominous, but with Steve Staunton and Gary Breen doing well in the middle of the defence, the fightback began and, to the delight of the big Irish presence in the stadium, it quickly grew in intensity. When Niall Quinn replaced Ian Harte 17 minutes from the end, McCarthy gambled all by going with a 3-4-3 formation, and after their impressive fluency earlier in the game, the opposition suddenly began to wobble. Yet, it was not until the third minute of injury time, at a stage when Danish referee Kim Milton Nielson was looking at his watch with increasing frequency, that the breakthrough came. Steve Finnan's long cross was knocked by Quinn into the path of Robbie Keane, and while Kahn got a firm hand to the ball, the shot had sufficient weight to finish in the net.

The third game against Saudi Arabia at Yokohama was always likely to prove the easiest of the three, and so it proved with Robbie Keane, Gary Breen and the irrepressible Damien Duff delivering the goals in an emphatic 3–0 victory. Now it was Spain who stood between Ireland and a place in the quarter-finals and with Duff's mesmeric skills on the ball emerging as one of the features of the championship, it was a case of onwards and upwards when the Irish contingent moved to Suwan in South Korea for the round of 16 test which would define the quality of McCarthy's squad.

Like Ireland, the Spaniards did not lose a game in the preliminary phase of the competition and had taken much of that form to the Far East in search of their first World Cup title. Steve Staunton, captaining the team in the absence of Roy Keane, became the first player from the Republic to make 100 international appearances when he led out his team in front of an attendance of almost 40,000, but within eight minutes of the kick-off, he could only look on in anguish as Spain jumped into the lead.

Carles Puyol, one of the great names in Spanish football, provided the cross which saw Fernando Morientes slip in ahead of Gary Breen to score with the near-post header and render McCarthy's Plan A redundant. For all the latent threat presented by Robbie Keane and Damien Duff, Fernando Hierro and Ivan Helguera were still dominating their penalty area, but then, just after the hour, came the opportunity to get back on level terms. Juanfran, tormented by Duff's sleight of foot, eventually took his legs inside the 18-yard area but to the dismay of the Irish bench, Ian Harte, normally so dependable, saw his penalty saved by goalkeeper Iker Casillas. That miss threatened to haunt McCarthy for the rest of his days, but with time almost up, Ireland were awarded a second penalty and this time Robbie Keane deceived the goalkeeper to send the game into extra time and, ultimately, a penalty shootout.

Sadly, David Connolly, who had been dismissed in the World Cup play-off in Brussels four years earlier, missed his penalty, and when Kevin Kilbane replicated that error minutes later, the dream was indeed over for McCarthy and his squad. Not surprisingly, the game marked the end of the road for Steve Staunton and Niall Quinn, the last survivor from the squad which Jack Charlton took to Italy for the first of his World Cup escapades 12 years earlier; but back in Ireland, people were sufficiently moved by the experience to turn out in their thousands for the homecoming, presided over by McCarthy in the Phoenix Park. For all the heartache of Saipan and the unlucky nature of their demise in Suwan, the manager was still the darling of the crowds. And as he stood there with the applause of the masses ringing in his ears, nobody could have foreseen that within another four months he would be out of a job.

Russia and Switzerland were generally perceived as the biggest threats in Ireland's group for the preliminaries of the 2004 European championship, and adhering to the proven formula, the manager chose to meet them at the top of his qualifying programme, taking on the Russians in Moscow on 9 September 2002 and the Swiss in Dublin five weeks later. Flushed by what he had witnessed in the Far East, he decided to confront the Russian team with an attacking formation – and paid for that audacity by conceding two first-half goals. Gary Doherty got one back with 20 minutes to go, but when Alexander Kerzhakov scored again almost immediately, the hosts were on their way to a 4–2 win.

It needed a big performance in the home game against Switzerland to get the title challenge back on track, and a difficult task became even more intimidating when Stéphane Chapuisat put the Swiss ahead before half-time. It required an own goal by Ludovic Magnin to level the scores with 13 minutes to go, but it prompted McCarthy to go for broke, withdrawing a defender, Ian Harte, and sending on the utility player, Gary Doherty, up front. The plan misfired spectacularly, however, and with the home team committed to the search for a winner, substitute Fabio Celestini, on the counter-charge, exploited a huge gap in the home defence to plunder the goal that effectively ended McCarthy's proud Ireland connection. Within the week, he was summoned to Dublin by the FAI to be told that they were preparing to appoint a new manager.

Chapter Twenty-Nine

The Way Forward

Two big issues dominated the FAI's agenda in late 2002. The first centred on the choice of Mick McCarthy's successor as national team manager; the second and more complex task was to streamline the administrative structure of the Association, having first identified the adjustments needed to discharge the commercial and social responsibilities of an organisation intent on projecting a fresh image in the early years of the new millennium.

Among the names touted for the managerial vacancy were some of those unsuccessful in the process which led to McCarthy's appointment almost seven years earlier. Eventually, the list was reduced to just two contenders, Brian Kerr, the then technical director, and Bryan Robson, the former Manchester United and England player who had been linked with the corresponding England job some time earlier. Robson, a galvanic force in the prime of his playing career, was seen as a man who would command international as well as national respect, but a relatively modest managerial career in English club football did little to help his cause.

In that situation, there was a big consensus for Kerr to become the first home-based Ireland manager since Eoin Hand. For one thing, he had proved himself a winner in his time in charge of St Patrick's Athletic and the national under-age teams, and he was highly regarded in his role of national technical director. His appointment was interpreted as another boost for the game at local level, and in time he named Chris Hughton as his assistant, with Noel O'Reilly taking over the coaching brief.

Following the earlier report by Ray Cass calling for changes in the way the FAI did its business, the Scottish-based consultancy firm Genesis was appointed to examine the administrative practices at 80 Merrion Square as they related to the support structures in place to help the national team achieve further success. The main thrust of its recommendations, however, centred not so much on this aspect of the Association's operations as on the need to slim down the numerical composition of the Board of Management from 22 to 10. Inevitably, perhaps, this led to allegations that the new regime, as proposed, would be distanced still further from the voluntary element at grass-roots level, with greater power being vested in fewer individuals, while others viewed it as the advent of long-overdue change.

Into this controversial arena stepped Fran Rooney, a successful business entrepreneur with a background in football. Rooney became the first chief executive of the Association following the resignation of the General Secretary, Brendan Menton jnr., but scarcely stayed long enough to effect significant change. That was the lot of his successor, John Delaney, who like Menton was continuing a family relationship with the FAI. In time, Delaney would leave an indelible mark on the Association, overseeing the move which took the administrative headquarters of the Association from Merrion Square to Abbotstown in west Dublin and, more importantly, filling the lead role in the negotiations which, in 2010, saw the Association become equal partners with the Irish Rugby Football Union, in ownership of the pristine National Stadium on the site of the old Lansdowne Road arena. The project was made possible only after a substantial funding from the Government headed by Bertie Ahern, but it meant that after long years of frustration, international football at last had a home of its own in the capital.

That was still no more than a fond aspiration when Kerr took charge of the senior squad for the first time, in a non-competitive fixture with Scotland at Glasgow's Hampden Park on 12 February 2003. Friendly or non-competitive fixtures are notoriously unreliable when it comes to establishing markers for the real business of World Cup or European championship matches, but in this instance a 2–0 victory was sweet. Meetings with England were invariably at the top of the want list of Ireland teams, north and south, but in a different context it was always gratifying to secure a good result against the Scots.

Ultimately, however, Kerr's tenure in charge would be judged by his record in the bigger matches and, in the wake of the European championship defeats by Russia and Switzerland, he was into this defining challenge almost immediately. McCarthy was the first Irish manager to leave in the middle of a competitive programme, and after the sombre lessons of his last two games in charge, the climate of expectation born of that heart-warming stand against Germany at Ibaraki just nine months earlier was now but a distant memory.

One of Kerr's first moves on his appointment was to reopen negotiations with Roy Keane on a possible return to international football. After the infamous spat in Saipan, Keane had decided to end his connection with the FAI, and it is a measure of the enduring passion engendered by the incident that Kerr's action immediately landed him in controversy. To some, the manager's decision was seen as constructive at a time when the national team was travelling on a high tide of uncertainty. For others, the recall of a player who was viewed as having debased the currency of Irish international caps by walking out of the World Cup was construed as a gaffe of unprecedented proportions.

To his credit, Kerr lost no time in restoring the morale of his players, and European victories home and away over Georgia and Albania ended the 2002–03 season on an encouraging note, but he knew, deep down, that he would be judged on the return meetings with the Russians and the Swiss. Even at the summit of the Soviet Union's reign in international sport, their football teams had always been vulnerable away from home, so there was every hope that the indignities visited on the Irish in Moscow the previous year could be avenged at Lansdowne Road. To the disappointment of a capacity attendance, however, the home team could not improve on a 1–1 scoreline, and when Hakan Yakin and Alexander Frei scored to give Switzerland a 2–0 success at Basle shortly afterwards, it was the end of the trail for the Irish.

It meant that the pressure was on to qualify for the finals of the 2006 World Cup, the next major international event, and in a group including France, Switzerland and Israel as well as Cyprus and the Faroe Islands, Kerr may have sensed that the task would be even more difficult than in the preceding campaign. His response was to plot the two best performances of his time with Ireland, drawing 1–1 with the Swiss at Basle and following that achievement with a goalless draw against France at Paris. With

Switzerland and France due in Dublin for the last two qualifying games, those results appeared to tilt the odds in Ireland's favour, but after twice failing to beat Israel, they tripped up again in dropping two home points to the Swiss and, even more expensively, losing out to Thierry Henry's goal in the French match. In overall terms, Kerr's percentage record was the best of any Irish manager, but judged on competitive fixtures alone, it wasn't deemed good enough to allow him to keep his job.

Aside from the declining fortunes of the national senior squad, there was much to encourage the FAI, not least the news that after all the procrastination of the previous five years the question of building a new home for international football and rugby in the capital was finally resolved. The Government had decided to enter into a partnership with the FAI and IRFU to construct a new 50,000-capacity all-seater stadium on the site of the existing facility at Lansdowne Road. For much of the previous twenty years, the two sporting bodies had lived cheek by jowl, in a commercial arrangement which enabled the football body to escape the consequences of their inertia in failing to build a stadium of their own, after doubts about the suitability of Dalymount Park for big matches began to be voiced as far back as the 1950s.

A time frame of three and a half years was envisaged for the demolition of the old structure and the construction of the new one, posing the problem of finding a temporary home for the national rugby and football teams during that period. At different times, Parkhead in Glasgow, Old Trafford in Manchester and Anfield in Liverpool were mooted as possible venues for the football team's home matches, while Twickenham and Cardiff's Millennium Stadium were seen as the most likely settings for Ireland's rugby games. That raised a number of pertinent issues, including the loss of prestige in having to export home international games, as well as the economic repercussions in terms of damage to the tourist industry.

In the end, the solution was improbable but all the more welcome for it. Throughout its early history, the Gaelic Athletic Association had been hostile to both the football and rugby organisations, not only for ideological reasons but also, and perhaps more pertinently, because they were in competition with them for the minds and bodies of the younger generations. This was particularly valid in the more densely populated urban areas, but the ground rules began to change in 1971 after delegates to the GAA's Annual Congress voted to repeal the infamous ban on their members playing or watching what were termed "foreign" games. The gospel of ecumenism required time to percolate but, unmistakably, the ethos of young people in rural areas mixing their sporting interests began to take root. In 2002 there was another straw in the wind when, among the messages of goodwill for the football squad taking part in the finals of the World Cup in the Far East, was one from Danny Lynch, Public Relations Officer for the GAA. That ran counter to the Association's earlier policies of ignoring all such events, and the move to promote improved relationships with other sporting bodies gathered pace with the election of another Kerry man, Sean Kelly, as President of the GAA.

While holding to traditional values in other areas of the GAA's operations, Kelly was quick to acknowledge the commercial benefits of opening up Croke Park, their state-of-the-art arena – which, like the new National Stadium at Lansdowne Road, was funded in part by the Exchequer – to sports which historically had been perceived as alien to Irish culture. It turned out to be a masterstroke which, in addition to showcasing the stadium internationally, enriched the GAA to the tune of something in the region of €1.25m per game. The biggest spin-off by far, however, was the bonding effect it had on the nation and the preparedness of Irish people to move forward with a common sense of purpose. In a very real way that decision to open the stadium to football and rugby for as long as it took to construct the new Lansdowne Road arena was one of the more significant developments in Irish society at the start of the new millennium.

By the time the country's qualifying programme for the 2008 European championship began, with a game against Germany in Stuttgart, on 2 September 2006, a new manager was in place. Steve Staunton had been the first player to win 100 caps for the Republic and, in the course of a protracted playing career, nobody had been more dedicated to the national cause than the Dundalk man. However, with no managerial experience to recommend his appointment, it was quickly interpreted as a huge gamble. Two home defeats at the hands of Chile and Holland, in the build-up to the European campaign, merely served to emphasise the dimensions of that leap of faith, and from this disturbing base, his time in charge of Ireland was frequently beset by controversy.

He might well have achieved what he set out to do in the Stuttgart game, had it not been for an unlucky break which saw Michael Ballack's close-range free-kick deflected past Shay Given by Robbie Keane's leg, but there were no excuses readily available after lowly Cyprus had emerged with a comprehensive 5–2 victory in Nicosia. And that shattering result was put in even bleaker perspective by the fact that Stephen Ireland had put the visitors ahead after only eight minutes. Later, in the game against Wales, the same player would have the distinction of securing the first ever international football goal at Croke Park, but before the European programme had run its course, he announced that he was quitting international football.

For most of the team's supporters, however, that was no more than an irritating postscript to a campaign which saw Ireland drop to their lowest rating in almost twenty years. Inevitably, in such situations, the finger is pointed at the man in charge, and after one of the shortest Ireland managerial reigns on record, Staunton was ousted. In view of the quality of the unsuccessful candidates in the search to replace Brian Kerr two years earlier, it was no surprise when the FAI, in its wisdom, decided to look beyond Ireland and Britain in their search for the person best fitted by pedigree to point the way back to the good times.

To assist in the trawl, they named a three-man recruiting panel comprised of Don Givens, Ray Houghton and Don Howe, and after considering the qualifications of at least two other candidates, they eventually found their man in Italy. At 68, Giovanni Trapattoni didn't fall within the conventional age limits for such appointments, but in every other respect his qualifications were beyond question. In spells in charge of AC Milan, Juventus, Inter Milan, Benfica, Bayern Munich and Red Bull Salzburg, among others, he accumulated seven Italian championship titles, six of them with Juventus, as well as masterminding championship triumphs in three other countries, Germany, Portugal and Austria. A highly respected player in his younger days, he went on to manage his native country and was widely respected throughout international football as a master of his trade.

Chapter Twenty-Nine

Thanks to the assistance of a sponsorship provided by the entrepreneur Denis O'Brien, a suitable financial package was put in place; and with Marco Tardelli and Liam Brady assisting him in the dug-out, the man with a reputation for parking his easy-going manner to become a hard-headed coach for the duration of a match, took on the job of restoring Ireland's image as one of Europe's better teams. In a group which included Italy, Bulgaria, Serbia, Montenegro, Georgia and Cyprus, it was obvious that he had little leeway for error in his attempt to emulate the achievements of Jack Charlton and Mick McCarthy by leading his squad to the finals of the 2010 World Cup championship. As it transpired, it took a late goal from Robbie Keane to earn an important success in Cyprus, but inevitably the defining games would be those against the World Cup holders, Italy.

There was no better way for Trapattoni to announce his return to international management than with a good performance against his native country, and it duly materialised in Bari's San Nicola stadium on 1 April 2009. It helped that Giampaolo Pazzini was red-carded for a foul on John O'Shea just four minutes into the game, but when Vincenzo Iaquinta launched the home team into the lead just six minutes later, it looked as if the champions would be capable of disguising their numerical disadvantage. The trend of the match told a different story, however, and after several near misses, the Irish got no more than they deserved with Robbie Keane's equaliser three minutes from the end.

The return match, in front of an attendance of 70,000 at Croke Park six months later, would prove equally taut. Twice Ireland led through goals from Glenn Whelan and Sean St Ledger, the latter hitting the target only four minutes from the end. For all their frustration, however, the Italians were not in the mood to capitulate and a minute into injury time Alberto Gilardino, on as a second-half replacement for Antonio Di Natale, silenced the home crowd with an equaliser. To all intents and purposes, that confirmed the champions as the group winners, but a goalless draw at home to Montenegro sufficed to put the Irish into a play-off with France for a place in the finals in South Africa the following summer.

Few needed reminding that four years earlier it was France and Thierry Henry who had ended Ireland's hopes of building on their 2002 achievement by qualifying for the 2006 World Cup finals. The French went on to reach the final against Italy in Germany the following year, but with Henry and some of his senior colleagues past their prime, there was genuine hope that Trapattoni could now succeed where Brian Kerr had so agonisingly failed. A crowd of 74,000 fans, representing the biggest ever attendance for a football game in Ireland, had belief too, as they converged on Croke Park for the first leg of the tie. Alas, there was again a sting in the tail for the Irish, with Nicolas Anelka's deflected shot breaking the deadlock for France late in the game.

The Irish, nothing if not competitive, still entertained hope of survival in the return game in Paris, however, and after Robbie Keane linked with Damien Duff to level the scores on aggregate approaching the interval, the tie eventually went into extra time. Then, in moments of enduring controversy, Thierry Henry again broke Irish hearts by deliberately handling the ball to enable William Gallas to equalise on the night and book his team's place in the finals. Henry stood indicted of an act of cheating which compared with Diego Maradona's infamous Hand of God goal against England in Mexico City in 1986, but the score stood and Ireland were out of the competition. That was a bitter pill to swallow for the hordes which accompanied the team to Paris, but the upside was that it confirmed the admirable progress Trapattoni had made in his two years in charge of the team.

For the FAI, it was undoubtedly a lost opportunity of sharing in a financial windfall. However, they must have been gratified by the statistic which showed that, at its peak, the telecast of the Paris match had attracted an audience of 2.2 million, the highest for any sporting event shown by RTE in the previous 15 years. It reflected yet again the unrivalled mass appeal of football at this level and was probably the decisive factor in securing a sponsorship deal worth €7.5m over a four-year period with the communications company, 3 Mobile.

It required time and some encouraging performances in an extensive preparatory programme to soothe the pain inflicted by Henry's audacity in Paris, but the average Irish football supporter is nothing if not resilient. And by the time Trapattoni and his players were ready to start their qualification programme for the preliminaries of the 2012 European championship, all the old passion was back in evidence.

Chapter Twenty-Nine

The Irish team got off to the perfect start with a 1–0 victory in Armenia, later to emerge as the most improved team in the group, followed by a home win over Andorra, only to give top-seeded Russia a three-goal start and lose 3–2 at Lansdowne Road just four days later. For all Russia's latent power, that was a difficult defeat to explain away in the light of the Republic's supremacy in the second half, and it meant that Trapattoni simply could not countenance the prospect of another loss when they travelled to Moscow for the return match in September 2011.

Previous expeditions to Russia had all ended in heartache for the Irish, but encouraged by success in the inaugural four-nation tournament involving Scotland, Wales and Northern Ireland in Dublin earlier in the year, the Republic team dug deep for the resilience they needed. Their reward was to leave the Luzhniki Stadium with the scoreless draw which kept them in contention for the runners-up position in their group – and qualification for the play-offs to determine the remaining finalists for the 2012 European championship.

Subsequent wins over Andorra and Armenia ensured that objective, and when Robbie Keane scored twice to bring his record goals haul to an astonishing 53 in the first leg of the play-off against Estonia in Tallinn, Ireland were on their way to another football extravaganza, this time in Poland and Ukraine. Fittingly, Shay Given, one of Europe's longest-serving international goalkeepers, established another first by winning his 120th cap in the return game in which a 1–1 draw formally established their place among the championship finalists.

After an interval of 12 years, the Republic of Ireland had reclaimed their status as one of Europe's better teams, and when the final whistle blew in the National Stadium, Michael D. Higgins, the newly elected Irish President, presided over some euphoric scenes.

Among other things, the achievement testified to the role of the national team as the financial engine driving the Football Association of Ireland. It was this consideration which prompted the commissioning of the Genesis report and, by extension, produced the root and branch changes which have modernised the organisation and positioned it more advantageously to act as one of the larger influences in the shaping of the new Ireland. We have seen how its role on the stage of the biggest international field sport was a major factor in projecting the image of the Irish Free State in its infancy in the 1920s. It was essentially the same formula which seventy years later announced the arrival of the Celtic Tiger era in the carnival times which marked Jack Charlton's term in charge, and now, with the dramatic expansion in communications, its brief is probably still more important in helping the nation surf some difficult times.

In Northern Ireland, Billy Bingham's achievement in taking his team to the World Cup finals in Spain in 1982 and again in Mexico four years later is recalled as one of the few joyous interludes in a singularly difficult era for the province. Sadly, Mexico and the retirement of the inspirational Pat Jennings from international football marked the start of a sharp decline in the team's fortunes, and for much of the next 25 years they toiled in the slipstream of their southern counterparts.

It was not until the arrival of David Healy, a modest player at club level but an outstanding striker in international football, that the outline of recovery began to take shape under manager Nigel Worthington in 2005. For years, Colin Clarke, like Healy a relatively little-known club player in spells with Queen's Park Rangers, Southampton and Portsmouth in the 1980s and early 1990s, had been Northern Ireland's leading scorer with 13 goals. Healy's achievement was to reach that total during the preliminaries of the 2006 European championship, the highest by any player in that competition, and by 2011 he had raised the Northern Ireland record to 35 goals.

Resilience and a penchant for survival in the lean times have been the badge of Irish football and those who administered it for 130 years. No less than the Irish Football Association in the north-east of the island, the Football Association of Ireland has been forced to operate in the shadow of a much more powerful neighbour across the Irish Sea and compete with the saturation television coverage of British games and, increasingly, those on mainland Europe. That is a hazard which, in an oblique way, also threatens the GAA, an organisation which until recently faced relatively little competition outside the bigger urban areas. To that extent, all Irish sporting organisations are having to address the public relations aspect of their operations, in the ongoing struggle for column inches.

Alert to that situation, Irish football, particularly in the south, is acutely aware of the need to adjust to the new demands in the marketplace and ensure that its structures are designed to cope with fresh challenges. In terms of numbers playing the game, the FAI has never had it so good, but the reality is that in providing a new home for the national team, its finances have, inevitably, been dangerously stretched. And it is in that context that the level of the national team's performances in major competitions is now more crucial than at any time in the past.

For the IFA, too, the next decade is fraught with urgency. After the stable stewardship provided by Billy Drennan and David Bowen, who between them clocked up almost fifty years in the role of General Secretary, the Association has run into some difficulties in the recent past, resulting in the resignation of its President, Raymond Kennedy, and the subsequent appointment of Jim Shaw at the head of the organisation. On the credit side, however, there is now genuine hope that Belfast will soon have a new all-seater stadium, probably a refurbished Windsor Park, capable of catering for some 22,000 spectators. This is substantially less than half the number that Northern Ireland's meetings with England once attracted to Windsor Park, but as a result of the civil unrest which beset the northern capital for more than thirty years, the attendance figures for big games there have dwindled significantly.

As a consequence of the Northern Ireland troubles, at least some of the nationalist element in the IFA's support defected to the southern team, but with a new stadium in place and an improved relationship with Dublin, the hope is that the IFA's international teams will again command broad support across the community. In a sharp reversal of the old order, the northern Association recently saw fit to seek a ruling in the International Court of Arbitration for Sport, following the FAI's decision to include players born north of the border in their national team, but that was regarded as no more than a blip in the improved relationship between the two administrations.

One of Michael O'Neill's first actions on being appointed to succeed Nigel Worthington as manager of the Northern Ireland team in January 2012, was to appeal to players to resist the temptation of following the example of Darron Gibson and Marc Wilson, both born in the jurisdiction of the IFA, in making themselves available for selection by the FAI.

O'Neill, a highly articulate manager who was widely praised for his achievement in leading Shamrock Rovers to the group stages of the Europa League, the first Irish club to do so, believes that even with a relatively small group of players, Northern Ireland can still be a force in international football.

In a changing world, the more pragmatic decision makers now see the future of Irish football as a joint venture, each Association holding to traditional values but still prepared to co-operate in areas requiring a mutual response. The introduction of the four-nation tournament in 2011 was in line with that new, progressive mindset; and even more significantly, perhaps, there are indications that the FAI and IFA may come together to make a joint bid to stage the European championship within the next ten years. And with the pristine Aviva stadium at Lansdowne Road open for business, it is possible that, at some point in the future, the IFA may even be tempted to look to Dublin as a venue for its bigger competitive games.

Coupled with the trickle of northern players currently crossing the border in search of international football, it could even raise the prospect of a return to the days, almost a century ago, when the island was last represented in international competition by just one team. That is a subject which even the most dedicated ecumenists are loath to discuss, but given its historic role as a nation builder, the likelihood is that Irish football will, as ever, figure at the centre of any moves to bridge the great divide of north and south.

In the meanwhile, there is the inviting prospect of supporters, on either side of the border, joining forces to sing the Republic's team to some big performances in the Euro 2012 finals in the summer. Over a bridge of forty years, Eamon de Valera's evaluation of football's role in projecting Ireland's image abroad is still as valid as ever.

Index

Index

Index

Index

Index